I'D TRADE HIM AGAIN

ON GRETZKY, POLITICS, AND THE PURSUIT OF THE PERFECT DEAL

**TERRY McCONNELL & J'LYN NYE
WITH PETER POCKLINGTON**

FOREWORD BY WAYNE GRETZKY

BOLTON, ONTARIO

For Marley Busenius. Without her,
this book would never have been written.

A Fenn Publishing Book / First Published 2009

Library and Archives Canada Cataloguing in Publication

Pocklington, Peter
    I'd trade him again : On Gretzky, politics and the
pursuit of the perfect deal / Peter Pocklington with Terry McConnell and
J'lyn Nye ; foreword by Wayne Gretzky.

ISBN 978-1-55168-366-9

1. Pocklington, Peter. 2. Businessmen—Canada—Biography.
3. Businessmen—United States—Biography. 4. Edmonton Oilers (Hockey
team)—Biography. 5. National Hockey League—Biography. 6. Progressive
Conservative Party of Canada—Biography. 7. Edmonton (Alta.)—Biography.
I. McConnell, Terry, 1952- II. Nye, J'lyn III. Title.
HC112.5.P62A3 2009   338.092   C2009-902088-2

ONTARIO ARTS COUNCIL
CONSEIL DES ARTS DE L'ONTARIO

The publisher gratefully acknowledges the support of the Canada Council for the Arts and the Ontario Arts Council for its publishing program. We acknowledge the support of the Government of Ontario through the Ontario Media Development Corporation's Ontario Book Initiative.

We acknowledge the financial support of the Government of Canada through the Book Publishing Industry Development Program (BPIDP) for our publishing activities.

Fenn Publishing Company Ltd.
Six Adelaide Street East, Tenth Floor
Toronto, Ontario
Canada M5C 1H6
www.hbfenn.com

Text design and electronic formatting: Martin Gould

Printed and bound in Canada

09 10 11 12 13 5 4 3 2 1

NOTE FROM THE AUTHORS

Peter Pocklington has been a public figure in Canada for more than 30 years and, in that time, volumes have been written and reported about him.

So when we chose to make him the topic for this book, we asked ourselves: what is there about Peter Pocklington that has not been written, not been reported?

The answer was striking in its simplicity: it was Peter Pocklington's point of view.

Certainly, in the 20 years since Peter's reputation fell into such remarkable disrepute, his critics have pretty well had a free hand to say whatever they wished about him, the vast majority of which has not been terribly flattering. For that, Peter deserves his share of the responsibility. He was usually hesitant to express his thinking or divulge his motives—and if, as a consequence, he was lambasted by the media, he usually responded in kind. A mutual distrust between Peter and the pundits took root and festered—and neither party was well-served as a result.

Yet, while he has often been portrayed as everything from a heartless scoundrel to a common criminal, we suspected there was another side to the man waiting to be explored. After all, there were too many anecdotal tales making the rounds that cast Peter as someone other than a scoundrel and a crook—tales that portrayed him as a daring community builder, unheralded philanthropist and bold entrepreneur.

If there was any truth to these stories, and that aspect of the man was to be brought to light, we were going to need his cooperation—and fortunately, he trusted us enough to provide it. And while we made the decision we were not going to shy away from some of the more unsavory aspects of Peter Pocklington's life story, we were not going to build our book around them, either. After all, those negatives have been exhaustively documented over these past 20 or so years. Rather, we would strive to paint a more complete picture of the man—as much as that was possible—and be sure to include more than a few surprises as well.

In that pursuit, we chose to give Peter his own voice within these pages. The reader will find his narrative in columns that are typeset in narrower margins and smaller type size than the rest of the book. We trust the reader will not find it difficult to discern the difference, and the Peter's voice can be heard clearly in these verbatim passages.

We hope you enjoy the book.

CONTENTS

ACKNOWLEDGEMENTS

'There is serendipity at play here'

Glen Sather says he was stunned to think we would even attempt to summarize in words a character as complex as Peter Pocklington. "How will you ever capture this guy in one book?" he asked.

Life is a great adventure and, for us, writing this book has been one of its more compelling chapters. It began with a phone call to Peter Pocklington in the summer of 2006 and everything that has happened since has unfolded in a way that has, at times, seemed amazing—yet always felt right.

There is serendipity at play here, and we try not to lose sight of that.

So many people have contributed to helping us bring this project to fruition. First, we must thank those who consented to share with us their opinions and recollections, and to have them appear within these pages: Glen Sather, Kevin Lowe, Charlie Huddy, Rod Phillips, Bob Kinasewich, the Right Honourable Brian Mulroney, Nelson Skalbania, Jim Matheson, Michael Gobuty, Don Berry and, especially, Wayne Gretzky.

We thank our colleagues at Global Television and the *Edmonton Journal*: Lynda Steele, Gord Steinke, Liane Faulder, James Baxter, David Staples, Jac Macdonald, Darcy Henton, Pat Beuerlein, Sheila Pratt, Graham Thomson and David Evans—for their continuing support, encouragement, assistance and advice. In particular, we must also thank Terry's boss Allan Mayer, the *Journal*'s editor-in-chief, who supported this project from the outset and ensured we were able to devote the time and energy needed to see it through.

Our gratitude as well to Brian McAndrew at the *Toronto Star* for his insight and guidance, to Don Metz and Ashley Busko at Aquila Productions for technical assistance and advice that was beyond what we could have asked, and to cartoonists Gerry Rasmussen and Gary Delainey for their talent and humour. Special thanks also to David Baines at the *Vancouver Sun*, Jeff Holbrook and Kevin Crawley from the Phoenix Coyotes, and Darren Krill and J.J. Hebert from the Edmonton Oilers for their helping hands.

An endeavour such as this cannot succeed without the support of family and loved ones. For J'lyn, it's her parents, Bob and Patty Nye, for instilling in her a love of reading and writing, Trish Fedeyko-Millard and Kim Misik for their love and for always being ready with a bottle of red and plenty of laughs, "the boy" for his friendship and advice, and her puppies, Neil and Ted, for the comic relief. Terry must first of all thank his wife Vicki Charron, without whose love and understanding this book would never have been started, for sharing the burden, and for providing valuable proofreading and editing services; and his children, Carson, Mac, Jamie, Lauren and Shannon, for providing the inspiration and the motivation. Our dear friends and neighbours—they know who they are—also merit special mention, though we dare not list them all here.

Special thanks, as well, go to our agents, Bill and Frances Hanna of Acacia House Publishing Services in Brantford. They believe in us, provide precious hand-holding when needed, a pat on the back when it's called for and a kick in the ass when that, too, is appropriate. Also sincere thanks to Jordan Fenn, Michael Mouland and everyone at Key Porter Books and H.B. Fenn & Company for taking this leap of faith with us.

Finally, we would be remiss if we did not thank the man himself, Peter Pocklington. Through five trips in the span of 24 months to his home in Palm Springs, California, countless hours of phone calls, and emails too numerous to mention, he has been unfailingly helpful, patient, forthcoming, candid, understanding and trusting. Moreover, he has taught us much about seeking out what Abraham Lincoln once referred to as the better angels of our nature, and we have learned at his knee about the virtues of a positive outlook and a sunny disposition. Truly, his life stands as testament to the words of Winston Churchill: "When you're going through hell, keep going."

—*Terry McConnell and J'lyn Nye*
Edmonton, Alberta
July 2009

Truly, for some men, nothing is written unless *they* write it

—Sherif Ali to Col. T.E. Lawrence
in the 1962 David Lean film Lawrence of Arabia

FOREWORD

'I consider Peter a friend, and I hope he feels the same way'

The Edmonton Oilers' greatest player reflects on a happy time he thought would last forever. The fact that it didn't does not change his feelings of affection for the man he came to think of as a second father.

August 9, 1988: my final day as an Edmonton Oiler. It was an emotional day for me, as anyone who saw the news conference knows. But it was really emotional for Peter Pocklington, too. This was a big thing he did, trading me to the Los Angeles Kings.

It was so big that when I flew back to Edmonton that day for the announcement, both Peter and Glen Sather told me one more time they would kill the deal to send me to L.A., if I wanted it killed. And I was this close—this close—to killing the deal.

I got to Edmonton that day and I started remembering how great it was, and I began to ask myself, "What are you thinking?" The reality was that had I killed the deal, had I remained an Oiler, I would probably have signed the contract extension Peter wanted me to sign, that afternoon. Peter would have said, "What do you want? I'll give it to you," because that's the kind of guy he was. That's the kind of guy he is.

I know that because for 10 years of my life I could pick up the phone if I ever had a problem and call Peter and he was always very nice, very accommodating. He was like a father to me.

Peter never interfered with the team, but every now and then he'd come into the locker room, and he'd talk to the players. Well, he came in one day—I'll never forget this as long as I live—and he said, "How are you feeling, Wayne?" I said, "I'm feeling good." I'm getting dressed for the warmup and he said, "You think you can get three goals and seven points tonight?" What do you say when your owner says this? So I said, "Yeah, yeah I feel good." So he said, "Okay, I'll give you 10-to-1 odds on a hundred bucks." All right. Again, what are you going to say? No?

Anyway, one of my teammates beside me said, "Hey Peter, can I have the same bet?" And Peter looked right at the kid and said, "Yeah, absolutely." And the kid went, "Well, how many points?" And Peter said, "Same bet, right?"

And the kid went, "Hold on a sec, I've got 15 goals. I can't have the same bet as Gretz." And Peter looked at him and said, "Fifteen goals! Why do we still have you here?" And he walked away.

The whole room just fell over laughing. And I'm thinking, did he really mean that or was that just his way of saying, "You better get going"? I couldn't figure it out. But I did get the three goals and the seven points that night.

Peter has always had a great mind. And he was really, well, eccentric. I mean, he loved having a chef in his office, a barber in his office and all those things. But his theory was this: if you have money and you don't spend it, you might as well be poor.

But he did so many great things for Edmonton, business-wise, charity-wise. He was proud to be an Edmontonian. He liked living here, and he used to tell me he'd never leave. The problem is fans are passionate, whatever city they're in. But Edmonton is smaller than New York or Chicago, and so they live and breathe the Edmonton Oilers. That's their feel-good story, that's what they do to relieve the pressures in their own lives, to cheer and root for the Oilers. So, the people in this town felt that he let them down. But the reality is it was a business decision.

It's just that in the end, the business side of things kind of got carried away. At the time, there were a lot of things about the business of sports I didn't grasp, because I was just a kid. Now that I'm on the other side of it, I totally understand. And I'm at peace with it.

Peter is tough. He's a tough businessman, but he's not a jerk. He's a good person. He has to be a good person, because he married one of the nicest ladies in the world—and she wouldn't marry a jerk. It's as simple as that, you know what I mean?

Peter is the kind of guy that when things were going great, he sort of stayed in the background. But when things got tough, he was the first guy to get in the locker room, he would meet with the players, and it was all positive. He had this whole philosophy. When Peter would leave the room, I used to say, "We can fly!" because his theory in life was always so positive. The glass was always half full, never half empty. That's how he lived his life. He still does.

It wasn't just the day I left Edmonton that was emotional for me. I get that way just thinking about my 10 years in Edmonton, with Peter and Glen and my teammates and all the friends we made and the championships we won together. It was all good, you know. I wouldn't trade it for the world. I wish it would have lasted another 20 years.

But I have no hard feelings whatsoever. I consider Peter a friend, and I hope he feels the same way.

—Wayne Gretzky
Edmonton, Alberta,
August 2007

PART I

'For some reason, I wanted to be noticed'

Peter and Eva Pocklington go for dinner at their favourite restaurant, little suspecting that, by the time the evening is over, Peter will own part of a hockey team and Eva's jewellery collection will be short one ring.

The pursuit of "the deal" has been Peter Pocklington's mission in life for much of his 67 years. The deal is the cornerstone of the marketplace, the trigger that allows free enterprise to flourish, its favours bestowed on those with unshakeable faith in its grace. If you happen to enjoy the art of crafting "the deal"—well, that's just icing on the cake.

And Peter Pocklington—Peter Puck to his friends and detractors alike—does enjoy crafting the deal.

But here was a deal that seemed different. It beckoned to him in a way Peter hadn't felt for years—in a way he hadn't allowed himself to feel. Never fall in love with any deal, he often reminded himself. After all, he needed to be able to walk away if it didn't ring the right bells. His head understood that, but this time his heart wasn't sure it wanted to listen. If this deal was different, it was because he didn't want to walk away.

Peter Pocklington, former owner of the Edmonton Oilers, the most successful hockey franchise of the modern age, wanted back in the game.

• • •

The date was Monday, June 19, 2006, a time of year when California's Coachella Valley is very hot and very dry; hardly hockey weather. But hockey was very much on Peter's mind that night.

For, in his heart, Peter knew his passion for hockey had been rekindled. On that June night, the Edmonton Oilers were one win away from capturing the Stanley Cup, just as they had five times before during the 22 seasons he had been their owner and patron. But this was the first time the team had come so close since those glory days—and damned if he didn't miss being a part of it.

Peter hadn't missed much about life as an NHL owner since he had stopped being one eight years earlier. It had become a job that was not for the faint of wallet. Nor was it much fun, even if you could afford it. Players' salaries had risen dramatically through the 1990s and a labour dispute that wiped out much of the 1994–95 season didn't fix the problem. Indeed, a new deal struck with the players only made the problem worse. By late in the decade, some owners were paying their players more money than their clubs were taking in— and the rest of their expenses were on top of that. It had reached the point that any owner who expected his team to be competitive had better be prepared to lose money—a lot of money.

Peter wasn't that kind of owner. Nor was Edmonton the kind of town where there were a lot of wealthy individuals willing to be that kind of owner. Already, the league had evolved into a partnership of "haves" and "have-nots." The clubs in larger, more lucrative markets such as New York, Toronto or Detroit boasted player payrolls three to four times greater than those in small-market Edmonton, Pittsburgh or Buffalo.

By 2006, however, the economics had changed. The year before, the owners had locked out the players for an entire year, wiping out the 2004–05 season. The new collective bargaining agreement with the players that brought labour peace also restored a business discipline that the NHL had been sorely lacking. Financially, being an owner was beginning to make sense again. Hell, it might even be fun again. And for the first time in a very long time, Peter Pocklington allowed himself the luxury of wondering "what if?"—as well as remembering what once was.

• • •

On that night, Peter drove his BMW southeast on U.S. Route 111 out of Palm Springs, past the gated neighbourhoods of Cathedral City, Rancho Mirage and Palm Desert, and into Indian Wells, the small but well-heeled desert oasis he and his wife Eva had been calling home since leaving Edmonton eight years earlier.

Those years had been good for him, good for his health. His closely trimmed hair and beard had long since turned white, but he was a tanned and fit 5-foot-9, and his blue eyes sparkled. His relaxed manner made it easy for him to get along with others, and that held him in good stead with people in the often-converging worlds of business, politics and entertainment. People have always taken a liking to Peter Pocklington, and for him, the feeling is mutual—most of the time, anyway.

He swung the Beemer south onto Cook Street, waved to the guard at the security checkpoint for the Vintage Club, then cruised along the picturesque, palm-lined boulevard. He turned east onto Vintage Drive, past the golf course, the manicured lawns and the desert homes of some of America's elite, including Bill Gates and Lee Iacocca. He pulled into the parking garage for his condo.

A few minutes later, Peter poured himself a glass of vodka and soda, sank into his chair, reached for the remote and turned on the television. There, live from Raleigh, North Carolina, NBC was carrying game seven of the Stanley Cup Finals: the Oilers and the Carolina Hurricanes—winner takes all.

Against the backdrop of national anthems and pre-game chatter, Peter let his mind drift back to another night, a night that was laden with equal significance. In his mind's eye, he could see his old buddy Nelson Skalbania lead a pack of reporters into the restaurant where he and Eva were dining. He smiled at the recollection. For it was on this night that car dealer Peter Pocklington became the owner of the Edmonton Oilers.

• • •

As serendipity would have it, Peter and Eva were at the Steak Loft on Jasper Avenue on that October evening 30 years earlier. They were just settling in when Skalbania walked in, followed by 20 or so members of the local media. That captured Peter's attention. "Holy shit, what goes on here?" he wondered. So, as was his manner, he asked.

"I got hooked into buying the Oilers," mused Skalbania, who at that time wasn't much more than an acquaintance. Skalbania made his home in Vancouver, but he did seem to spend a lot of time in Edmonton, making his fortune in real estate.

"Well," said Peter impulsively, "sell me half." On the spot, Skalbania agreed. He had good reason.

It was 1976, and the Oilers were about to embark on their fifth season in the World Hockey Association, an upstart league with designs on challenging the NHL for the North American hockey dollar. Up to that point, the club had been owned by a three-man partnership. The money man was Dr. Charles Allard, a surgeon who made his fortune in real estate and radio. Two years earlier, he had gained national prominence for launching the legendary Edmonton television station ITV, whose signal was broadcast by satellite to cable systems across the country—a rare thing for TV in those days. The other owners were Zane Feldman, the proprietor of Crosstown Motors, a Chrysler dealership in Edmonton, and "Wild" Bill Hunter, the club's founder. Yet, while Allard's and Feldman's other businesses had been enormously successful, the Oilers had been hemorrhaging money from the get-go. By this point, they had compiled an accumulated debt of $1.6 million.

Skalbania certainly wasn't looking to get into the hockey business. He had come to know Allard through North West Trust, a company owned by the Allard family that had been financing many of Skalbania's real estate deals. Stories have circulated for years that Allard told Skalbania if they were going to continue doing business, Skalbania would have to agree to take over the Oilers and assume their debt.

Whatever the reason he came to own the Oilers, Skalbania knew enlisting a partner was a good idea. When he bought the club, he had

asked Allard how much money he would need to run it. Allard said
he'd lose no more than $300,000 that first year. Instead, Skalbania
would lose $300,000 in the first week. "I thought, 'Gosh, I think I
need a partner,'" he says. "I figured the less you own of the club, the
less money you lose."

So if Peter wanted half the club, that was fine, but Peter would
have to be good for half of the debt, too.

"We wrote out the deal on the back of a napkin," Peter remembers.
This was a time in Edmonton when handshakes often sealed deals,
and due diligence was a rare thing. But Skalbania did ask for a gesture
of goodwill. Peter looked at the 12-karat diamond his wife was
wearing. "I pulled it off her finger and said, 'Here's the deposit,'" recalls
Peter.

From that moment, Peter Puck became part of Skalbania's news
conference.

According to the Douglas Hunter book *The Glory Barons*, the ring
was worth $150,000. But Peter insists Eva didn't mind that it became
part of her husband's latest deal. "She knew she'd get a better one."

There is some dispute about the remaining terms of the deal.
Skalbania says Peter also turned over three Rolls Royce convertibles,
including a vintage 1928 Phaeton used in the Robert Redford movie
The Great Gatsby. Peter insists the Phaeton was the only car involved.
In any event, Skalbania drove it back to Vancouver himself, despite its
bad brakes and stiff gearbox. Four years later, his first wife would get
the car as part of their divorce settlement—she got Eva Pocklington's
ring, too—and would later sell it. "Too bad. It was kind of a neat car,"
Skalbania recalls. He says that six paintings, including works by
Maurice Utrillo, A.Y. Jackson and Nicholas de Grandmaison were
also part of the deal. Peter says that's not the case. They do agree on
the total value of the swap: $700,000, though Peter recalls assuming
much of it as debt owed to the Bank of Montreal.

It was a lot of money for a business that had never so much as
made a dime.

But Peter knew what he was buying. Certainly his business
acumen concluded that, as a small-market club in a four-year-old

rogue league, the Oilers weren't such a great deal. But there was value in the name, value in the club as a going concern, value in the publicity the Oilers could generate for Peter Pocklington, his other businesses, and the city. And he knew it wouldn't do "my crazy ego" any harm either. "I looked at it as, 'Wow, what can I do with this?'" he says.

"For some reason, I wanted to be noticed."

Peter would get noticed all right, especially once he bought out Skalbania. But being sole owner had its challenges, too. "Every game the Oilers played, it cost me 20 grand. The first year wasn't much fun."

The club's fortunes did improve, albeit slowly, over the next two years. Then came the day in October 1978 when they would improve dramatically. Once again, Skalbania had a role to play, this time with an opportunity much more valuable than the one Peter so rashly seized in the Steak Loft.

By this point, Skalbania was the owner of the Racers, the WHA team in Indianapolis. His marquee player was a 17-year-old Wayne Gretzky.

"Indianapolis was going nowhere and Nelson said they were ready to hang him," Peter recalls. Skalbania had taken a lot of season-ticket money but had run out of the cash needed to run the club. "Obviously, the fans weren't too happy."

Eight games into the season, Skalbania decided Gretzky would have to go if he was to generate the cash needed to keep the club afloat.

In the end, the cost for acquiring hockey's future legend was around $400,000. "But that was the magic that turned Edmonton on," Peter says.

Within a year, the Oilers—as well as the WHA teams in Hartford, Quebec City and Winnipeg—were playing in the NHL. Peter says that if it weren't for Gretzky, none of it would have happened.

The NHL would have probably shoved us out. The Cincinnati team was going under, Indianapolis went under, Birmingham was in trouble. Nobody was doing well.

But once we had Gretzky, Edmonton really supported the Oilers in a big way—and the NHL saw the dollars we were taking in at the gate.

People were shocked. Our crowds were bigger than in Chicago. We were leading the league in attendance, up there with the New York Rangers.

I decided it wouldn't be the last time Edmonton would shock the hockey world. From then on, it was a rocketship ride.

PART II

'As a kid, I used to buy and sell apartments'

Owning the Oilers is the realization of a dream that began in London, Ontario, where the young Peter Pocklington grew up. Before the age of 30, Peter was well on his way to amassing a fortune.

Peter Pocklington developed his entrepreneurial flair for salesmanship at an early age—to hear his parents tell it, perhaps too early.

He was born to Basil and Eileen Pocklington in London, Ontario, on November 18, 1941, a time when mid-war rationing and hardship were common. Yet there was something uncommon about Peter's early experiences. When he was five years old, while other kids were trading marbles and baseball cards, "I picked cherries and put them in jars with water, selling them to our neighbours as my mother's preserves," he wrote in his online biography. So enamoured was he with his newly discovered zeal for capitalism, he sold his Christmas presents to friends.

But the greatest influence on Peter's early life came when he was 14, and he discovered the motivational teachings of legendary broadcaster Earl Nightingale. What he heard changed his life forever and set him on a course he follows to this day.

My dad brought home Earl's record *The Strangest Secret*, recorded in 1956. I still have it.

I memorized the damn thing. It literally stated, "You become what you think about," and gave examples. You had to write about the kind of person you wanted to be, and then keep it with you. Earl said that over a period of 30 days, you'd become what you thought about—and it works.

I pretty much figured I was part of the energy that we're all granted—and away I went.

However as he grew older, and emboldened by his new outlook on life, Peter's relationship with his father became more and more strained. "Well, my dad was an Englishman. You can always tell an Englishman, but you can't tell him much," Peter laughs.

Basil Pocklington was born in 1913, emigrated to Manitoba when he was 19, and went to work for the Bank of Montreal in Carberry, near Brandon. It was there he met Peter's mother. They married and settled in London to raise a family—Peter and his sister, Nancy.

After a stint in the RCAF, Basil became the manager of the Dominion Life Insurance Company in London.

In later years, Dad and I got along well, but we didn't when I was young, or at least I didn't get along with him. He was brought up in a private school in England where youngsters were to be seen and not heard. It was a pretty structured society he was born into, and he tried to do the same with me.

Actually, I think something changed him. Up until I was five or six, he was really positive, and he really got me up on the stump. He'd let me spiel off about whatever was on my mind. But he turned negative and I don't know what happened to him. He was no longer the confident, strong person I wish he could have been. He was smart, he was a real gentleman, he was honest, he was all the good things. He just didn't have the derring-do to do the things that he wished he probably could have done.

In his adolescence, Peter also learned to develop a thick skin, something that would come in handy in later years.

The one good thing I learned when I was 12 is that school kids will talk about one another. And I finally came home one night after something happened and said to my mother, "You know, it doesn't matter what people say. They're going to say it anyway." And from then on, I didn't really care what people said. I can't control them.

And years later, when the press used to tear me a new backside in Edmonton, you know, it bothered my wife. But I learned early on to let it go.

Peter soon discovered the car business was the best way to scratch his free-enterprise itch. "When he was 14, he traded his bicycle and $100 cash for a 1928 Model-A Roadster, then sold the Roadster for $500," wrote Peter Gzowski in the April 1982 issue of *Saturday Night* magazine. "At 15, he went on holiday to his grandfather's home in Carberry, and discovered that cars on the Prairies were in better shape than those that had been driven on the salted roads of Ontario." Peter would find the cars, which were anywhere from 25 to 40 years old, behind the barns and in the farmyards that dotted southwestern Manitoba. He'd buy them for $25 each, ship them east by train, and sell them in Ontario for $500.

When he was 16, Peter sold the family automobile—while his dad was out of town.

It was a 1956 Olds 98, a great car, only two years old. In those days, dealers wanted $1,300 to trade up from a two-year-old car to a new one, but I got him a deal for an even grand, and had the new one delivered—a '58 Olds. And when my dad took the train home from Toronto and saw the new car on the road, he damn near died.

At 17, Peter bought his first apartment building, a 16-unit complex. Of course, he wasn't old enough to sign the legal papers, so he had his mother do it. "She already knew I was crazy," he says.

It was about this time that there was also a parting of ways between Peter and his high school education. Peter was summoned to a meeting with his teachers where, he says, he was "fired from school."

I'm not even sure I made it until the end of Grade 12—but I didn't care what they thought. It was their system. Once I learned to read and write and think, I was done. I loved history, I always got 90 or 100 in history. And math. And I loved science. And English. To this day, I get upset with people who don't speak properly in our language because your language is what you think in. But the rest of that crap was nuts.

Peter now says part of his problem was an undiagnosed case of dyslexia. But that did not diminish the expectations he had for himself. He became a voracious reader, a habit he continues to this day, as a way to educate himself. His curiosity about the world also nurtured a keen sense of wanderlust.

As a young man, in my dreams I always thought I was flying around. I would get up from my bed and fly to see places. I know that sounds nuts, but that's how free a spirit I was, and still am. At night, I still dream that I can fly anywhere I want and see whatever I want. It's a great feeling, which I love to be—a free spirit, as all of us are, if you believe it.

Most people, though, would tell me, "You're fucking crazy."

Crazy or not, Peter soon was making a career selling cars and real estate. Though he had mixed results with the latter in London, the former proved especially lucrative. Then one day in 1967, his mother saw an ad in the *London Free Press*, an opportunity she thought might hold her son's interest: "Ford dealership for sale. Westown Motor Sales, Tilbury, Ontario."

• • •

Tilbury in those days was a small agricultural town of around 3,500 people—it hasn't grown much since—located on Highway 401 between Chatham and Windsor. For Peter, it represented a golden business opportunity, and it was only a 75-minute drive from London.

He made the trip that same afternoon to meet with Westown's owner, Bob Daigneault.

By the time Peter was done talking, Daigneault agreed to take $5,000 down and to hold a note for the rest: $20,000. Peter then negotiated a loan and a line of credit at the local Provincial Bank and paid off the balance. Daigneault then departed and suddenly, at the age of 25, Peter found himself the Ford Motor Company of Canada's youngest dealer.

> But that was okay because I just started selling cars. That little dealership took off like crazy. Sales quadrupled. Ford didn't know anything about it at first, so I was really selling cars under Bob's franchise. It was four months before Ford gave me the dealership, but once they saw how many cars I was selling, they were pretty happy.

Peter adopted the Westown name. Two years later, he would take that name with him to nearby Chatham, population 35,000, when Ford offered him the dealership there.

> I liked being a Ford dealer. It was fun. Ford must have thought this guy was doing something right, too. But Chatham was a tough little market. I suppose it was too small for my thinking, though I did fairly well there. But I liked Tilbury more. In Tilbury, I had no overhead.
>
> And then I went to Edmonton where business was just exploding, and I became the biggest Ford dealer in the country. I was very successful.

Peter was so successful, he was selling 5,000 new cars and trucks a year. That's roughly one every half-hour.

• • •

The first time Peter saw Edmonton was in July of 1971. "It was hotter than hell," he remembers. He stayed downtown at the Chateau

Lacombe while he sized up his newest business opportunity, a dealership of some distinction called Shirley Ford.

Peter was Ford's up-and-coming star and Ralph Shirley's store offered him his ticket to the big time—and he took a liking to the town right away. "My first impression was of a sleepy little western city, ripe to take off in."

And that's exactly what happened. It would be Westown Ford's phenomenal success that would provide him with the cash flow he needed five years later to buy Edmonton's failing franchise in the World Hockey Association.

As it turns out, Peter's decision to move west changed not only his own life's course, but that of the city he would come to love—for both good and bad.

Peter Pocklington was all of 29 years old.

PART III

'If you make me the coach, you're going to lose your job'

The World Hockey Association has a well-earned reputation as a league where anything can happen, and often does—be it the result of crackpot coaches, eccentric players or anomalous owners. But it also provides the foundation Peter Pocklington needs to build a first-class hockey organization—and to charge Glen Sather with the responsibility for forging a championship team.

In Peter Pocklington's first season as co-owner of the Edmonton Oilers, the team was going nowhere and impressing no one. There was, however, one bright light: the captain, Glen Sather.

After nine seasons and 658 games in the National Hockey League, Sather had joined the WHA's Oilers for the 1976–77 campaign after his contract with the Minnesota North Stars expired. Evidently, coming back to the city where he had played his junior hockey was doing wonders for the man who earned the nickname "Slats" because of his gritty play: at the age of 32, Sather was having his most productive season ever, and was leading the team in scoring.

Sather might suggest that such a statistic was more a testament to the shallow pool of talent on the Oilers that season, but they did boast some veteran hands—Norm Ullman, Al Hamilton and Bob Nevin among them. Nevertheless, the team was floundering—11 games under .500. With only 18 games left to play, Peter told general manager and coach Bep Guidolin to hand over the coaching reins to Sather.

As Douglas Hunter states in *The Glory Barons*, Guidolin felt making Sather the coach meant someone other than him would take the heat for the team's failures. It didn't quite work out that way.

"When Bep gave me the news, I told him, 'If you make me the coach, you're going to lose your job,'" Sather remembers. "And he sort of laughed it off. But I had been around by then, I knew what was going on."

The team responded under Sather, went 9–7–2 the rest of the season and squeaked into the playoffs three points ahead of the Calgary Cowboys. And just as Sather predicted, Peter fired Guidolin at season's end. Larry Gordon was hired as the new general manager.

By then, Peter had bought out Nelson Skalbania—who was headed for Indianapolis and the Racers—for half a million dollars. Soon after, he called Sather into his office to appoint him his full-time coach, and an enduring friendship took root.

"When I went into Peter's office, he had jeans on and a sports jacket, longer hair, beard—a progressive kind of guy. I liked him right away," Sather remembers of their first encounter. "He had a good attitude—although he didn't give me any more money to be the coach!"

But Sather was confident Peter Pocklington was a good fit for the Oilers. "Peter was exactly the kind of owner we needed, somebody who wasn't afraid to take a chance. He was an upbeat, positive, aggressive kind of guy, and he had a great sense of humour. I liked being around him."

Oilers play-by-play broadcaster Rod Phillips was equally impressed with the team's new owner. "I remember thinking this [was] a really good move for the hockey team because Peter was dynamic. And he was really pumped about owning the team. He was a very likable guy, the minute you met him. Very personable and friendly and outgoing."

From that point, Peter embarked on building an organization that would not only be elevated to the upper ranks of the WHA, but would one day become an elite franchise in the NHL. Because the hockey community is a small one, it didn't take long for word of what was happening in Edmonton to get around. "The players that played under Peter for a lot of years—I guess it starts with the owner and it trickles down—liked to play in Edmonton," says Phillips. "The Oilers have always been a very good organization, and highly regarded by the NHLPA. They treat the players very well.

"And that goes back to the WHA; nobody ever missed a paycheque. They always had good dressing rooms and the travel was always as good as it could be in those days when you were on commercial airlines and everything.

"Peter treated everybody well, even the front office staff. He was a very good owner."

For his part, Peter was a big supporter of Glen Sather: "Glen was good, a great coach," says Peter. "No question." Sather was taking his cue from the Winnipeg Jets, who enjoyed much success in the WHA. Teams used to see a lot of each other during the course of a season, and as Sather watched from the bench, he studied the free-flow, speedy transition game the Jets employed, inspired by the play of their top line of Bobby Hull, Anders Hedberg and Ulf Nilsson. He knew from the way the Jets could shift quickly from defence to offence that he wanted the same from his Oilers.

"At the time, no one played that way," Sather told Ed Willes in *The Rebel League.*

• • •

The summer before the 1977–78 season also saw the first serious attempt at a merger with the National Hockey League. The plan was eminently reasonable, which of course is why it failed.

Six WHA teams—the Oilers, the Jets, Houston, New England, Quebec and Cincinnati—were to be admitted to the NHL. They would play in their own division for five years while slowly being integrated into the older league. The WHA's owners thought they had a deal. But there were forces within the NHL—led by Toronto's Harold Ballard, Chicago's Bill Wirtz and Boston's Paul Mooney—that had always opposed peace with the WHA. They rallied the troops and the merger failed by one vote.

In retrospect, the merger's defeat was a fortuitous development for the Oilers. Determined to punish the NHL for its stubbornness, the WHA aggressively began to recruit underage players, including future superstar Wayne Gretzky. Had the WHA ceased to exist in 1977, he might never have come to Edmonton.

But it also gave Sather and Gordon, the new general manager, the time to begin building the team that would soon challenge for the WHA championship. They did so with players who would become familiar faces in Edmonton: Ron Chipperfield, who arrived from the Cowboys after they closed up shop; Paul Schmyr, who did the same when the San Diego Mariners failed; Brett Callighen and Blair McDonald, who a year later would become Gretzky's linemates; and a draft choice who would become one of the most popular Oilers of all time, Dave Semenko.

•   •   •

Twenty months later, Wayne Gretzky had emerged as the most exciting player in any league, a development that finally made the merger between the NHL and the WHA inevitable—no matter how bitterly Harold Ballard and his equally cranky cronies opposed it.

By this point, the WHA was on its last legs. Not only was the league down to six teams, but two of them, Cincinnati and Birmingham, were struggling to survive.

Gretzky admits a schedule that had each WHA team playing the others as many as 17 times was wearing thin on fans and players alike. "But the NHL had its own struggles, too," he points out. "People kind of forget that. The NHL had some teams that were really hurting."

In 1976, for instance, the expansion Kansas City Scouts moved to Denver after just two seasons and became the Colorado Rockies. In 1978, the Cleveland Barons, a team that had entered the league in the 1967 expansion as the California Seals, folded and merged with the Minnesota North Stars, who were also struggling at the gate.

The NHL had shrunk to 17 teams, but the turmoil was hardly over. Within another year, the Atlanta Flames would finally abandon the U.S. Deep South and move to Calgary. Two years after that, the Rockies would forgo Denver for suburban New Jersey. Professional hockey had sunk to its weakest point since the 1930s.

So it was with an instinct for self-preservation, as much as anything, that on March 22, 1979, the NHL board of governors finally agreed to accept four WHA teams into the fold: the Oilers, the Jets, the Quebec Nordiques and the New England Whalers.

It was the third time the merger had come to a vote, and it proved to be the charm. Not only had the NHL rejected the WHA proposal two years earlier, a second vote, held just two weeks before, had also failed to achieve the required three-quarters approval. But a couple of developments happened to persuade two of the "no" clubs, Montreal and Vancouver, to change their vote and support the merger. There had been an immediate backlash against Molson Brewery, the owners of the Canadiens, in the three Canadian WHA cities. In Winnipeg, even the Molson Three Stars became simply known as the Three Stars. Convinced that fighting a WHA merger was bad for the beer business, Molson changed their vote.

Vancouver was also placated with promises of a balanced schedule, which alleviated concerns of increased travel costs.

When the third vote was held, only Toronto, Boston and Los Angeles voted against the merger. Alas, they alone could not kill the deal. Ballard was outraged. "Who the hell are the Edmonton Oilers?" he asked with his customary bluster.

Each WHA team was assessed a franchise fee of $6 million, with each one paying an additional $1.5 million to Birmingham and Cincinnati to go away.

• • •

There was considerable player movement once the two leagues' seasons were over. Each existing NHL club was allowed to reclaim WHA players for whom they held the NHL rights. An expansion draft followed to restock the new teams. Through it all, each WHA team was allowed to protect two players from their rosters. The Oilers protected Bengt Gustafsson and Wayne Gretzky. "It was Glen and Peter who fought for that," says Wayne. "As it turned out, we only ended up protecting one player—me, because the NHL ruled Gustafsson had to go to Washington."

Still, the Oilers were able to embark on their first NHL season with 13 players from the team that went to the finals in the WHA's final year. They lost that series to—who else?—the Winnipeg Jets.

The Jets, whose roster was gutted as their best players were reclaimed by their new NHL partners, would never get the better of the Oilers again.

• • •

The NHL version of the Edmonton Oilers made their home debut at Northlands Coliseum on Saturday, October 13, 1979, a 3–3 tie with the Detroit Red Wings.

It was a triumphal moment for Peter Pocklington, but one he insists would never have happened were it not for Wayne Gretzky. "The WHA was in trouble," he says. "If it weren't for Wayne, the NHL would have shoved us out."

But to hear others tell it, that moment would never have happened without the patience and determination of the Oilers owner. In their collective opinion, Edmonton made it to the big leagues because of one man, Peter Pocklington:

"Peter got the Oilers into the NHL. He's the guy that did it. It was his money that kept the WHA team alive—and he gets no credit for that at all."

—Rod Phillips

"Peter brought Edmonton the most exciting team to ever play in the NHL, and that includes the Montreal Canadiens of the '50s, the Canadiens of the '70s, the Islanders of the '80s, and the Penguins of the early '90s. Whether we won or lost, the fan left the arena saying, 'That was the most exciting game I've ever seen.' So I've always said he put together the most exciting hockey organization the NHL has ever seen. It's as simple as that. And he treated them all like his own kids."

—Wayne Gretzky

"Peter was a dreamer and he was a big idea guy. And probably if it wasn't for his big ideas, you know, Edmonton might not have ever had Gretzky. And as much as I want to say the Oilers were more than just Gretzky—you need a lot of good players to win a championship— let's face it, Gretzky put us all in that position to win that many championships."

—Kevin Lowe

"People talk about Bill Hunter and Zane Feldman bringing the Oilers to Edmonton, but it was a WHA team that they brought, not the NHL team. Peter brought the NHL team there. Peter was the one who stuck his neck out."

—Glen Sather

"Peter has a lot of knockers, because sometimes he's a little short and abrasive and cocky and whatever the hell you want to call it. But there is only one reason the Oilers won five Stanley Cups and that franchise was successful, and it's because of Peter. I know the sacrifices he made to pay for the team, to manage it until it got somewhere. No one else would have done that—to sell his assets, sell his diamonds, and take the gamble that he did. Peter took a helluva shot that no one else would have taken. I don't know anybody who would sacrifice the way he did to keep that club there."

—Nelson Skalbania

PART IV

'Hockey's newest superstar. He's 11.'

Peter Pocklington says he probably paid too much to acquire the rights to Wayne Gretzky. So why does he do it, especially after the Winnipeg Jets had already cast doubt on the kid's worth? "Why do I do a lot of things?" he asks. "If your mind is open and you're ready to take the risk, what's the downside?"

Nelson Skalbania knew he was in serious trouble.

Looking for the one player whose skill and star power could attract fans and save his failing hockey franchise in Indianapolis, Skalbania settled on a skinny 17-year-old by the name of Wayne Gretzky. He signed the kid to a seven-year, $1.75-million contract.

And in response, the number of season tickets in Indianapolis did increase . . . by 200, barely a blip from the pathetically low 2,000 bums already in the seats. To say Skalbania was disappointed would be an understatement. "I've got to get out of this business," he muttered to himself.

If the sporting public in Indianapolis was underwhelmed by Skalbania's signing of a teenage hockey phenom, it wasn't because the kid lacked the credentials. Wayne Gretzky began to draw attention to himself in his native Brantford, Ontario, when he was only six— holding his own while playing against kids who were four years older. When he was 11, he scored 378 goals in just 82 games. A subsequent appearance in the *Star Weekly* and *Canadian* magazines, inserted in weekend newspapers across Canada, made Wayne a nationwide hockey celebrity (one of the cover headlines: "Hockey's Newest Superstar. He's 11"). Wayne would leave home at 14 to play Junior B hockey in Toronto, then at 16 he was drafted by the Sault Ste. Marie Greyhounds of the Ontario Hockey League.

Wayne's dad wasn't sure he wanted his boy going to the Soo—it was a lot farther from Brantford than was Toronto—but it turned out to be a good move. In Wayne's one and only year in Major Junior hockey, he set the OHL's rookie scoring record with 70 goals. He was also a star for Team Canada that year at the World Junior Hockey championships in Montreal, scoring 17 points in six games and winning the tournament's scoring title.

By season's end, Wayne Gretzky felt it was time to turn pro—and though the NHL didn't draft any player younger than 18, the WHA had no such qualms.

• • •

Nelson Skalbania didn't view Indianapolis as a hotbed of hockey in the American Midwest, just waiting for someone to come along and stoke the coals. Rather, the World Hockey Association had asked him to save the team that was already there but headed for failure—and thereby keep the league from shrinking from eight teams to seven. "I got sucker-punched into stepping in," he says.

When he stepped forward in 1977, Skalbania became the Indianapolis Racers' fourth owner in four years. At the time, he still owned a piece of the Edmonton Oilers—but watching the two teams play each other, he says, "was like watching grass grow." He sold his share of the Oilers to his partner, Peter Pocklington, so he could turn his full attention to the Racers.

It didn't help. Indianapolis, he says, wasn't much fun. "One big rule you learn is that you shouldn't buy a sports team unless it's in a city that you either live in or spend an awful lot of time in." He may have spent a lot of time in Edmonton in those days but, clearly, Indianapolis did not qualify on that count. Skalbania says that sometimes it seemed he only travelled to Indy to bring more money for the club's creditors, a lot more money than what the fans were forking over at the gate.

Skalbania initially hoped to keep the Racers alive long enough to either gain admission to the NHL or to be compensated if they were left out. But there were no guarantees. The Houston Aeros—arguably the most successful of the WHA's American franchises—would suspend operations after the 1977–78 season because the owners had been told that if there was a merger, they wouldn't be included. So in the end, for its seventh and final campaign, the WHA was down to the seven teams the league had desperately enlisted Skalbania to avoid.

For Nelson Skalbania, signing Wayne Gretzky to play in Indianapolis was the hockey equivalent of a Hail Mary pass.

• • •

On June 10, 1978, Skalbania and Gretzky flew from Skalbania's home in Vancouver to, ironically, Edmonton, so that the "saviour" of Indianapolis hockey could be introduced to the Canadian media— well, two members of the media, anyway. Rod Phillips, the play-by-play voice of the Oilers and a sportscaster at the time for CFRN Television, and *Edmonton Journal* hockey writer Jim Matheson were the only ones in attendance.

"Rod and I were at the municipal airport to meet Skalbania's plane," recalls Matheson. "Skalbania had phoned me a few days earlier to ask what I thought of this kid Gretzky. Rod was over for dinner at the time." Matheson remembers booking a room at the Chateau Louis Hotel, not far from the airport, "and we spirited Gretzky there to keep him away from any other media who happened by."

At least the 17-year-old Gretzky knew where he was and could find Edmonton on a map. He wasn't so sure about Indianapolis. Wayne would pay his first visit to his new home a month later for an autograph session at Ayers Department Store. Hardly anyone showed up.

The beginning of the season was equally inauspicious—for the Racers and for Wayne. The team wasn't winning, the rookie star wasn't scoring. "It wasn't a very good team," Wayne recalls, "and we were drawing only about 6,000 people a game." Skalbania was running out of money, fast.

Skalbania quickly decided he had to cut his losses, and the fastest way would be by parting with his prized asset and the six-figure salary that came with him. Maybe there was even a little bit of money to be made, too. "I was kind of pissed off with the hockey business by that time," Skalbania admits.

The Indy owner may have been ready to part with Gretzky, but the kid was hardly on the Oilers' radar at the time. Peter says he didn't know anything about Gretzky. Sather remembers he didn't know much more, other than what he and the rest of the country had read in *Star Weekly* and what he had heard about the kid through the league rumour mill.

But the Oilers were about to pay their first visit of the season to Indianapolis. No one could have guessed at the time but that game, on October 20, 1978, was to be a date with destiny for Sather, for Gretzky—and for Pocklington.

• • •

On the morning of the 20th, Glen Sather showed up at the Market Square Arena in Indianapolis to watch his counterpart, Racers' coach Pat Stapleton—a veteran of both the NHL and the WHA—put his team through its paces. Sather particularly had his eye out for this kid Gretzky, but since the players' names weren't engraved on the back of their practice sweaters, he wasn't sure who to look for.

There was one thing Sather was sure of, however: that the skinny kid he saw circling around the ice wasn't the player he was looking for.

"I thought this kid was the son of one of the players on the team," Sather says with a laugh. "He just looked like an ordinary young boy. He could have been 14 or 15." When he was told the kid was indeed the phenom he was looking for, the coach wondered to himself what the fuss was about.

That night, Sather found out. The Oilers won the game 4–3, but that's not what the coach remembers best. Instead, it's that Wayne Gretzky scored two goals against his team—the first goals of his professional career.

On the second goal, "he came from behind the net—Dave Dryden was the goaltender—and scored on this classic little move" that fans later came to know so well. But it was the first goal that really opened Sather's eyes. "Wayne went around Paul Schmyr, who was one of the best defencemen in the WHA in those days, and he made him look silly."

Sather returned to Edmonton convinced Gretzky was going to be a star. What he couldn't have known at the time was that star would burn brightest in Edmonton.

* * *

In the end, Wayne Gretzky would play only eight games in a Racers' uniform. His last game was on October 28, a 3–2 win over the Winnipeg Jets. Skalbania was in Indianapolis that night, watching the game with Michael Gobuty, one of the Jets' new owners. Then together they flew to Winnipeg on Gobuty's plane for a rematch between the two teams the following night.

The topic of discussion? Making Wayne Gretzky a Winnipeg Jet.

* * *

The day before, Skalbania invited Gretzky for lunch. By that time, the kid already knew his first experience with pro hockey wasn't turning out quite the way he'd hoped.

"I'm only 17. I'm in the middle of nowhere," Wayne says of Indianapolis. It's a figurative reference, relative to the hockey universe. Even in a market of 2 million people, it was evident not many of them were hockey fans, and it didn't take Wayne long to figure his coaches were not really thrilled to have him on the team. "They wanted to go with their veterans," he says of Stapleton's staff. "They wanted to win.

They were all fighting for their own jobs.

"It just really wasn't a perfect marriage."

Skalbania began to explain to his young star how pro hockey wasn't working in Indianapolis, but all Wayne could remember thinking was, "Wow, I'm only 17 and already I'm being traded." Then Skalbania gave him a choice: you can go to Edmonton, or you can go to Winnipeg.

In an instant, Wayne was all for Winnipeg. "Oh, I was a big Jets fan," he recalls. Playing in Sault Ste. Marie the year before, he knew the Jets well, and had been thrilled by the exploits of what was probably the best line in hockey: the Jets' Hull, Hedberg and Nilsson. Though Hull had since retired, and the two Swedes had moved on to play for the New York Rangers, their line's reputation for using the entire ice for their highly skilled playmaking had continued in Winnipeg. "This is the fit for me," Wayne thought. "This is my kind of hockey."

It was a good thing he felt that way because Skalbania and Gobuty were already close to making a deal. In fact, by the time Gobuty's plane left for Winnipeg, the deal was done. All that was needed to put Gretzky in a Jets' uniform was for Gobuty's general manager, Rudy Pilous, to give the transaction his blessing.

● ● ●

As difficult to imagine as it may be today, there was hardly a consensus in the late 1970s that Wayne Gretzky was destined for stardom.

His goal output in Indianapolis—six points in eight games—was not bad for a rookie, but it was a far cry from the success he had enjoyed at lower levels on the competitive rungs of hockey. Had Gretzky finally advanced beyond his skill level? Had he perhaps peaked too early? It wouldn't, after all, be the first time a shining star of junior hockey flamed out when he got to the show.

Jets' coach Tom McVie was among the skeptics. "Everyone else will probably tell you, 'Oh yeah, I saw it right away,'" McVie told author Ed Willes for the book *The Rebel League.* "They're lying. To me, he looked like somebody's little brother. It looked like he was going to get fucking killed."

None of this mattered to Peter Pocklington. By now, he knew plenty about Gretzky and if his friend Nelson Skalbania gave him the chance to sign the kid, Peter intended to make good on it—and the cost be damned. And the asking price was not cheap. Not only would Wayne's new team have to assume his contract, which paid an average $250,000 a season, but they'd have to pony up the cost of obtaining his rights: Skalbania was asking $750,000. For a club like the Oilers, whose total gate at the time was only $2 million a season, that was a pretty steep price. Contrary to the conventional wisdom that comes with hindsight, Wayne Gretzky was hardly a bargain—or, for that matter, a sure thing.

"He was a skinny little kid," Peter says, "but you know what? I didn't give a damn. I knew he could play."

• • •

Pilous was waiting at the Winnipeg airport when Gobuty's plane landed. His assessment of the Gretzky deal? A 17-year-old with three career goals was no bargain—and just like that, the deal was off. According to Gobuty, Wayne Gretzky was considered by Pilous to be too young, too skinny and too inexperienced to play professional hockey.

It may have been one of the final times Gobuty or his partner Barry Shenkarow listened to Rudy Pilous. He was soon replaced by John Ferguson.

Ever the dealmaker, Skalbania then picked up a phone at the Winnipeg airport and called his friend and old business partner in Edmonton. "Peter," he said, "I've got a deal for you." They agreed to meet the next morning.

• • •

The Winnipeg Jets were the royalty of the WHA. Their reputation for winning was compared favourably with the legendary Montreal

Canadiens, and they won the league championship three times in the
league's seven-year existence, more than any other club. But their
fortunes were destined to be the polar opposite in the NHL. The Jets
wound up as perennial also-rans, lovable losers for the most part who
failed to qualify for the playoffs six times in their 17 seasons and, in the
other 11 years, advanced past the first round only twice. The franchise
ultimately failed, and in 1996 it was sold and moved to Phoenix.

Would Wayne Gretzky have made a critical difference to the Jets'
NHL fortunes? Would he have ensured the Jets' tradition of excellence
survived their transition from the WHA? It's hard to imagine that he
wouldn't. But would the Jets still be in Winnipeg had he played there?
That's a tougher call, though Peter Pocklington thinks they very well
might be. Whatever scenarios Jets' fans care to conjure up, the one
irrefutable fact they can ruminate over is that their team left town for
the Arizona desert, while the Oilers still call Edmonton home.

Gobuty, who remains close friends with Peter, freely admits he
should never have deferred to Pilous on the day he tried to bring
Wayne Gretzky to Winnipeg. "I should have done what you did and
just signed him," he recently told Peter.

.   .   .

Once Nelson Skalbania arrived at Peter's Westown Ford office, the
deal to bring Wayne Gretzky to Edmonton didn't take long. Peter
would pay considerably more for Gretzky than the $250,000 price
Skalbania had settled on with the Jets, but Skalbania agreed to a down
payment: for $200,000 down, the Oilers acquired the rights to Gretzky,
forward Peter Driscoll and goaltender Eddie Mio. In return, Peter
agreed to let Skalbania buy back 50 per cent of the Oilers any time he
wanted—a prudent negotiating point for Skalbania, given that the
Oilers could be one of the teams gaining admission to the NHL.
However, he gave up that right a month later when Peter agreed to
pay him another $200,000, and the two men considered the
transaction completed.

After Skalbania left his office, Peter called Sather to share the news.

I said to Glen, "I just bought this kid Gretzky. What do you think?" Glen said, "Yeah? Well, let me get back to you." I said, "Excuse me, what do you mean 'get back to me'? I just bought him. You own him."

Anyway, Glen was obviously very excited because to a coach, it was like having God join your team. This guy Gretzky was unbelievable.

And of course the rest is history; how we made out in the WHA, and then on into the NHL and winning four Stanley Cups in five years. And we only missed the other one because of a fluke, Steve Smith knocking in a goal on Grant Fuhr that probably should never have happened, but did.

But as it turned out, it was wonderful for everybody, everybody. Wayne obviously has succeeded in life, and had a great career and is still having an interesting career. It worked out for everybody, worked for Edmonton, worked for the league, and it worked for Wayne.

• • •

While Skalbania was busily trying to make a deal, Gretzky, Mio and Driscoll were headed to the Indianapolis airport to catch a chartered plane. Destination: unknown.

"When we got on the plane we didn't know where we were going, Winnipeg or Edmonton," Gretzky recalls. It was an hour into the flight, he says, before they learned they were headed for the Alberta capital. "I was the throw-in," Wayne laughs of the deal that made him an Oiler. "They wanted a goalie and they wanted Peter Driscoll. Glen loved Peter Driscoll."

What the pilot wanted was money, and according to *The Rebel League*, no one had arranged for him to be paid. Mio produced his wife's credit card.

Only after the plane landed in Edmonton and the pilot wanted full payment was a phone call put in to Peter and assurance given the flight would be paid for. The cost was $7,900. Mio's credit card receipt was torn in half. "I should have kept it," Mio told author Willes. "That would have made a great souvenir."

. . .

When the plane carrying the players from Indianapolis arrived at the Edmonton International Airport, Glen Sather was there to greet them. The media were 35 kilometres away, at Edmonton's municipal airport, having been given the benefit of a bum steer. Wayne remembers his new coach's first words: "The first thing Glen said to me was, 'You're playing professional hockey?' I was 151 pounds!" Wayne laughs. "He kind of adopted me as sort of his son that year and really made sure everybody realized that not only was I a teammate, but I was still a kid."

Gretzky would play his first game for the Oilers five days later, a 4–3 overtime win for his new squad. The opponent? In what was probably the final irony, it was the Winnipeg Jets.

. . .

In the end, selling Wayne Gretzky didn't save Skalbania's hockey team any more than signing him did. Nor did it prevent the WHA from shrinking to six teams. The Racers folded on December 15, 1978, just 25 games into the league's final season. They were quickly forgotten. Not so Wayne Gretzky.

. . .

The Edmonton Oilers turned out to be the fit Gretzky thought the Winnipeg Jets could be, and hoped the Indianapolis Racers would be. He made an impact straight away, and it wasn't long before the hockey fans in Edmonton began to take notice.

Before Gretzky's arrival, the Oilers were off to a slow start, winning only three of their first eight games. But with No. 99 in the lineup, they won 19 of their next 29 and by Wayne's eighteenth birthday on January 26, 1979, the Oilers were within eight points of first place.

"He had exceptional skill," Sather says of his young protege. "He was quick, he was smart, he was a very dynamic player at that age and there was no question he was going to be a real star. And he was intelligent. I always said the best players are always the most intelligent players."

Wayne took a liking to his new environment as well, and to his new bosses. He lived with Glen and Ann Sather during his first month in Edmonton, before moving in with a family across the street for the rest of the year. And Peter gave him a car. "I remember when I first got here, one of the first things Peter said to me was, 'Come over to Westown and pick out a car.'"

It didn't take Peter long to decide he wanted to keep Wayne around for a long time to come, either. He offered to tear up the Skalbania contract and give his bonus baby a new deal, a 20-year contract that would keep Wayne in an Oilers' uniform until the end of the 1999 season. The deal was rumoured to be worth between $4 million and $5 million. Gretzky says it averaged around $300,000 a year for the first nine years.

"It was huge money back then for a kid who up to that point scored 15 goals in professional hockey," Wayne recalls.

Everyone around Wayne—his teammates, lawyers, even his agent—told him not to sign the contract. "The only two people who were saying, 'You're nuts not to sign this,' were myself and my dad. And I was like, 'My dad says sign it, I want to sign it, I'm signing it.' So I signed the contract."

The signing ceremony is one of the most celebrated in hockey history. On his eighteenth birthday, before a game against the Cincinnati Stingers, Wayne signed the contract at centre ice. His family, who had been flown in for the occasion, and his new boss looked on.

Still, he almost didn't put his name to the legal document, says Rod Phillips, the Oilers' broadcaster.

"Wayne told me that just before he signed his name, he thought about signing somebody else's name instead," Phillips recalls. "He wasn't really sure that he was doing the right thing. Then I guess he said to himself, 'Aw, I'll sign it.'"

Wayne finished the season with 46 goals and 110 points—solid numbers, even for a grizzled veteran. For a teenager, they were astounding—and Peter credits Wayne with transforming not just the Oilers into contenders, but for reinvigorating the game itself.

> Wayne was a great acquisition, and a fun guy to be around, too. He raised the performance of every member of the team by at least 5, 10 per cent. You get that much more action out of 25 guys, that's huge. So he literally, just by his own talent, raised the level of play in everybody else—because they all thought, watching him, "God, I can do that." Not that they could, but they thought they could and that's all that matters.
>
> With Wayne, it was his passion to be like an artist. He was like Picasso. He could do things nobody else even thought of doing. He could pass to himself! He could put the puck off the boards here, and skate to where the puck was going to come to him.
>
> He went beyond anything I've ever seen. He had great skill. He was unbelievable. I guess that's why they call him the Great One.
>
> Wayne Gretzky was like the ballet dancer, Nureyev. He was magic, he was all those things.

PART V

'Whatever your passion, you have to go for it'

Peter Pocklington's business empire grows in both size and stature, while he clings to the parts of his life that are most important to him: his wife, his family, his friends, and the occasional friendly game of backgammon. Yet in the end, it's his ownership of the Oilers that gets him that elusive reservation at a popular restaurant.

Peter Pocklington was in the business of business. The nature or purpose of that business wasn't nearly as important to him as the satisfaction he derived from building it, from buying it or from selling it.

For Peter, business was all about crafting the elusive deal—and the deal only worked for him if he could be passionate about it. He derived much of that passion from his family.

> I find in life there are three things you have to have: You have to love, you have to be able to accept love, and you have to create. If one of those is out of whack, you're a pretty sad person. If you can put those in balance and you have a strong belief you can conquer those things, then life is pretty exciting.
>
> Knowing my wife loves me makes me stronger than steel, and that gives me the freedom to love everything else I do. If I don't love it, I don't do it. It has to be a passion.

Peter has always felt deeply about his family: his beloved wife, Eva, six children, 12 grandchildren. Today, his attention is focused on ensuring his grandchildren have the benefit of a college education. Twenty-five years ago, his concerns were more pressing.

> When our youngest, Zach, was five or six, he used to get beat up at school because he was my kid. So my wife decided she would go see the school principal, but I said, "No, we're not."
>
> There is no sense moaning and groaning about this sort of thing. You deal with life the way it's presented. I could have been angry about it but what was I going to do, go beat the [other] kid up? No. I had to show Zach how to look after himself.
>
> So I found him a Golden Gloves fighter from Edmonton, Dennis Belair, and we'd go down to the Canadian Native Friendship Centre three times a week to learn how to box. In six months, Zach beat the shit out of a kid in Grade 4 and that was it. Nobody ever bothered him again and to this day, he walks with his chest out.
>
> After all, I believe strongly that a brave man dies only once, but a coward dies every day.

It's a lesson he tried to impart to all his children with the hope they would, in turn, pass it on to their children. He believes his kids have all become good parents.

> But that's mainly because of my wife. My wife is the greatest mother in the whole world. She's great and that's passed on to them.
>
> She's a strong lady. She's my best pal. And supportive. That's when marriages last, when you have that unconditional love both ways. If you don't have that, forget it.

Eva Pocklington was born in Yellowknife and moved to Edmonton with her parents when she was 12. When she met Peter, she was divorced from Brian Hughes, proprietor of Hughes Petroleum, a chain of Edmonton gas stations. She and Hughes had two children, Darren and Jill.

Eva and Peter were introduced by a mutual friend while they were en route to inspect an apartment building Peter had just bought. Peter was instantly smitten. But after a week of dating, he learned Eva had suddenly left on a vacation to Hawaii.

I went to work at Westown Ford on that Friday morning, and I thought, goddamn it, why would she go to Hawaii like that? So I phoned the airline, drove straight to the airport, got on the plane and bought whatever I needed when I got to Hawaii. It was true love.

Three months later, they were married. That was in 1974. Zach was born two years after that.

The marriage was also Peter's second. His first marriage, to Rosalie Tomlinson, lasted eight years. She was born in Ingersoll, Ontario, and grew up in Toronto. Together, she and Peter had three children: Leslie, Molly and Peter, Jr.

When Peter and Rosalie divorced, she returned to Ontario with the children. Not having the kids near as they were growing up remains one of his lifelong regrets.

I was too young the first time I got married. I was 22 and I didn't know myself. I imagine I was pretty tough to get along with. I'm sure I wasn't very understanding. I was lucky to have found the girl I have now.

Life is tough and it makes it a lot easier if you've got a great partner. But you've got to work at it, it doesn't just happen. I think chemistry gets you together, then after that if you have similar dreams and desires, you can make it work. But life isn't simple.

•   •   •

As Peter's business empire grew, so did the Pocklingtons' circle of friends. They did a lot of socializing and it became evident to guests just how close Peter and Eva were.

"I never noticed them being touchy-feely or anything like that," recalls Bob Kinasewich, a friend and one-time lawyer in Peter's office. "You just knew the respect and the dedication and the love was there. They were always very pleasant—and you could tell, you feel the positive vibes from that."

Oilers' broadcaster Rod Phillips can remember he and his wife Debbie being invited to the Pocklington home when their daughter Quinn was just an infant. "I remember Peter carrying Quinn around the house. She was only six months old at the time."

Phillips particularly recalls the works of art in the Pocklington home. "Oh yeah, it was full of paintings—like he had really fine artwork. I don't know shit from Shineola about art, but I remember looking at these paintings, and they were like $700,000 paintings."

Peter often travelled with the Oilers, and he particularly enjoyed New York City. "A couple of times in New York, we had some absolutely fabulous parties after games," remembers Phillips. "In those days, the schedule was a little more lenient, and we'd be in New York for two or three days—and it was always scary to go to dinner at a restaurant with Peter because you know, he would think nothing of ordering a $300 or $400 bottle of wine." That could get dicey when it came time to divvy up the bill. "'Peter, you bought the $400 bottle of wine. I think you'd better pay for that one.' But he was fabulous."

• • •

As Peter set out in the 1970s to forge his business empire, he couldn't have picked more fertile territory in which to do it than Edmonton. Alberta's oil reserves were concentrated primarily on Edmonton's doorstep in central and northern Alberta, and most of the province's oil industry at the time was based in the city. The oil-fuelled boom of the 1970s and early '80s brought the sort of prosperous activity Edmonton hadn't seen since the halcyon days of the two world wars. The city doubled in size, attracting newcomers by the hundreds of thousands, primarily from Saskatchewan, Ontario and the Atlantic provinces.

What Edmonton offered them was an opportunity to build a northern metropolis on the banks of the North Saskatchewan River—perhaps the last great opportunity in North America to build a city from the ground up and finally get it right.

Embracing that opportunity was a cadre of freshly minted entrepreneurs—people like Pat Bowlen, Tim Melton, Don Stanley, Bob Stollery, Bill Comrie, Dr. Charles Allard, Cal Nichols, Jim Hole, Nelson Skalbania, and Peter Pocklington.

"Edmonton then was a cowboy town, a lot of fun," Skalbania remembers. "It was easy to do business. It was done with handshakes, and you didn't need a lot of documents. You could raise money easily."

Most fortunes were made in real estate as every scrap of available land was acquired, serviced and developed. The trading on existing properties resembled activity on a giant Monopoly™ board.

"We were in a business that was kind of simple in those days," remembers Skalbania. "When you bought some real estate in a growing market, even a bad deal was good in six months. In those days, it didn't require a lot of due diligence, a lot of learning curve to be in the real estate business.

"You know, real estate is a leverage game," he adds. "It doesn't take much to figure out if you buy a house for $100,000, all cash, it's got to sell for $200,000 to double your money. But if you buy a house for $100,000 with a dollar down, to double your money you only have to go to $100,000 plus one dollar. So that's where the leverage comes in. That's why many of the big real estate companies in the '70s in North America were all Canadian because they could leverage it, they could get money from the banks to buy things.

"So I had a lot of fun in Edmonton. The ease of doing business, the quickness of doing business, that kind of stuff, made it fun."

Peter was very much engaged in the real estate business, through his company Patrician Land Corp., which owned apartment buildings across Canada, as well as vast tracts of undeveloped land in Edmonton, Calgary and the Rocky Mountain playground of Canmore. "I must have bought half-a-billion dollars in real estate from Nelson Skalbania over 10 years," says Peter. He bought his own "bank," Fidelity Trust, to help finance his real estate acquisitions; owned the largest Ford store in the country, Westown, and a second dealership in Toronto, Elgin Ford; he was a player in the Alberta oil patch with Patrician Oil and Capri Drilling, which leased rigs to oil companies; and he owned a chain of gyms, Club Fit.

Peter also built his sports empire, which included not only the Oilers but the Edmonton Drillers of the North American Soccer League and the Edmonton Trappers, of minor-league baseball's triple-A Pacific Coast League.

Later, there would be Peter's food-related businesses, some profitable, others not so much: Palm Dairies, one of the largest retailers of dairy products in the West; Cambra Foods, a Lethbridge-based manufacturer of canola oil; Magic Pantry, which sold prepared foods that did not require refrigeration; Kretschmar Foods, which serviced restaurants; Green Acre Farms, a chicken-processing company with plants in Texas and Mississippi; and, of course, the Edmonton beef- and pork-packing operation, Gainers.

At its peak, the Pocklington empire exceeded $2 billion in sales.

. . .

Peter admits, however, that there were missed opportunities as well. One was the chance to bring a National Basketball Association franchise to Edmonton.

My friend Jerry Buss offered me an NBA franchise for Edmonton in the early '80s. He owned the Los Angeles Lakers then—well, he still does—and because the Oilers were so successful, he said I could have an NBA team for $6 million.

I turned it down. I thought who in Edmonton would come and watch seven-foot guys chasing a basketball? If you sit in the first three or four rows, it's fine. After that, you go up and look down at that little wee court, and a bunch of tall guys running back and forth . . . it's not my idea of a sport. That's why I didn't take the opportunity from Jerry.

He was right in one way. There probably wasn't a market in Edmonton for an NBA franchise—at least in the long term. But he could have invested the $6 million, then sold the team or moved it to a more lucrative market a few years later. In 2002, Charlotte secured a new NBA franchise called the Bobcats. The price tag: $300 million.

Some years later, Peter was offered 10 per cent of the diamond-mining company Diamet—for $100,000.

> The guy was on the board of the Shoctor Theatre with me. He pleaded with me, he and his brother needed a hundred grand to finally find these crazy diamonds in the Northwest Territories. I said, "You guys are out of your fucking minds. There are no diamonds in Yellowknife or anywhere else up there."
>
> Unbelievable. It was just a helluva deal. My $100,000 would be worth $100 million today.

Diamet eventually joined forces with Australia's BHP Minerals, and together they mine about 3 million to 5 million karats annually. One diamond recently recovered from the mine was 182 karats.

Then there was the aforementioned 3,000 acres Peter owned in Canmore, just outside the gates of Banff National Park.

> I bought for $5 million and sold for $7 million. It's probably worth $500 million now. That's just crazy.

• • •

Peter may have been asset rich, but he was often cash poor. Like many wealthy business people, he seldom carried much cash—though he did have a wallet full of credit cards, so anyone who tried to outwrestle him for a restaurant tab did so at their peril.

He does tell a story, though, of a time in 1976 when his company was out of cash, overextended on its credit, and facing a $200,000 payroll. Just about then, a $200,000 cheque came into the office and was promptly deposited.

Only after the money was safely in his bank account was Peter told the cheque had been sent to him in error. Nevertheless that money still enabled him to meet his payroll, and he paid it back later—with interest.

It was exactly this sort of run-and-gun approach that endeared Peter to some people—primarily those who did business the way he did—while frustrating, even infuriating, others.

"Peter was a shooter," says Skalbania. "I guess I was a shooter, too." He remembers two incidents that illustrate his point—and they both involve Peter's love of backgammon.

"I sold Peter a very large building in Edmonton, 775 suites. And we were something like $200,000 apart in price, in adjustments of this and that. We were in the boardroom with lawyers and everybody else around, so we said we'd play a game of backgammon to 10 points, and the winner would get the $200,000 advantage.

"We actually played a game of backgammon for $200,000.

"Peter ended up jumping out to a lead of something like 9 to 2, so I kinda had written the money off. I thought, 'God, I guess I'm going to blow 200 grand.' Son of a gun, I got it up to 9–all, and we looked at each other, and simultaneously said, 'Split!' We shook hands and divided the $200,000 by half. We each absorbed $100,000."

A week later, Peter and Skalbania were back in Peter's office, and back playing backgammon. "Peter ended up losing about $12,000 on this game," Skalbania recalls.

Then Peter told Skalbania, "You know, I don't have any cheques."

"Here he is in his corporate office, and he owes me 12 grand, and he doesn't have any cheques? I think the problem is he may have had the cheques, but maybe there was no money in the account," recalls Skalbania. "So I said, 'You know that painting over there, I'll take that instead. Is that okay?' And he said, 'Fine.'

"I took it off his wall and it was a Frederick A. Verner, late 1800s. He is a very famous Canadian painter now." Skalbania still has the painting. He says it's probably worth about $70,000 in today's market.

Not everyone did business that way, nor did they appreciate those like Peter who did.

"Peter was a grinder," says Kinasewich who, as Peter's lawyer in the early 1980s handled a lot of his business transactions. "Peter was a car salesman. He'd be throwing numbers, here, there and everywhere—'Look at that, see? Easy. Sign and do it.' And some people would sign what he was selling, and then the grinding would start. But even when he was buying, he would grind. I had some friends who were involved in real estate deals with him, and just hated it because he'd want concessions. 'Oh yeah, but if you want to get it done, I need this concession now.' So people really didn't respect that."

But for Peter, that was part of the dealmaking. "When you're buying, always give people more than they're asking and get it back on the terms," he told Peter Gzowski in the April 1982 issue of *Saturday Night* magazine. "If you offer what sounds like enough, you can give them zero interest."

Sometimes, however, even his closest friends wouldn't respond to his overtures the way he'd hope.

Recalls Kinasewich: "Smart business people like Tim Melton would just look at Peter and say, 'Peter, I'm not agreeing to anything with you right now. Send me a letter, tell me what you want to do and I'll give it some consideration.' Well, that would frustrate Peter to no end. 'What are you talking about, Tim, you're smarter than that. Just do it.' That's because Peter would 'just do it.'"

• • •

There is no arguing with success, however, and Peter was successful.

Business, he says, is the same, irrespective of its size. "The only difference is the number of zeros," he says. "You should sell when everyone else is buying, and buy when everyone else is selling."

The secret to succeeding in business is having enough capital, hiring good people and, obviously, having a market. Whatever it is you're putting the money into, be sure the people want it, because you can always find the money and you can always find the people to run it.

But even if you can spot the market, and you can deliver the product or the service, and you have good management, if you don't have enough capital, you're still big-time screwed. Normally, you will need twice as much money as you think you do.

• • •

Success in business is also dictated by the business-friendliness of government. Peter says if the people who create wealth are given the latitude to do what they do best, everyone can benefit. If not, everyone ultimately suffers.

Wealth creation is pretty simple to explain. I told a lot of kids in Junior Achievement this story when I was giving talks.

If you're building a $5-million building, and $5 million of energy and other people's work and products go into that building, at the end of the day they've all been paid their $5 million and you have your $5-million building. That's $10 million and that's wealth creation. You rent out that building, go get another mortgage and do it again.

But the socialists figure you shouldn't be allowed to do that unless they tax you 50, 60, 70 per cent. Well, then you don't have enough to go put up another building. You spike the wealth creation, you kill the goose that laid the golden egg. And it's nuts.

No one really discovered that on a grand scale until America became a republic in 1776, and said all men are free and equal to go do what you have to do and be responsible—and they created more wealth than the world had seen since the dawn of time. Private enterprise exploded. Now people live to 80 and are healthy and get holidays and they can eat and drink and have a car or two, and send their kids to be educated.

This is the message we have to get out to people: "Don't kill the goose that laid the golden egg." Lincoln said it best when he said you don't help the poor by taxing the rich.

• • •

That said, Peter insists he always tried to do business with a measure of civility.

> I learned in the car business the guy who beat you up on a deal and had to have this and had to have that, was not pleasant to be around. It would always be better to say, "Deal with the guy down the street, okay? I don't want to do business with you." The guy who hurt you the most and twisted your arm the most and wouldn't let you make a profit, also bugged the hell out of my people when he came back for service. Nothing was any good with him. In fact, his life was probably screwed up.
>
> Now the guy you made a fair profit on, he always had a smile when he was back to get his car fixed or whatever. It was a pleasure doing business with those people.
>
> So I find now I won't do a deal if it's with people I don't want to be involved with. Life really is too short, and the easier the deal, normally the more successful they are.

• • •

For all his reputation for bluster, threat and invective, Peter did not have an appetite for confrontation, and only reluctantly would he engage in a relationship he considered toxic.

"I will not allow myself to be around people who are negative," he says. "It's toxic as blazes. It's painful to be there."

It was not solely in the car business he encountered such people, however. Kinasewich remembers one adversary from Calgary who caused headaches for his boss.

"Peter bought this piece of property in northeast Calgary, I don't know how many acres it was," Kinasewich recalls. The price was in the neighbourhood of $10 million, but there were problems with the transaction and neither side was very happy with the other. The man Peter had to deal with was Harold Stark. Kinasewich remembers him as small in frame, but with a big voice. "Harold Stark here," he'd boom.

"And then he'd threaten to do all kinds of dastardly deeds to Peter," says Kinasewich.

"One day, Peter calls me into the office and says, 'Bob, Harold Stark is going to be in Calgary today. You gotta come down and meet him with me.' I say, 'Peter, I can't.' 'Why not?' 'It's my anniversary today and I've got a dinner reservation with my wife and, sorry, I'm taking my wife to dinner. You can handle Harold.' He says, 'We'll figure it out.'

"An hour later I got a phone call from my wife: 'Why am I going to Calgary with Eva and Peter for dinner?'

"I go to see Peter. 'You're a real ass,' I say. He says, 'C'mon, we'll have some fun.' So we take the plane down to Calgary, we go to Hy's Steak Loft and we're having dinner. Then halfway through the dinner, Peter says, 'Okay, Bob and I have got to go across the street to meet with Harold Stark.' We're there for an hour—don't even ask me what the outcome was—then we come back and fly home."

At least Peter picked up the cheque. "'When you travel with the Puck, the Puck pays.' He always said that to me," says Kinasewich. "And when you travel on behalf of the Puck, you go first class. And I remember saying, 'Peter, I don't have to fly first class.' But he would insist."

.   .   .

Anybody who has worked for me—with a few exceptions, I fired the odd one—who was productive and creative knew they would have more opportunity with me than with anybody else.

One such person was Glen Sather, who had not only the responsibility of running Peter's hockey team, but the authority to run it his way—"with one notable exception," Sather once said.

"We never really had any problems," says Sather. "Peter would hire somebody to do the job, and expect them to do it, and he was good at delegating responsibility that way. He didn't interfere an awful lot, though he had an opinion about all sorts of things."

Sather says Peter had a huge ego in those days, but is quick to add: "Most successful people have a huge ego. How can you be successful if you don't?

"Peter was a classic. He could walk into a room, he had a great presence, people knew who he was."

Peter also had a streak of mischievousness that was often misunderstood by people—especially those who were inclined to think the worst of him.

"I can remember some of the dinners we had in Edmonton, he'd start throwing buns around because he got bored," Sather recalls. "Pretty soon, half the restaurant was doing the same thing—and he was just having fun! But you have to have pretty good self-presence to be able to do that, you know, not thinking that you are going to offend people."

One other incident that has stayed with Sather came during the NHL All-Star Game in Quebec City in 1987. Instead of the usual conference matchup, the event involved a two-game series against the Soviet Union national team that was called Rendezvous '87.

There was a parade of NHL executives through downtown Old Quebec, and everybody was in a horse and carriage. NHL president John Ziegler led the procession while the representatives of the Oilers—Peter and Eva Pocklington and Glen and Ann Sather—were in a carriage near the back of the line.

"So we paid the driver $50 to go by everybody to the front of the line. Well, to us it was funny. I mean it was a hoot. But a lot of the guys in that little chain of horses, they were pissed. How could this guy do something like that? Well, we thought it was great, it was a good joke, it was fun. But if you didn't know Peter, you might take it the other way. And I think a lot of times that's what happened."

So, was it a case of rubbing people the wrong way? "I wouldn't say that. I think a lot of people didn't have the sense of humour to handle the things he was capable of handling," says Sather. "Misunderstood may be a better way of putting it."

All of which leads to another popular perception: Peter Pocklington cheats at golf.

The stories are legion around Edmonton, but many sound the same. "I've heard it enough times to know where there's smoke there's fire," notes Oilers executive Kevin Lowe. One that has been circulating for years involves a foursome that paired off into teams playing for cash per hole. Peter was on one of the teams and as he and his teammate approached the green, Peter slyly nudged an opponent's ball into a nearby bunker. One of his opponents called him on it. Peter's response? According to the story, he didn't deny nudging the ball, he just expressed surprise that anyone saw him do it.

Peter doesn't dismiss the story, though he doesn't recollect it in detail either. What he does say is he was often playful, but never dishonest, on the golf course. "I don't cheat," he said.

. . .

Peter does have his soft spots. For many years, he would take kids from Edmonton's inner city to the Oilers' games, even if those games were on the road.

> I took youngsters to other cities in my plane—and had a policeman come with us. The police picked the kids who went—it was always the toughest little buggers in the city, kids that weren't going anywhere, and probably had no chance for success.
>
> I wanted to treat them to something they'd otherwise never have the opportunity to ever think about, let alone do. I enjoyed taking these youngsters into the dressing room to meet the players, but I always left them with a little message that every one of them could become whatever they wish to be. But first, they had to sign a letter that they wouldn't do drugs and would be morally ethical.
>
> Probably over 300 of those kids made the trip over 10 years, and I still hear from some of them. A few of them became quite successful over the years, so it was fun to watch.

. . .

But what family, friends and business associates always agree on is that Peter was his own man—and that man was always in a positive frame of mind.

> I'm my own drummer. So many naysayers in life tell you what you can't do, so don't even try it. I learned early to tune them out. It's like I told the young guys I took to the hockey games: Turn off your hearing aid to the rest of the world and follow your own star, whatever it is. Whatever passion you have, go for it.

"Peter is an exceptional guy, entrepreneurial, vigorous, he is very courageous," says his friend Brian Mulroney. "He doesn't waver, and he pursues his objectives with tenacity."

Says another friend, Wayne Gretzky: "He was like a father—you know, very helpful to all the players."

•   •   •

So with everything on his plate—the car dealerships, the real estate, the trust company, the numerous food-related businesses, why would Peter bother with sports teams? Aside from being the subject of praise by former prime ministers and famous hockey players, that is.

Peter admits he cherished the limelight. Sather points out that there is an element of truth in that. Sports owners have a notoriety other multimillionaires don't.

"You can have all the money in the world, but you'll still stand in line and wait like everybody else to get a reservation in a restaurant," says Sather. "But if you're some kind of a sports celebrity, the doors open a lot easier for you.

"Peter had made plenty of money by the time he bought the hockey team, yet most of the people in Edmonton didn't have a clue who he was. And I'm sure Darryl Katz is the same way. You know, until he bought the Oilers in 2008, nobody knew who he was either.

"Peter wanted to be part of something great, and there is nothing wrong with that."

PART VI

'Holy mackerel, these guys have potential'

Q: Dear Hockey Nut, who is the best right-winger in hockey?
A: Without a doubt, it's Peter Pocklington.
            —*Columnist Chris Zelkovich in the Toronto Maple Leafs'*
                        hockey program, November 12, 1983

Peter Pocklington's stewardship of the Edmonton Oilers did not get off to a good start. Until the day he and Nelson Skalbania bought the Oilers, Peter had been to only one professional hockey game in his life. On his first trip to Northlands Coliseum as the new Oilers' boss, he ended up getting lost.

Peter would find his way soon enough, however, and it didn't take long for he and his players to begin drawing attention to themselves within the rarefied circles of the National Hockey League.

After all, the Oilers had the best player in the NHL, they were among the league leaders in attendance, and they boasted a flamboyant owner who did not hesitate to ruffle feathers—even when the plumage was as colourful as that sported by legendary *Globe and Mail* sportswriter Dick Beddoes.

On November 21, 1979, during the Oilers' first-ever game against the Maple Leafs in Toronto, Peter met the colourful Beddoes in the press box at Maple Leaf Gardens. "He was a cocky old prick," Peter recalls. "He came in with this funny little hat and said something about how could we even think about beating the Leafs."

When Beddoes persisted in casting doubts on the young Oilers and their prospects for success, Peter got his back up—and he made a bold prediction. "Look," he told Beddoes, "we'll win the Stanley Cup in five years, guaranteed."

It was not the customary boast one expects to hear from the owner of an expansion team—especially when expansion teams are notorious for being habitual losers that consider themselves fortunate to make the playoffs after five years. Just ask the Columbus Blue Jackets, who laboured for eight seasons in the league before earning a crack at the post-season. Talk of a championship was beyond the pale, even for Peter.

Not surprisingly, the boast attracted a lot of media attention, and critics began to portray Peter as a lot of hot wind blowing out of the West. But he meant what he said. "I was naive enough to believe it," he remembers. "I just knew it would happen."

Indeed it did—and as the Oilers hoisted the Stanley Cup five years later, the media repeatedly reminded hockey fans of Peter's prediction. It wouldn't be the first time conventional wisdom would underestimate Peter Pocklington.

• • •

The Oilers and the Leafs played to a 4–4 tie on that November night in Toronto, with Wayne Gretzky figuring in all of the Edmonton scoring. That would be as close as the Leafs would get to beating the Oilers for a while. Two months later, in Edmonton, the Oilers defeated Toronto 8–3. Two months after that, back in the Gardens, they dumped the Leafs again, 8–5. That night, before a national television audience, Gretzky posted six points to take over the league scoring race—and he probably would have had more had his wingers not whiffed on so many of his perfect passes.

Gretzky's sixth point came on a beauty goal that left Toronto netminder Mike Palmateer looking foolish. "Has he made a believer out of you yet, Bill?" *Hockey Night in Canada* colour commentator Gary Dornhoefer asked play-by-play man Bill Hewitt.

"He absolutely has," Hewitt responded, the wonder of Gretzky evident in his voice.

• • •

Someone else who was becoming a believer was none other than Harold Ballard, the cantankerous Leafs' owner who had famously asked, "Who the hell are the Edmonton Oilers?" when they were admitted to the NHL. But it wasn't just Gretzky who had Ballard intrigued, or any of the other Oilers for that matter. It was all of them, their entire operation, the building they played in, and the city they called home.

Ballard approached Peter to see if a deal involving Gretzky could be struck—but it wasn't the usual sort of deal that's made in hockey.

• • •

It should be noted that in 1996, Wayne Gretzky came very close to becoming a Toronto Maple Leaf.

At that time, his agent, Michael Barnett, had agreed to terms with Cliff Fletcher, the Leafs' general manager, on a deal that would bring Wayne to Toronto to play out the string on what was, by then, a truly remarkable career.

But according to the *Toronto Star*, Steve Stavro, the Leafs' principal owner of the day—in a move so cynical, it would surely have made Harold Ballard proud—nixed the deal. His reason for saying no? He asked Fletcher, "Would signing Gretzky put any more bums in the seats?"

Well, no, it wouldn't. The Leafs, after all, were sold out for every game. While selling more tickets would hardly be the point of acquiring Gretzky, killing the deal for that reason is but one example of the sort of thinking that lamentably has kept the Maple Leafs mired in mediocrity for the better part of 40-plus years.

Yet 1996 was not the only time No. 99 almost became a Maple Leaf. In 1980, Harold Ballard made a proposal to Peter Pocklington that would have brought not only Gretzky to Toronto, but Mark Messier, Paul Coffey, Jari Kurri, Glenn Anderson, Kevin Lowe—and the rest of the young Oilers.

In what would have been a blockbuster transaction that makes Gretzky's subsequent move to Los Angeles pale by comparison, Ballard and Peter planned for their hockey teams to swap markets. Ballard would move his quickly fading Leafs to boomtown Edmonton, while Peter would bring his up-and-coming Oilers to Toronto— provided, of course, that he also wrote Ballard a cheque for $50 million.

Peter was ready to do the deal in a heartbeat.

"I was actually pretty excited about it," Peter recalls. "I did the numbers. Christ, I would have made a fortune in Toronto."

It was a done deal as far as Peter was concerned—and it was one that no doubt would have thrilled most Toronto hockey fans. At the time, the Leafs' roster was being gutted by general manager Punch Imlach after some relatively successful playoff runs in the mid-to-late '70s under coaches Red Kelly and Roger Neilson. The team still had some talent: Darryl Sittler, Wilf Paiement, Bill Derlago and Rick Vaive led the forwards, while Borje Salming and Ian Turnbull anchored the defence. Czechoslovakian Jiri Crha was taking over in goal after Palmateer bolted for Washington, backed by league veterans Jim Rutherford and Michel (Bunny) Larocque.

But the team was losing ground in the standings after Imlach traded fan favourites Lanny McDonald and Tiger Williams, among a host of others. In 1980–81, they won only 28 games and finished last in their division. They still made the playoffs—only five of the 21 teams didn't in those days—but meekly exited the first round in just three games against the eventual Stanley Cup champion New York Islanders. They were outscored 20–4 in the series.

And while Leaf fans didn't know it at the time, by midway through the next season Sittler, the long-serving captain, would be gone as well—traded to the Philadelphia Flyers.

Yet if ardent Toronto hockey fans would have been disappointed to see Sittler go to Edmonton, they might have recovered in a hurry once Gretzky skated onto the Gardens ice wearing the blue and white of the Maple Leafs. After all, as No. 99 himself argued in the *New York Times* after the 1980–81 season, when a sportswriter suggested to him that Sittler was the NHL's best player: "I outscored Sittler by 50 points. That has to mean something." Actually, he outpaced Sittler by 68 points, but he made his point.

And while Gretzky was already living up to his "great" billing—55 goals and 164 points in his second NHL season—he was just one player on a team of rising young stars that was destined to win the Stanley Cup five times by 1990. By comparison, the Leafs were getting old and going nowhere. Their top players were all older than the Oilers' stars—Sittler was 30, Gretzky only 20. The Leafs would miss the playoffs for three of the next four seasons, and it would be another dozen years before they would even post a winning record.

But if trading the old Leafs for the new Oilers was a good deal for Toronto hockey fans—especially if it also meant bidding adieu to the much-loathed Ballard—it was a really sweet deal for Peter. He was about to be handed the keys to Maple Leaf Gardens—the so-called Carlton Street cashbox—for a "mere" $50 million. That same year, the Atlanta Flames were sold and moved to Calgary for $16 million, and Atlanta was no Toronto. The Leafs played in the biggest hockey market in the world. Given what the Flames were worth, the value of the Toronto franchise would still be a bargain at three times the price.

But aside from the money, why would Ballard do it? What was in it for him?

Peter says he never really knew for sure. But public records from the time suggest Ballard, whose stewardship of the Leafs had been—at best—checkered, desperately needed the cash.

By the beginning of the 1980–81 season, the 77-year-old Ballard's chronic mismanagement of the Leafs had seriously weakened the franchise. He had already been sent to prison for a year for defrauding other company shareholders. Moreover, he had borrowed heavily from the Toronto–Dominion Bank in the early 1970s to buy out his partners—first John Bassett and then the estate for Stafford Smythe; by the 1980s, the cost of that debt was crippling his business. High inflation, stratospheric interest rates and inadequate dividend income left him in danger of losing the Maple Leafs and the Gardens to the bank.

Beyond the $50 million he'd get from Pocklington—money that would make Ballard's cash problems vanish—the Edmonton deal offered other attractions for the Leafs' owner. The Oilers were league leaders in attendance, rivalling the perennially sold-out New York Rangers. They played in a new building with favourable rental terms and considerably more seating than there was in Maple Leaf Gardens, which, by that time, was 50 years old and falling into disrepair. And Edmonton was in the midst of an unprecedented oil boom that meant an expanding customer base of hockey-mad fans with cash in their pockets.

For Pocklington, the benefits were more long term. For Ballard, they were immediate. For fans in Toronto, it might have meant a bunch of Stanley Cups on the horizon. The only ones bound to lose out were the fans in Edmonton. It can only be speculated how they'd have taken to Wilf Paiement wearing No. 99 instead of Gretzky.

Gretzky says he was aware of the deal, though he admits to being hazy on the details. He thought the swap involved the Detroit Red Wings, who by that point were being run into the ground by the Norris family.

But if it was a done deal, as Peter claims, where did it go wrong? "I don't know," Peter says. "Ballard backed out. He was a crazy old bugger."

More probable is that Ballard found another source for the cash. It was around the same time that he recruited Molson Brewery as a partner in the Leafs. According to a history of the Toronto hockey club compiled by Maple Leaf Sports and Entertainment, the Montreal-based brewer paid off the TD loan in exchange for an option to buy up to 20 per cent of Maple Leaf Gardens Ltd. It was a deal that would lead to a decade of power struggles, strife and familial lawsuits within the Ballard family, to be resolved only after Ballard died in 1990.

And, as it turns out, it was the deal that kept Wayne Gretzky out of a Leafs' uniform.

• • •

So Gretzky would stay in Edmonton; so, too, the other Oilers; and so would Peter Pocklington. That suited him just fine. He could just as easily build the NHL's elite organization in Edmonton as he could in Toronto.

Besides, Peter knew the hockey crowds in Toronto weren't the "folks," as he likes to call them—the regular hockey fans he wanted to attract. To his mind, the seats at Maple Leaf Gardens were taken up with too many corporate executives and their fur-bearing mistresses. And the high ticket prices at the Gardens were a reflection of that blue-ribbon clientele.

> You end up with "suits" in the crowd. Those aren't the real hockey fans. The real hockey fans are the folks. In my opinion, if you want to sustain something, and get the folks involved, and cause a ripple effect through the community, you can't do that by making anything elitist.
>
> Look at Walmart. Right now they're the biggest retailer in the world. They do $45 billion in sales because they are good at it, they make you feel good. You walk into their store, and things are not only good value, but they make you feel welcome.
>
> We tried to do that with the Oilers. We always tried to make people feel good and give them a good product and not overcharge them. And it worked.
>
> My friend Jerry Buss—who used to own the Los Angeles Kings and still owns the Lakers—said you should offer value that's equal to three hours of a man's labour. He's going to buy two tickets, and a parking spot, a couple of hot dogs, and maybe a beer. So if a guy's making $20 an hour, you charge him 60 bucks. That's fair value.
>
> So I always tried to price the tickets so a guy could afford to bring his kid to a game. I did play a little bit of Robin Hood though, charging more for the guys that could afford it, the lawyers making $300 an hour.

For players like Gretzky, that approach meant seeing a lot of familiar faces game in and game out.

"You play in Maple Leaf Gardens or you play in the Montreal Forum, you look around the arena and see 15,000, 17,000 fans, and it's different people every game," says Gretzky. "In Edmonton, it was the same 15,000 people almost every night. And so I would look across the ice and if somebody wasn't sitting in their seats, I'd think, wow, maybe they're sick or maybe they're in Hawaii. So you develop this friendship with the community, more so maybe than in any other city."

And what the fans saw was a team that was winning on a consistent basis.

The Oilers made the playoffs in their first year in the NHL. In their second season, they knocked off the Montreal Canadiens in the first round.

"We weren't supposed to do anything against that team," remembers the coach, Glen Sather. "We had all these young guys." But the one young player who made the greatest difference in that series was Andy Moog, the goalie. He had spent most of the season playing for John Muckler on the Oilers' farm team in Wichita. "The Canadiens didn't have a clue who he was—and he's the one who won that series. And the team just got better and better."

Indeed.

"You could start to see it, that 'Holy mackerel these guys have potential,'" recalls Oilers broadcaster Rod Phillips.

The next year, only their third in the league, the Oilers earned 111 points in the standings. The year after that, they went all the way to the Stanley Cup finals before being swept in four straight by the New York Islanders.

"It was like being crushed, not winning," Peter remembers of coming so close, only to be denied. "A lot of us cried."

But the next year, their fifth in the NHL, the Oilers won it all. Their first Cup was clinched on May 19 with a 5–2 win over those same Islanders, who were seeking their fifth straight championship. They took the series in five games, and made good on Peter's prediction five years earlier to the prideful Dick Beddoes.

Oh, it was pretty heady stuff, winning the Stanley Cup. I don't think there's any higher win of anything in Canada than the Stanley Cup, especially after only five years. The whole city went nuts. It was madness, just madness. You experience something like that, you just want to go there again and again.

And the Oilers were truly impressive in their achievement. Gretzky topped 87 goals and 205 points for the season, a performance unmatched by any player, before or since. But he was far from alone. Paul Coffey, a defenceman, had 126 points; Jari Kurri, 113; Mark Messier, 101; and Glenn Anderson, 99. Other teams would consider themselves blessed if they had just one of these guys.

Phillips gives the credit to Sather and Pocklington—and a healthy dollop of good fortune.

"I think probably both Peter and Glen will tell you, when you drafted the way they did, when they started to build the team, you've got to get a little bit lucky," says Phillips. "And I think they would say there were some guys they drafted that turned out to be a helluva lot better than they expected.

"I don't think anybody had any idea what a great player Jari Kurri was going to be. I don't think anybody thought Andy Moog was going to be the goaltender that he was. Mark Messier, they had no idea. He had scored one goal in the WHA the year before they drafted him. Glenn Anderson is another; they had no idea he was going to be as good a player as he was. They were all great players. And then you had Gretz.

"To get four or five guys like that, that's catching lightning in a bottle. It doesn't happen very often and it hasn't happened since."

But the performance of future Hall of Famers didn't diminish the importance of the supporting cast, argues Charlie Huddy, a defenceman for that team. He says other players such as Ken Linseman, Dave Lumley, Willy Lindstrom and, yes, Charlie Huddy were critical to the team's success. "If you ask Gretz, he'd say we had all those great players, but you can't do it without the role players," says Huddy who, 16 years later, would become an Oilers' assistant coach.

"Those guys have to be able to know their roles and do their jobs out there, night in and night out.

"I was fortunate to be in the right place at the right time during my career and be able to come in here and be a role player."

. . .

It was in the glorious aftermath of that first championship that a big part of the Stanley Cup celebration was born. It is now customary for each member of a Cup-winning team to have some one-on-one time with the mug, to take it home to share with friends. That custom began on Peter Pocklington's watch.

"Peter and Glen started that tradition of the players taking the Cup," says Gretzky, recalling the celebration after winning that first championship. "Here we are in the locker room, it's a frenzy for three hours—family, friends, cameras and everything—and everybody starts slowly weeding out and going over to the convention centre for a big party. And I was sort of the last guy there, and I said to Glen and Peter, who were standing there, 'What do we do with the Stanley Cup?' Because in those days, when they handed you the Cup—the Montreal Canadiens and the Islanders—you know, they'd put it up on a mantle or whatever.

"And Glen said, 'Heck, you guys won it, take it.' And so, we took it. And that's how the tradition started." As time went on, the NHL hired someone whose full-time job it is to take care of the Cup, to escort it everywhere, and to see that each player gets it for one day.

The Oilers didn't do it quite that way. "We would just take it as a group—players, teammates, friends—and we'd go all over the city," Gretzky remembers.

"We lost it one time. Well, we didn't really lose it, it was in the trunk of one of the guys' cars. Someone wanted to take the Cup to the children's hospital, and we were all like, 'Do you have the Cup?' 'I don't have the Cup.' So we were all looking for it, and it turned up in one of the guys' trunk from the day before."

. . .

His team's continuing successes left Peter Pocklington feeling pretty good about himself. "Overwhelming confidence," is the way he describes it.

Moreover, he began to develop a bond with many of his young players. In the April 1982 issue of *Saturday Night* magazine, Peter Gzowski describes the interplay Peter shared with Gretzky and Sather:

"In the Edmonton Oilers' dressing room, Pocklington approaches his young star, Wayne Gretzky. The Oilers have just defeated the Quebec Nordiques 11–4, and Gretzky has scored two goals. . . . There is real affection between the two men.

"However there is something else on his mind. Pocklington likes to make small bets with Gretzky, offering long odds against scoring accomplishments. . . . Tonight, he's bet that Gretzky will not score a hat trick—three goals. The young phenomenon has been held to two, and Pocklington has come to collect. Gretzky has no cash in his underwear.

"'Write me a cheque,' Pocklington says.

"'Oh, come on Peter,' says Gretzky.

"'Write me a cheque,' Pocklington insists. 'You've got to learn to pay when you lose.'

"Gretzky takes a chequebook from his jacket. He writes the cheque. . . . [Peter] goes back to the team's office, where he finds Glen Sather, the Oilers' coach, general manager and president. Sather, whom Pocklington describes as his closest friend, is unafraid of Pocklington and enjoys chivvying him. . . . 'Let's see the evidence,' Sather says. Pocklington hands him Gretzky's cheque. Sather takes it and tears it into eight pieces. He throws the pieces on the floor and, chortling, leaves the office.

"Later, Pocklington drives another friend downtown. 'I guess Sather got you this time,' says the friend.

"'Oh yeah?' says Pocklington, and from his pocket produces the cheque, painstakingly Scotch-taped together."

. . .

Peter did not spend a lot of time in the Oilers' dressing room, but when he was there, it was memorable.

> I remember one time before we played L.A., I put $100,000 in cash in a duffel bag and poured it on the ping-pong table before the game. I said, "All right you assholes, this is your loot if you win." Well, they definitely won, but of course somebody told and it got into the press, and I got fined by the NHL. I don't recall how much but, oh, there was a to-do.

"I didn't know the exact amount," remembers Gretzky. "I've never seen $100,000. But Peter was always doing stuff like that. Like the first year we won the Cup, he said, 'If you guys win, I'm going to buy you all brand new golf clubs.' So he got these golf clubs made by Ping with the Oilers logo on them. I still have mine. I hung them up. A lot of guys used theirs but I said, 'I'm not going to use these.'"

"I'm still using mine," laughs Huddy. "They're not worth shit anymore, but I'm using 'em."

After another Cup, says Gretzky, Peter bought everybody a trip for two to Hawaii. "He was always very generous."

There was also the Christmas when Huddy remembers Peter giving every player a sheepskin coat. "This was before we won any Cups, but they all had a little patch on the inside that said: 'Stanley Cup champions,' and then it had '198_' and a question mark. That was pretty cool."

The players would often get a kick out of seeing the owner in the dressing room, says Huddy. "He would come in almost as a friend, really, and have a conversation with you about the game or about your home life or whatever the case may be. But it was always good. He would come out of that owner's lounge with his glass of wine and, as young kids, we'd always get a kick out of that."

"He was always dressed immaculately," remembers Gretzky. "He used to kid about it, too, saying Eva dressed him. We'd say, 'That's a nice suit you got.' He'd say, 'Eva got it.'"

. . .

Of all the players, Peter was closest to his superstar.

"Peter was very good to Wayne, and I don't think Wayne would say anything different," Phillips remembers.

Peter once gave Wayne a Ferrari—presented at centre ice, Peter says. Wayne remembers Peter giving Vicki Moss, Wayne's girlfriend, a car after she quit smoking. Peter also remembers giving Wayne a gold-plated hockey stick when, in 1990, the Great One surpassed the 2,000-point mark.

But Peter best remembers the night of February 24, 1982, when Gretzky broke Phil Esposito's single-season scoring record in Buffalo.

> At the end of the second period, he hadn't broken the record yet, so I said, "You know if you break this record, I will give your girlfriend a new Mustang convertible." Damn if he didn't go and get three goals and beat Esposito's record. And the next day back in Edmonton, he brought Vicki to the showroom at Westown Ford, and I gave her a new Mustang convertible.

On hand that night at Buffalo's War Memorial Auditorium to witness Wayne's 77th, 78th and 79th goals of the season were Canadian movie director Norman Jewison, and actors Burt Reynolds and Goldie Hawn. They were in Buffalo filming the movie *Best Friends*.

The *Hockey News* was there, too. "I still have the pictures with Burt Reynolds and that funny little blond," says Peter.

But the star players didn't get all of Peter's attention, or Sather's. What's not as well known is how the two men reached out when one of their players was in trouble.

Dave Semenko, Dave Hunter and "Cowboy" Bill Flett are the publicly documented cases, but there were others, players with substance-abuse problems who were sent to the Betty Ford Center in Rancho Mirage, California, for treatment—all on Peter Pocklington's tab.

"Peter was the first guy to step up and send guys to the Betty Ford and pay for it," says Sather. "We sent quite a few guys there. Peter was front and centre with all that. He wanted to help them."

In Semenko's case, Peter did even more. According to Peter's lawyer Bob Kinasewich, the Oiler tough guy had been defrauded by someone he trusted, and it cost him more than half a million dollars. "Sather and Peter looked after him," says Kinasewich. "They put him on a budget and helped him work it out."

Of course, there wasn't a drug-testing program in those days, which meant players could get railroaded with little or no proof—and there was little Peter could do. Sather says that's what happened to goalie Grant Fuhr. He was suspended by NHL president John Ziegler after a story in *Sports Illustrated* said Fuhr was a cocaine user.

Sather was outraged. "When Ziegler suspended Fuhr, it was on hearsay from Grant's wife and from (hockey agent) Ritch Winter"— and Fuhr and his wife were divorcing, says Sather. "There was no proof that he'd done anything. He had never been tested, and we had to go to a kind of a kangaroo court in Toronto, where Ziegler was the main guy doing the interview. Grant got suspended for six months for that."

● ● ●

The Oilers were always Sather's responsibility, but if something was important to Peter, he made sure they knew about it.

His enthusiasm for positive thinking was one example. He wanted his players to believe they could be champions, and he called on a former president of the United States to help him:

I took the Oilers down to California every year to play golf with Jerry Ford, and have dinner with him and go to his home and go to his office, so they could hang out with the president. It was to make them feel that if you're an Oiler, you're one of the elite and you guys are going to win. And that all helped bring Stanley Cups.

I also brought in a program called Omega every year, put on by a man named John Boyle. He taught that if you raised your self-concept, your behaviour automatically follows. And this is what Wayne exemplified. His concept was way up here, and of course, his behaviour shot right up beside it.

It was a three-day program and at first, the players really rebelled against it. They'd say, "What the hell is this. We come to play hockey and not get our heads cracked." But believe me, within a year it started to show, when they were all dressed up and on the airplane, they all wore their suits and ties, and they held their heads high. And when it came to negotiating salaries, they'd say, "What do you mean I'm not worth it. I'm the best." So it was a two-edged sword, but it sure as heck won Stanley Cups.

To this day, few players admit they benefited from the experience, either because they already considered themselves positive thinkers or, in some cases, because they thought it was a blatant waste of time.

Gretzky tells a story that confirms the latter:

"We were all 19, 20 years old, right? Peter comes in and says, 'You guys are going to do a seminar for a couple of days.' And we're all like, 'You're kidding me.' So we're over at this hotel and this guy starts talking. Well, he stops about six and a half hours later, right? And I'm like, 'Oh my God.'

"And we got to go do it again the next day. So, we're sitting there— I'm sitting beside Kevin Lowe—and I say, 'Kevin, look at Coff over there.' The speaker gave everybody notebooks, right? And Paul is writing pages and pages. And I'm thinking the last guy I would think is going to get into this is Paul Coffey. So after about two hours, we get a break. And I go, 'Coff, have you been writing all this shit down?'

"'No,' he says. 'I just got Springsteen's new album and I'm writing down all the words to *Born in the U.S.A.*'

"Yeah, Peter really believed in that power of positive thinking."

Lowe admits finding the experience more valuable, but points out he already was a positive thinker. "I do all that stuff naturally," he says. "I envision things and I dream. I'm a positive person, not a negative person, so they don't work on anything I didn't already know. But it's good, there is always something you pick [up] from it."

He does tell the story, however, about a teammate who, like

Coffey, didn't find the talks so fascinating—the Oilers' one-time captain and former head coach, Craig MacTavish:

"We were at the Mayfield Inn. I think the guy's name was Lou Tice. Lou was in there with a pretty motivated group, Stanley Cup champions, and he's saying something about records are going to be broken. Anyway, right at the height of this guy's speech, MacT—he's a pretty black-and-white guy—is in the back and he feigns coughing and he goes, 'Cough, bullshit!' And the whole place just cracks up."

Though the players suggest they were indulging Peter's passion for positive thinking, Sather thinks that, in the end, the message did sink in.

"I think in the beginning, a lot of these guys just thought this is a bunch of crap. But as they got into it, they started to pay attention to it. I think a lot of it sunk in, even though they didn't understand it in the beginning. But you look at what those guys have done with their lives and how they run them today, I think most of it sank in."

He points to the success many of the players from the Stanley Cup era have enjoyed since their playing days ended. On the business side, Coffey, for example, owns two car dealerships. On the hockey side, the list is even longer: Lowe and Kelly Buchberger continue with the Oilers; MacTavish and Huddy have since left the organization, but are in demand elsewhere in the NHL; Gretzky and Fuhr work with the Phoenix Coyotes and Moog with the Dallas Stars; Kurri is the general manager of the Finnish national team; and Mike Krushelnyski coaches in Germany.

"That was Peter's philosophy," says Sather. "There wasn't anything you couldn't do if you believed you were going to do it. It was all positive thinking. A lot of these players may not have bought into it on the surface, but I think privately a lot of them did."

• • •

The players also drew remarkably close. Kinasewich remembers how Gretzky, if invited somewhere, would insist his teammates be invited along.

"Gretzky would get a call to go see Muhammad Ali in L.A. or do something like that, and he'd say, 'You invite me, my boys come with me,'" says Kinasewich. "He was no prima donna, he wasn't a Barry Bonds. You invite Gretz, you invite the whole team."

Gretzky, says Kinasewich, "was a wonderful, wonderful person. Taught by example and the way he lived his life."

He also recalls how all the players were growing up at the same time they were winning championships—and he credits Gretzky and Lowe for the influence they brought to bear. "If it hadn't been for Gretzky and Lowe, guys like Mark Messier, Glenn Anderson, Grant Fuhr, they wouldn't have survived. I really, really believe that. They showed them how to become adults, young adults."

That was especially evident at playoff time, when Peter would host a team dinner before each series and a little party after the games—"nothing too grand," says Kinasewich.

"And these young guys, all of them to a T, were very respectful of anybody who was in the room. They listened to people, they had their pizza or whatever it was and maybe a beer or two, and off to bed they went. I don't think any of them ever drifted off anywhere to do anything. I don't think Gretzky would have allowed it. When it is serious business, it is serious business."

But when it was time to party, they knew how to do that, too, says Kinasewich. "Anybody who thinks otherwise is stupid or naive or both," he laughs. "Seriously, they were young guys, they were virile guys, they were idols wherever they went. Are you kidding me? Give me a break. But they did it discreetly, they didn't flaunt it, publicly, and they were smart about it."

●　●　●

By the mid-1980s, the Oilers dominated the league in a way no team in the modern era has done. They had so much talent, and were coached so well, that teams of more modest means were afraid to play them.

In some cases, the gap between the Oilers and the league's lesser teams was embarrassing. Edmonton finished the 1984–85 season with 119 points; New Jersey had 41; Pittsburgh only 38.

As the radio voice of the Oilers, Phillips remembers what it was like for some of the other teams to come into Edmonton. "They said it was just terrifying from a player's point of view," he recalls. "They'd say, 'We'd come in here ranting and raving about how we can beat these guys, and by the end of the first period, we're thinking we shouldn't even be·on the same ice as them.' They were just so good. It was a nightmare for other teams."

Gretzky remembers thinking their winning ways would go on forever.

"We grew up together, we were frickin' teammates for life, we thought we were going to be here forever," the Great One recalls. He remembers looking at the championship banners hanging from the rafters at Northlands and thinking, "We're going to win eight or nine cups and challenge Montreal and all that kind of stuff."

It didn't happen, of course, and Sather remembers well the day he felt the first inkling the ride was coming to an end. The Oilers had just finished a game in New York and boarded a bus for Philadelphia.

"Wayne was reading an article in the *Sporting News* that compared all the best players in every sport. And hockey was at the bottom, and he was at the bottom of all these superstars." Sather turned to Bill Tuele, the Oilers' public-relations director. "The thing that is going to destroy this team is going to be money," he told Tuele, "because we're a small-market team, and we can't afford to pay what they're going to be worth some day." And that's what happened.

"The first guy to go was Coffey."

Paul Coffey was a dazzling player and the springboard for the Oilers' potent offence. A fluid skater with an eye for putting the puck on a teammate's stick, he was often the player who set up the forwards for their offensive forays. And the statistics reflected that. He regularly posted more than 100 points a season.

Coffey was also a prolific scorer, setting an NHL record for goals by a defenceman, 48 in 1985, and he won the Norris Trophy as the league's best defenceman in both '84 and '85.

"Paul was very innovative and very smart," says Gretzky. "We forget how good Paul Coffey was. Maybe only one other defenceman was better than him and that was Bobby Orr. He was that good."

He was also profoundly unhappy. Coffey and Sather had reached an impasse over Coffey's demand for his contract to be renegotiated, and the defenceman made it known he wanted out of Edmonton.

But first came the 1987 Canada Cup tournament. Coffey was one of five Oilers on Team Canada, and he was instrumental in their victory over the Soviets in the three-game final. The day before the tournament's last game, Gretzky asked his buddy when he'd be returning to Edmonton for training camp. "I'm not," Coffey answered.

"That was the first I heard of it," Gretzky remembers. "And my mouth dropped. And I asked, 'What do you mean, you're not going to Edmonton?' And he said, 'I won't be back as an Oiler.' And I just remember thinking, 'Wow.'"

Sather flew into Hamilton before that final game, and pulled Gretzky aside. "He said, 'Look, we've got to sit down and get Paul onside.' And I think he tried, but Paul just basically said, 'I want out. I'm moving.'"

Coffey refused to play. By mid-season, Sather traded him to the Pittsburgh Penguins, along with Dave Hunter and Wayne Van Dorp. In return, the Oilers received Craig Simpson—who would have his own 50-goal season in Edmonton and was instrumental in the Oilers' Stanley Cup victories in 1988 and 1990—Chris Joseph, Dave Hannan and Moe Mantha. But without Coffey, the Oilers never again moved the puck out of their own zone quite so efficiently.

"Ironically, when I got traded, I remember thinking, 'Geez, I wonder if the guys feel the same way that I felt when Paul Coffey got traded?'" says Gretzky. "But the reason they were able to pick up the pieces was because of their leadership: Kevin, Mark, Jari Kurri, Grant Fuhr. That's why they were able to prolong it."

They were indeed. Broadcaster Phillips thinks they were the best team ever assembled in the NHL. "For five years in a row, that team scored over 400 goals every year," he says. "Now a high-scoring team gets 300. They were, well, a dynasty."

• • •

Throughout those championships years, the bond between Peter Pocklington and Glen Sather strengthened. At times, onlookers said they bickered like an old married couple, but the respect and affection they shared was genuine.

"We were very good friends," Sather recalls from that time. "Peter and Ann and Eva and I, we would do a lot of things together. We were around them a lot, our kids liked them. It was a good relationship."

Rarely did they have serious differences. After all, Sather exercised control of the club, and Peter was loath to change that. "Peter didn't interfere with that stuff," says Sather. "I would consult with him and let him know what was going on, what I was going to do, but he never said, 'No, don't do it.'"

But in 1984, they did have a disagreement over Wayne Gretzky—one that would portend a more serious argument four years later.

Sather was never involved in Gretzky's contracts—they were the only ones he did not negotiate himself. Instead, Peter handled them—as he did when he assumed the contract Nelson Skalbania had drawn up in 1978, and the famous 20-year contract that was signed the following year.

By 1984, a new contract was not only desirable—it would more than double Gretzky's salary—but necessary. Because Gretzky's 1979 deal was a personal services contract with Peter, it did not conform to NHL guidelines and the league wanted it redone. Moreover, Peter had ambitions to take the Oilers public, and a standard NHL contract for Gretzky was required. Only after the negotiations were completed, however, did Peter share the details with Sather. "I can remember him telling me 'Boy, this is a great deal,'" Sather says.

But the general manager was shocked at what he found when he read it. Unlike other Oiler contracts, this one did not include an option clause. When the contract expired in 1989, Wayne Gretzky would be a free agent.

• • •

Whatever trouble lay hidden in Gretzky's contract, it was but a bump in the road in what was otherwise a continuing effort on Peter's part to build up his team.

President Kennedy said, "A rising tide lifts all boats." And any time I could pump up anybody on the Oilers, I did it. That was my job as owner, to get everybody lifted. You can knock off the tall fruit if you're up there with it.

In the process, Peter Pocklington earned the respect of most of his players. "Peter should be proud of what he did," says Huddy. "I was proud to be a player for a team that he owned."

PART VII

'I thought I was bulletproof—until I was shot'

Peter Pocklington thinks he leads a charmed existence. Fate and a Yugoslav immigrant with a gun, an attitude and a plan are about to prove him wrong.

By the time Peter turned 40, every venture he took on had prospered, just as he knew it would. Through a combination of experience, expertise and his own unerring instinct for crafting successful deals, he had amassed a personal fortune worth as much as $150 million. He was the newest golden boy of Canadian commerce.

His triumphs, and particularly in the hothouse of Canadian hockey, had earned him a growing reputation for shrewdness. Not only did he own one of the National Hockey League's best teams, but also the game's most dynamic player. Peter was even travelling in the same circles as his exceptionally talented protege. Celebrity had embraced Peter—and he was returning its mercurial affections.

In his own mind, Peter Pocklington had come to believe he was not only infallible, he was invincible. All that changed on April 20, 1982: Hitler's birthday, as Peter recalls with a laugh.

• • •

I really thought I was God's gift to mankind until the day I met Mirko Petrovic, the Yugoslav immigrant who was about to prove I wasn't so invincible after all. He was 29, a former contractor who broke into our home with a plan to kidnap my wife Eva. That was poor judgment on his part, but it set off a chain of events that would eventually leave me lying on the kitchen floor, covered in blood—shot by the very police who were sent there to save me.

When that happened, I thought "Me? This is happening to me?" Talk about an egotist. But it proved to be a defining moment in my life. Nothing would be the same, or seem so simple, ever again.

I thought I was bulletproof—until I was shot.

. . .

The Pocklingtons lived in a seven-bedroom Tudor-style mansion at 8638 Saskatchewan Drive in Edmonton. All the homes in the tony south-side neighbourhood possess a majestic view of the North Saskatchewan River as it flows through the heart of the city and on toward Hudson Bay.

It was a typical spring day for Edmonton. There was still snow on the ground in places, but the temperature was mild under a shining sun and an azure blue sky.

The Pocklingtons' 5-year-old son Zach had already left for school, accompanied by a 21-year-old American houseguest, Joseph Wright, who had become the boy's babysitter. By 9:45, Peter was in the kitchen finishing breakfast before making the short drive to his downtown office, located in the penthouse of the Sun Life Building. He kissed Eva and walked out to the attached garage. As he opened the door to his Rolls Royce, a figure—wearing a black balaclava over his head with green trim around the eyes—stepped from the shadows. There was a flash of metal and Peter gasped.

. . .

This guy cocked a chrome-plated .357 Magnum and held it to my head. "Do as I tell you," he said, "or I'm going to kill you."

My blood instantly ran cold. But I also realized, quickly, thank

God, that if I didn't take control of the situation, I would soon be dead. I paused for 10 seconds or so—though it seemed much longer—then said, "fine," and led the gunman back into the kitchen.

Eva had her back to me, talking on the phone. She turned and saw me standing by the door, a gun to my head. She screamed and dropped the phone. It fell hard, clanging as it hit the tile floor. She picked it up and put it back on its receiver.

The stranger told us to sit, but I wasn't about to let him tell me what to do. I screwed up my courage—or ignored my fears; I'm not sure which—and told him no.

"Obviously you're here for money," I said, "so the first thing I want you to do is uncock the gun, or we don't talk."

I looked into the gunman's eyes. They were beady as blazes. He was upset that I would dare tell him what to do, but when I pointed out that if anyone was hurt, there wouldn't be any money, he quickly changed his mind. He uncocked the weapon and put it on the table. He also put down the bag he was carrying, then pulled a knife from it, along with some wire.

"Is there anybody else in the house?" the gunman asked me in a Slavic accent. He had a stocky build, 5-foot-10, maybe 5-foot-11, about 190 pounds, still wearing the mask, dressed in blue jeans and an army jacket.

I told him about Joe, the young man who had returned after taking Zach to school, and our housekeeper, Carmen Mitchel. She was tidying up in the living room. They were brought into the kitchen, and together we all sat around the table.

"How much is it you want?" I asked. The man said $5 million. "Then you came to the wrong house," I quickly said, shaking my head. "I don't have $5 million."

That's when the gunman said he'd come to kidnap Eva and hold her for ransom—and he was determined to get his $5 million. "It isn't going to happen," I insisted.

The gunman glared. "What do you mean it isn't going to happen?"

By this time, I had decided to call the gunman Joe—"because I don't know who you are and I don't want to know." I told him I'd give him $1 million. Joe grew more agitated, insisting on the five. "Go somewhere else," I said. "I don't have five to give you."

At that point Eva spoke up in a nervous, squeaky voice that always reminds me of Edith Bunker: "Would you like a cup of coffee?" she asked the masked man.

I told her to stifle it. "Eva, be quiet," I said. "We're doing a deal here."

We dickered some more before finally settling on a $2-million ransom. "I think I have a couple of million in my bank account," I told him. Joe agreed he could live on that, and herded everyone into the living room. He told Joe Wright, Zach's babysitter, to use the wire to tie me to a chair—my hands behind his back—and then to do the same with Mrs. Mitchel. The gunman then tied up Joe. Then he told Eva to get dressed—she had been wearing only a dressing gown—and he led her upstairs to change into something else. He watched as she put on blue jeans and a T-shirt. It bore the words "I (Heart) NY" on the front.

As they came down the stairs together, the phone started to ring. It was my secretary, Irene Gunter.

• • •

When the gunman had first come into the house with Peter, Eva was on the phone with her best friend Marilyn Reynolds—"A bright girl, thank goodness," recalls Peter. When Eva screamed and dropped the phone, then hung up, Marilyn called Irene Gunter and told her she thought there was something seriously wrong at the Pocklington house. Irene in turn called her boss. Eva answered.

"Eva, is everything all right?" asked Irene.

"Claire, I just can't make lunch. Sorry, goodbye," Eva said abruptly. Then she hung up. Irene called the cops. Soon, the city police were headed to the Pocklington house—and so were the local media.

Harry Knutson, the president of Pocklington Financial and

Peter's right-hand man, flew out of his office and raced to the scene when Irene told him what had happened. Meanwhile, the police instructed Bob Kinasewich, Peter's corporate counsel, to say nothing to the media when they called.

"I was told to deny that we knew there was anything untoward going on," Kinasewich recalls. "I had reporters saying, 'Are you stupid?' I'd say, 'Maybe, I don't know.' 'Well, is Peter in the office?' 'No.' 'Well, doesn't that cause you concern?' I'd say, 'He's the boss!'

"I had to make up these stories because the police didn't want this guy getting any publicity."

It would soon be too late for that.

• • •

By the time Eva got off the phone with Irene, it was almost 10:30. "Look, this is the deal," the gunman told me. "I'm going to kidnap your wife and take her wherever, then I will phone you at 8 o'clock tonight and you'd better have the $2 million. I will tell you where you are going to deliver it."

The man held his gun on Eva. This time, I figured I wasn't in a position to argue.

There were two cars in the garage, my Rolls and Eva's Porsche. In the driveway was a Ford Bronco SUV. That was the vehicle the gunman wanted for his getaway. So he told Eva to back the Porsche out of the garage and bring the Bronco in. He planned to put her in the back seat and cover her with throw rugs he had her gather up from around the house. They walked out to the garage together, Joe's .357 on Eva the whole time. "If you try to escape, I'm going to kill you," he told her.

• • •

Eva did what she was told, and drove the Porsche to the end of the driveway. When she got there, she saw a police officer standing right behind her fender. She jumped out of her car, saw Knutson, and ran

towards him, screaming something about a guy in the house with a
gun. "You mean Peter shot somebody?" asked the cop.

Joe watched as Eva make good her escape, then flew into a rage.
Discovering the door into the house had locked automatically behind
him only made his mood worse. He broke a window to get back in,
then stormed into the living room. "Well," he declared to Peter, "I
guess I'm going to have to kill you and everybody else here."

. . .

If I was to save our lives, I was going to have to think fast. "Joe, this
is the best thing that's ever happened to you," I told him. "This is
your fortunate day. Have you ever heard of D.B. Cooper?"

"What do you mean by that?" asked Joe. He was still seething.

"Well, there was a fellow named D.B. Cooper who hijacked a
jet out of Washington state and parachuted out of the plane with a
couple of million." Actually, it was more like $200,000, but by this
time, I was on a roll. "He got away and nobody has heard from him
since."

Quickly, I hatched a plan. "Look, I have a jet at the airport.
We'll make sure the police deliver the $2 million, then you and I go
to the plane and we'll fly into the U.S. The Americans have military
airports all over the place; a lot of them are abandoned. We'll fly
low and get into one, drop you off and you're gone."

Joe thought that was a helluva deal—maybe because he had no
other choice. But whatever the reason, he said, "That's how we'll
play it."

The phone started ringing again. This time, the police were on
the line. It was Detective Jim Cessford, who I was to later learn
specialized in hostage negotiations. Joe held the phone to my ear.
"Hello," I said.

"I understand you have a problem," said the detective.

"Yeah, but I think it can be solved," I replied. "We are well on
the way to getting this deal put together."

I explained the details of my plan: the police should call my secretary, who would tell them how to contact my pilots. I also gave them instructions to contact the Royal Bank, where I did most of my business. "They will arrange the couple of million and get this in motion," I said.

"Fine," replied Cessford, who promised to call back. He was good for his word.

•   •   •

According to the *Edmonton Journal*, the police made 15 separate calls to the house that day, lasting anywhere from two minutes to an hour. Their plan was to stall the hostage negotiations for as long as possible, to force Peter and Joe to spend time together, thereby giving them enough time to bond. The plan seemed to be working.

•   •   •

By this point, it was 11 in the morning. Joe had moved me to the third floor, leaving the housekeeper and the babysitter downstairs. When the phone rang again, the police said they had made contact with the pilots. The next time it rang, they told him they were having trouble finding the $2 million in cash. "This is not a big city," I reminded Joe. On and on, the calls continued, the police stalling for time; 11 o'clock became 11:30, then noon. I grew frustrated with the constant delays, and told Cessford, "Let me talk to Eva."

They put my wife on the line. "Eva, tell these crazy SOBs this is what I do for a living. Tell them to listen to me, tell them to get this done, tell them to get us to the airport."

"Peter, you know what they're like," Eva told me.

"I know what they're like, but be strong. Tell them this is what's going to happen."

One of the police negotiators called back. "Now look," said the cop, "we have this under control."

"Yeah, sure," I replied.

Then Joe grabbed the phone. "I want this to happen by 1 o'clock," he said, "or I'm going to kill everyone."

A few minutes later, Cessford called Joe back. "If you want any co-operation from us, you've got to release the two people downstairs," he said. Joe agreed. He went downstairs, released Joe Wright and Mrs. Mitchel, and then came back. The calls continued. So did the negotiating. The 1 o'clock deadline was fast approaching and I don't mind admitting I was getting a little worried. I was sure this guy was manic depressive, and my only hope was to keep him calm enough and stable enough not to panic and start shooting.

Finally, the deadline came . . . and went. I knew I needed to remind my captor that everything was going to work out exactly as we planned. I also knew I couldn't let him see my own doubts. "Joe, this thing is going to go together," I said, assuring him—or maybe me. "There is no question we're going to get this handled. Besides, you don't have a helluva lot of choice, so cool your heels and let's get this done."

• • •

One o'clock became 1:30, then 1:45, then 2:00. A helicopter flew overhead. The police cordoned off the streets around the house, the Groat Road Bridge was closed to traffic, and joggers were even denied access to nearby Hawrelak Park.

By the time the afternoon rush hour began, traffic was backed up across the river and into the downtown area. It was taking motorists more than half an hour to get across the High Level Bridge to the south side.

Despite the precautions, a crowd had begun to gather. Some brought lawn chairs; others came equipped with cameras, binoculars, and telescopes. At one point, Peter looked out the window to see the street, boulevards and lawns covered with more than 1,500 people— and a caterer. The fellow was doing a brisk business, too, selling sandwiches, coffee and pop.

"I'm doing better in half a day than I usually do in two days," the intrepid caterer, Joe Ewing, told the *Journal*. He said he made about $700 in a few short hours.

. . .

"Hey Joe, I think there's a guy out there selling T-shirts," I said as I looked out the window. "Free enterprise sure does work."

But by this time I was getting tired, and the Stockholm Syndrome was beginning to take hold. It's this insidious emotional state named for an incident at a bank in Sweden where the captives—tellers and the other bank employees—began to develop sympathy, even a loyalty, towards their captors during the six days they were held hostage. I didn't know it at the time, but as I watched Joe go to the window, I grew concerned for his safety. "For God's sake, get down or they'll shoot you," I finally told him at one point.

As the hours continued to pass, I asked if Joe's mother would approve of what he was doing, and I gave it to him for resorting to extortion to get his money. "You could have come to me and we could have done a business deal and we probably would have made more," I said—and I meant it, too. Joe had been in the cement business in Fort McMurray before coming to Edmonton and falling on hard times.

"And now we're into this. My idea is to get you out of this and you keep your $2 million. You learn something and you can get away . . . we'll get it done," I vowed. I fervently believed it, too.

By 7 o'clock, I had been tied up for more than nine hours. Truth be told, I thought my bladder was about to burst. "Look, Joe, I've got to pee," I said. How he responded was not what I expected, and I admit it was embarrassing. It still is. But Joe grabbed a Coke bottle, unzipped my fly, pulled me out and told me to pee in the bottle.

At 8:30, nearly 11 hours after the hostage crisis had begun, the phone rang with the news the $2 million was downstairs in the kitchen and a ride to the airport was waiting for us. "Finally," I thought. I remember looking at the window, and thinking I had never seen a sunset so beautiful. It was the first time a sunset had made that kind of impression on me.

Joe pulled me to my feet by the wire binding my hands. It was digging into my skin. Then he stuck the Magnum into my back and we slowly started going down the stairs—the first flight, then the second—towards the main floor.

I could feel the tension in the house. It was incredible. It was only later that I learned a four-member team of Edmonton's elite police task force had snuck in some time around 6 o'clock—but I did know someone was there. You could just tell. I called out to them:

"I know you're here. For God's sake, this guy's got a gun in my back. Stay away."

We reached the bottom of the stairs. Joe looked in the front hall, the living room, the den. But he didn't look in the dining room; that's where the tactical team was hiding.

We went into the kitchen—and there was the suitcase, containing $2 million in 20-dollar bills. Joe ordered me to pick it up, but it was too heavy, especially since my hands were still tied behind my back. It must have weighed 90 pounds. I put it back down.

Just as I straightened up again, I saw one of the tactical cops burst through the door, his M16 rifle aimed at us. "Halt, police!" said the cop. And then he fired.

.   .   .

Several press accounts at the time said that the police shot Joe, and that the same bullet then struck Peter. "The bullet passed through the gunman's body and wounded Mr. Pocklington in the arm," reported the *New York Times* in a story filed by the Associated Press. The *Edmonton Sun* wrote that when the bullet hit both men, Joe was wounded in the arm, Peter in the arm and chest.

In fact, just the opposite happened. The police shot Peter. The same bullet then hit Joe.

• • •

The bullet from the M16 struck me in the arm. It was a .22-calibre bullet with a .30-calibre jacket, charging at me with 4,000 foot-pounds of pressure at the muzzle.

When a bullet like that hits flesh, it begins to tumble. It went through my arm, missing my bone by a hair. If it had hit the bone, my arm would have been gone because the bullet would have smashed it. Instead, the bullet started to spin, and I still have a scar in my back from where it came out.

The bullet then hit Joe in the arm, but at the time I can't say I noticed. The weight of the bullet is like being hit by a car, or maybe a sledgehammer. My ass was on the floor like "BANG!" My hands were still tied up, so my head hit the floor and I was knocked out for a minute.

What wasn't reported was that Joe's gun also went off. It was from the weight of me hitting him as I fell back. If I hadn't hit him, though, and he pulled the trigger, he would have shot me in the middle of the back and I'd be dead. Or the cop, if I had swung too far after I put down the money, he'd have hit me in the heart instead of the arm.

I came to, and suddenly felt the worst pain in my life. At first, I didn't know what had happened, but then the horror and shock of it all began to set in. I looked down—I was covered in blood. "Shit, I've been shot," I thought. "They hit *me*?" And then I started to belt out the worst obscenities to these cops I've ever heard myself use—just the frustration of the day, you know?

"Do you know who you just shot, you assholes?" I yelled.

The cops descended on Joe, who lay three or four feet behind me, his arm almost torn off by the M16's bullet.

• • •

In the aftermath of the shooting, one of the task force members was asked by a *Journal* reporter what was happening and if it was serious.

"There's so much blood and gore at the scene, I can't tell," the cop replied.

Meanwhile, the hostage drama unfolded live across Canada on television. It was particularly traumatic for Peter's three children in Ontario, who watched as events unfolded 4,000 kilometres away. The story led the nightly national newscasts, and dominated the next day's front pages.

In the States, Max Robinson gave a report of the incident on the supper-hour *ABC World News Tonight*, and Ted Koppel relayed the drama to his late-night viewers on *Nightline*.

Later, Peter was asked to do a re-enactment of the incident for a TV newsmagazine—"*20/20* or some damn thing, I forget"—but he declined. "I didn't need the publicity."

● ● ●

The University of Alberta Hospital is only six blocks from our house, so it didn't take long before two ambulances showed up. Poor Eva knew very little about what had happened to me. Like everyone else, she heard a shot, but she hadn't been told much more than "Peter's been hit." The police drove her to the hospital, where she waited for the first ambulance to arrive. But it wasn't me inside, it was Petrovic.

"Sorry, ma'am," he told her.

Eva had already phoned the Oilers' team doctor, Gordon Cameron, who was in the emergency ward by the time I arrived—along with what seemed like 25 other doctors, nurses and assorted onlookers. What happened after that is a bit of a blur, but I tell you, I was in a huge amount of pain and shock.

I was also pretty cranky. They put me on this table. Then some young intern came at me with this thing. I was covered with blood and they thought my chest cavity was full of blood, and they have a brace with a spike in it that they ram into you to suck the blood out so you won't die, so your lungs won't fill with blood.

Well, I took a swing at the intern, but I missed. "Get the hell

Centre ice at Northlands Coliseum provides the setting as Peter Pocklington signs Wayne Gretzky to a 20-year, $5-million contract on January 27, 1979. From the left are Wayne's mother, Phyllis, and father, Walter; Wayne; Peter; Oilers' general manager Larry Gordon; and public-address announcer Gord Ross.

— Ken Orr, *Edmonton Journal*

Glen Sather is nearly knocked out of Peter Pocklington's boat Free Enterprise during a world championship powerboat race on Alberta's Smoky River in 1978. Sather recalls he was so sore the next day, he couldn't move.

— Jim Cochrane, *Edmonton Journal*

On June 5, 1997, Peter Pocklington leaves the news conference where he announces the Alberta Treasury Branches is calling his loan, forcing him to put the Edmonton Oilers up for sale. — Larry Wong, *Edmonton Journal*

Mere weeks after announcing the ATB is calling its loan and forcing him to sell the Oilers, Peter presents graduation awards to students at McCauley School in Edmonton's inner city. Joining Peter and the prize-winners is Oilers' forward Dean McAmmond.

— Ed Kaiser, *Edmonton Journal*

Famed Italian tenor Luciano Pavarotti joins Peter to meet the media at the Hotel Macdonald in Edmonton on December 1, 1995. Pavarotti's sold-out performance in the Edmonton Coliseum is his first in Canada in more than a decade.　— Larry Wong, *Edmonton Journal*

Peter Pocklington and his captain Wayne Gretzky hug at centre ice on October 11, 1984, the night Peter presents the players with their first Stanley Cup rings.

— Chris Schwarz, *Edmonton Journal*

In the spring of 1983, the entrepreneur Peter Pocklington becomes the politician Peter Pocklington by announcing his candidacy for the leadership of the Progressive Conservative Party. He later likens the experience to "Don Quixote, tilting at windmills."

— Keith McNichol, *Edmonton Journal*

Peter bids goodbye to former British prime minister Margaret Thatcher after they have lunch together at the Westin Hotel in Edmonton on February 24, 1997. Thatcher is one of Peter's idols.

— Mario Pietramala, *Edmonton Journal*

Emotions run high in the summer of 1986 when Peter clashes with a militant union at his Edmonton meat-packing plant, Gainers. On July 16, strikebound protesters are waiting for Peter at the airport as he and a group of friends return to Edmonton from a fishing trip in the Northwest Territories.

— Mike Pinder, *Edmonton Journal*

out of my face with that goddamn thing," I yelled. "Gordon, get
everyone of these goddamn people out of here now."

Dr. Cameron asked everyone to leave. He and a nurse cleaned
the wound, gave me a tetanus shot and a painkiller and, well, I
pretty well floated out of there.

I was in the hospital for three days, though I admit I was a
little much as a patient. I even had Eva arrange to have food
brought in because I wasn't going to eat the crap they serve in
hospitals. But if I was a demanding patient, it was only because I
was so pissed off that someone would shoot me.

The night I was released from hospital, with my arm still in a
sling, Eva and I went to Renfrew Park to watch the Edmonton
Trappers, the minor league baseball team I owned. There were
5,000 or so people at the game and, God, they gave me a standing
ovation. I couldn't believe it.

•   •   •

Gretzky was in Finland at the time. The Oilers had been eliminated
from the Stanley Cup playoffs in the first round in 1982—remember
the Miracle on Manchester?—so he was playing with Team Canada at
the world hockey championships, along with his best friend and Oiler
teammate Kevin Lowe.

Distance proved to be no impediment in hearing the news. "Oh,
it was shocking to us," Gretzky recalls. "But to hear the stories of how
it unfolded, only Peter Pocklington could have done that.

"I've got to be honest with you, if I'm sitting there with a guy who
has a gun on me—first of all, I would have wet my pants, you know?
And Peter was negotiating with this guy with a gun to his head? I
remember thinking, 'You're nuts. I couldn't talk if a guy had a gun to
my head.'

"I wouldn't have the presence of mind to want to negotiate. I
would have just said, 'Please let me go.'"

•   •   •

A few weeks later, my insurance company flew in a former FBI agent to show us how to improve security around our home. While he was there, the FBI guy said something interesting: 4 per cent of the population is psychopathic, he said, and 6 per cent is sociopathic. In other words, 10 per cent of the population is nuts, just plain nuts. It shocked me that these people have no inner voice to say what's right and wrong. That's why we have crime, because these people don't understand right and wrong.

There was something else the FBI agent told me that I've never forgotten. Before Petrovic broke in, there had been a white van parked near our house for several days in a row. At the time I wondered why it kept showing up every day, but chalked it up to coincidence. "Look, whenever you see anything more than once, it is absolutely not a coincidence," said the FBI agent. "There are no coincidences in life, period. Guaranteed."

Mirko Petrovic was sentenced to 15 years in prison. I got a chuckle out of that. In the States, he'd get life.

So I wasn't surprised when, about five years later, the warden of the prison in Ponoka called to tell me Petrovic had been a model prisoner and they wanted to release him and send him back to Yugoslavia. I agreed, as long as he was never let back into Canada. But a few days before Petrovic was supposed to leave, he called me. "Mr. Peter"—he always called me that—"I need $10,000 so I can buy a gravel truck and I can become gainfully employed again." I agreed to help and wired him the money. What the hell, why not? Maybe it was the Stockholm Syndrome still working its power. Or maybe I felt sorry for old Mirko. And I suppose maybe it was a little insurance he'd never come back and go after me again. I don't know.

It was a year and a half or so before I heard from Petrovic again. He told me he was doing construction work in Yugoslavia and by that time had two trucks. After that, I never heard from him again. Nevertheless, I knew I had made a big impression—and perhaps a lasting one—on my one-time captor.

The secret to my ability to sell anything to anybody is to get as

close to them as I can, and I did my damnedest to get very close to
Mirko. He considered me a friend after that. He said I was the
nicest man he'd ever met.

• • •

Years later, one of the police negotiators told the *Edmonton Sun* he
believed Petrovic could have been lured out of the house without
gunfire. But, according to the newspaper, the cops negotiating with
Peter and Petrovic didn't know there were members of the elite team
inside the house. That breakdown in communication prompted a
review of the procedures for handling such circumstances, the
newspaper wrote, and the creation of the position of central
commander who is responsible for coordinating police actions in
this sort of crisis.

Though Peter has a high regard for the police in Edmonton, he
wasn't impressed with how his case was resolved.

• • •

I still believe it was handled badly. You don't have a cop roar in and
say "Halt, police!" then "Bang!" and shoot from the hip with an
M16—let alone use an M16.

I don't remember if the elite force members were outfitted like
the SWAT teams you see on TV, but I do remember the bulletproof
Kevlar vests, the brigs and boots. They looked like Hitler's
stormtroopers! And I sure as hell will never forget the shock and
pain that comes with realizing you've just been shot!

That mental side of it is huge. The venom coming from my
soul at that time—I was lying on the floor, it was the worst pain I
ever felt . . . something like that stays with a guy. You see somebody
shot on TV, and they get up again, right? Well that's impossible.

The X-ray showed that the bullet missed the bone in my arm
by maybe a millimetre. A millimetre! There has got to be a better
way to take out that kind of situation than shooting an M16. I still

resent how the police handled the situation. Here we live in a
peaceful civil society and you get shot by a cop?

Nevertheless, I do feel blessed, as if a guardian angel was
watching over me. If I hadn't been hit in the arm and pushed into
Petrovic, knocked him back so that his gun went off where it did, I
would have been dead anyway. So, you know, it turned out and I
still have my arm. I can still play golf.

About a week after the crisis, I invited Edmonton police chief
Robert Lunney to my office for lunch. The chief had told a news
conference after the shooting that it was the task force's duty to fire
a shot at first opportunity. I have to tell you, that didn't sit well with
me. I said to him, "Chief Lunney, I'd really like to try and
understand what happened. Why the hell didn't you listen to me?"

"Well, we thought maybe you were wired with explosives,"
Lunney replied.

"That's bullshit," I said. "I would have said something if I was.
You know, I'm a businessman. This is what I do for a living. I
negotiate deals. I negotiate everything I do.

"Everything in life is a deal. You should have listened to me."

PART VIII

'I was Don Quixote, tilting at windmills'

Despairing for his country given the "socialist" policies of Prime Minister Pierre Trudeau, and inspired by the prospects for the Progressive Conservative Party to form the next government, Peter Pocklington embraces politics and declares himself a candidate for the PC leadership. He brings with him a host of ideas that might not seem so unusual now but at the time were deemed too radical. He loses, yet in the process, he helps ensure that not only does Brian Mulroney win, but that Joe Clark loses.

In 1976, Peter and Eva Pocklington welcomed a special guest to the ski resort Peter owned on Tod Mountain, near Kamloops. The guest was the prime minister of Canada, Pierre Elliott Trudeau.

By all accounts, the skiing was enjoyable. The rest of the experience, at least for Peter, wasn't as great. What he did that day was listen—something that didn't always come easily. What he heard led him to the unshakeable conviction that the leader of Canada's government was more than just your NDP-friendly, pink Canadian socialist. To hear Peter Pocklington tell it, Pierre Trudeau was a Maoist.

"I will guide the ship of state with such skill, the destination will not be known until we arrive," Peter recalls Trudeau once saying. On this trip, which came shortly after the prime minister and his wife had returned from a state visit to Cuba, Trudeau expressed high regard for Fidel Castro, despite the fact the Cuban leader evidently "had a keen interest in my wife."

Peter heard enough that day to convince himself his country needed him.

I had always thought politics was something I would eventually want to be part of. I loved it, loved the politicians, the good ones anyway, the leaders who were successful.

I think politics is one of the highest callings a free society should place on anyone, especially selfless politics, as my friend President Ford had shown. And I so much admired Jerry Ford, and so much despised Trudeau—not the man, but his thoughts, his Maoism.

But it was only after Eva and I skied with Trudeau on Tod Mountain that I thought, "My God, I've got to do something about this SOB."

Then I saw what happened with the big jump in the prime lending rate and the almost complete collapse of Alberta's economy because of the National Energy Program. That showed me how politicians can destroy what businessmen create, including the jobs people need to survive. Without a strong economy we end up in a dictatorship—that's how critical it was to me.

That's why I took a crack at politics. If not me, I asked myself, then who?

• • •

By the fall of 1982, Peter had begun to cultivate a national reputation— thanks in part to Wayne Gretzky and his Oilers, but also due in part to the hostage crisis he and Eva endured the previous spring. But something else spurred him on, too.

With Trudeau's Liberals sinking in the polls, and his own profile growing, Peter felt this was the time to embark on a cross-country speaking tour to expose what he thought was Trudeau's destructive governance of the nation, while laying the groundwork for his own possible future in politics.

On November 4, he addressed a receptive audience at the Empire

Club in Toronto. "I'm not here to bash (Trudeau) the man, but his basic philosophy of state socialism," Peter told the crowd. "His solutions are bankrupting us."

Peter continued:

Thirteen years ago, Trudeau went on national television in a major press conference to talk to the Canadian people about inflation and the country's financial future. He said then, "We would be on the way to financial disaster if nothing were done to bring spending under control. To spend vast sums on welfare, education, and other programs while allowing inflation to continue would merely place hundreds of Canadians on a treadmill they could not escape."

The prime minister also committed his government to a substantial cut in the federal civil service.

What has happened since August 14, 1969? Government spending has increased by $65 billion—a 400-per-cent increase! The federal civil service has increased by 300,000 individuals. That's double what it was!

In the last 14 years, our government has created a collectivist or statist society where rights and privileges, freedoms and responsibilities, are being destroyed for the sake of rules, regulations and bureaucratic control.

In 1968, Canada was the third industrial power. Today, in 1982, Canada is the fourteenth industrial power. In 1968, the Liberal Party was a force to be reckoned with in Western Canada. It was the party of laissez-faire capitalism that also looked after the poor. Today, in 1982, the Liberal Party has destroyed itself west of Ontario and is headed to the far left of the political spectrum—in fact, left of the NDP platform of 1968.

In 1968, Canada produced a strong dollar, inviting foreign investment. We were a country on the verge of sailing into the future with little or no worry about jobs, inflation or energy. Today, in 1982, we have a government close to bankruptcy. Our ship is sinking!

This government has little regard for our basic liberties and no respect for the concept of private initiative, private opportunity, or private ownership. What this government understands is state socialism—a form of government in which government runs virtually everything, and what it doesn't run, it cripples by over-regulation. In effect, they are trying to change Canada, and we must ask ourselves, "Are we going to let them?"

As someone who never shied away from making headlines, Peter gained satisfaction from the positive press he was getting. But as someone who grew up in a Liberal household, and whose father was still an ardent Liberal supporter, Peter didn't find it easy to be so harsh.

Nevertheless, he had come to think of himself as a libertarian, someone who sought to minimize the state's involvement in people's lives. And the Liberals of the 1980s—despite Trudeau's earlier admonishment that "the state has no business in the bedrooms of the nation"—were certainly not that.

But if Peter was to fashion a future in politics, and it wasn't going to be with the Liberals, then who? The New Democratic Party was out of the question, despite a familial link. "Tommy Douglas was a cousin of my mother's, but he was a total commie," Peter says. No, if there was any party most closely aligned with his sympathies for less government and more wealth creation, it was the Progressive Conservatives.

There was only one problem. The Conservatives already had a leader, Joe Clark—and Peter didn't think much of Joe Clark.

"I thought Clark was a disaster," Peter recalls. "Nothing personal, he was just a bad guy for Canada. He was not even Conservative, and he certainly wasn't a libertarian. He was as socialist as Trudeau was, he just didn't let on." Peter soon found himself railing publicly against Clark as much as he did against Trudeau.

Not surprisingly, the next time Peter was in Ottawa, he was asked to visit Stornoway, the official residence of the leader of the Opposition.

I went to Stornoway and had breakfast with Clark and his wife. He asked me, "Peter, why are you doing this?"

I said, "Joe, what do you mean why am I doing this?" I said, "I love Canada, I want to make it great, you know, I want to change it. And if you want to change it, Joe, you're going to have to change your ways. You're going to have to become a Conservative."

Oh, was he pissed off with me for that. But he was nice about it.

In the world of politics, being nice wasn't always an asset. The Conservatives were planning a convention in Winnipeg in January of 1983, at which the delegates would be asked for a review of Clark's leadership. Peter saw opportunity in that vote.

Technically, all Clark needed to stay on as party leader was for a majority of the votes to be cast in his favour. Certainly, support of two-thirds of the delegates would have been seen by most Conservatives as a sufficient enough mandate for Clark to continue. Brian Mulroney, Clark's eventual successor as Tory leader and future prime minister, certainly felt that way.

If it was Mulroney who had earned the support of two-thirds of the delegates, "I would have looked out at a hall crowded with Tories and thanked them for such a wonderful validation of my leadership," he wrote in his *Memoirs*.

But Clark saw it differently.

Maureen McTeer, Clark's wife, wrote in her own autobiography, *In My Own Name*, that her husband felt he needed 75-per-cent support to continue in the job. In *Memoirs*, Mulroney wrote that Clark pegged the magic number at 70 per cent. Whichever one it was, Peter Pocklington was determined to do his part to ensure the Tory leader fell short of reaching it.

In the end, "Clark blew it in Winnipeg—and I helped him blow it," says Peter.

About a month before the convention, I had an opinion poll done by a friend of mine that asked, "What would happen if John Turner instead of Trudeau was the opposition to Joe Clark; which one would you vote for?" And people said, "Oh hell, we'd all vote for John Turner."

So I had a Gallup poll done—to give it a little more credibility—that asked the same question: Clark or Turner? Again, Turner won hands down. So on the night before the vote on Clark's leadership, I had my agent pass the results around the convention. It killed Joe.

I did that so I could run. I did it because I thought I could do some good.

As history would prove, there were other mitigating factors working against Clark. For one, as Mulroney wrote, delegate support from the seven Conservative provincial governments in Canada at the time was critically weak. But even Mulroney concedes the results of the Pocklington poll would have had a devastating influence on Clark's leadership prospects.

"Turner was very much viewed as the golden boy of Canadian politics, so he would have run way ahead of Joe," Mulroney says of Trudeau's eventual successor as Liberal leader. "That would have had a psychological effect on the convention."

Indeed. While the final tally showed 66.9 per cent of delegates voting in favour of Clark's continued leadership, and against a review—a significant number to be sure, it was short of what the Tory leader decided he needed. True to his word, Clark called for a leadership contest and declared he would be one of the candidates.

As it turns out, so would Peter Pocklington. "Running the country could be the crowning achievement of my life," he told Peter Gzowski in the April 1982 issue of *Saturday Night* magazine.

• • •

While support in the 67-per-cent range was not enough for Joe Clark to keep his job, Peter was keenly aware that the support of only 50.1 per cent of Conservative delegates would be needed to elect a new leader.

So he began to craft a platform around free trade with the United

States, privatizing Crown corporations, and retiring the national debt. All those proposals hinged on one central idea, the cornerstone of a platform that would set him apart from all the other candidates: a flat tax. Peter proposed a fixed rate of income tax that everyone would pay. Well, almost everyone. Low-income earners would be the exception.

At the time, Peter proposed that anyone earning less than $12,000 a year shouldn't have to pay any tax. He has since revised that number upward to $25,000. "Why bother taxing someone who can't afford to get out of bed in the morning, let alone pay taxes," he says.

Everyone else however—every individual, every company—would pay a flat tax of 20 per cent on everything they earned. If your personal income is $80,000 a year, you pay $16,000 in taxes. If your company earns a profit of $800,000, your tax bill would be $160,000. No tax shelters, no loopholes, no dodges. Everyone pays the same fair share.

"We could do away with tax lawyers," he told the Empire Club. "We could shrink the huge civil service involved in tax collection. We could do away with a tax form longer than a single sheet of paper. We could do away with millions of man-hours spent trying to figure out not only how much we owe, but how to beat it."

It would have worked, too. It should have worked. It does work. The flat tax works in Hong Kong and it's working in Russia. It works like a damn, because it gets rid of the culture of envy.

The culture of envy is what Peter considered the major affliction in Canadian society in the early '80s, and one he says persists to this day. In short, it means that if someone has something you don't—wealth most often tops the list—then they must have done something illegal or immoral to get it. Therefore, they don't deserve it, and it should be taken from them.

The captains of Canadian industry are most often the targets of this culture of envy, as are stars in the entertainment industry, but Peter says even successful small-town business people should be wary. He recalls something said to him by Mac McConnell, the publisher of the *Tilbury Times*, the small weekly newspaper in the town where Peter owned his first car dealership. Peter was one of the paper's largest advertisers, and the two men became friends. At one point, Peter offered to lease McConnell a new car every six months, after which he would turn it in so it could be sold as a demonstrator. The publisher agreed, but insisted he would never take an expensive car.

"If he had taken a Lincoln or a Thunderbird, maybe his other advertisers in Tillbury or his readers would have thought he was charging too much," Peter remembers. "You have to be careful in Canada; you don't want people to know you're doing too well." Peter says it's a lesson he came to learn only much, much later.

. . .

Peter didn't just want to simplify the tax system, but the rest of government, too. Ottawa, he said, was involved in too many things. He bemoaned the fact that, under the guise of Canadian National Railways, Air Canada, Petro-Canada and the CBC, government competed with private enterprise. And he was one of the first public figures to suggest Canada's Crown corporations should be sold off. In 1982, he spoke at length to Gzowski about it:

> The first thing you have to do is get government out of all business. Milton Friedman speculated that government should not be involved with the business of doing things. So you'd give away all the corporations in which government is now involved—the CBC, the post office, Petro-Can, railroads, Air Canada. Government is simply the seat of power that stops you from using force on me and me from using force on you. It sets up the law courts and administers the armed services. It shouldn't be anything else.

Privatization of public health care was also on Peter's agenda. He would scrap medicare in favour of a system modelled on the Mayo Clinic, with the doctors owning a share in their facilities.

If you want to have a health-care system that works, the government should look after the 5 per cent who can't look after themselves. Forget the other 95 per cent; let the market look after them. And it works. You know, you can buy health insurance and instead of paying 80 per cent of your income in taxes, you pay 20 as I proposed, then pay for your own health insurance.

People say health insurance, particularly in the U.S., is not perfect, but nobody dies in the States because they don't have insurance. Poor old Canada, that's why you've got a two-tiered system coming on so strong.

There was more. Peter wanted to repay the national debt "to avoid us becoming another Mexico or Argentina," he told the Empire Club. To help do that, he would sell surplus natural gas and water to the Americans, coal and other natural resources to Pacific Rim nations. To stop inflation, he would stop printing money. If Quebec wanted to separate, he would let it. He would restore the original branches of the by-then-unified Armed Forces: army, navy, air force. Criminals would be sent to Arctic penal colonies.

He was not without compassion, however. He told the Empire Club those in genuine need would be helped:

There are those who have been stricken with illness or accident, those who have chronic or permanent disabilities, those with nowhere to turn. I believe we are our brother's keeper, and we must help these people in any way we can. Whatever the task requires, it should be freely and creatively given by us all.

But I do not believe in making the safety net too comfortable. I do not believe you motivate people by offering to take care of them from cradle to grave. That isn't helping them, that's enslaving them. When a person is down, you give them opportunity, encouragement, a bridge to another job—not a lifetime of handouts.

Mostly, though, Peter felt charity begins at home, that in a libertarian system, among people who believe in free enterprise, some of the responsibility for those in need must be assumed by the family, the church and the community. Government, he says, is for the protection of borders and to run law enforcement and the courts, to ensure the rule of law—"law that we all make, not law made by judges."

And so Peter Pocklington embarked on his leadership campaign secure in the conviction that the skills he mastered in the marketplace would serve him well in government. He felt it was almost his duty to offer himself to his country.

• • •

To say that Peter wasn't taken seriously as a bona fide candidate would be understating the reaction of the Canadian political establishment. Gzowski reported that Keith Davey, the Liberal senator and power broker, suggested the real world of politics was too sophisticated for the likes of an Edmonton car dealer. Even Peter's friend, Peter Lougheed, the Alberta premier of the day and an intermittent Pocklington guest at Oilers' games, was not encouraging. Asked if Peter should be regarded as a serious political factor, the premier offered a curt, one-word response: "No."

There were, however, people who believed fervently in Peter's cause. Bob Kinasewich, Peter's lawyer at the time, remembers one such supporter—an Edmonton building contractor named George Whissel.

"Whissel and Peter were friends—and they hated each other at the same time," remembers Kinasewich. "They each considered the other an idiot."

The pair were also litigants, according to Kinasewich. Whissel had bought some property from Peter, who was holding the mortgage, and Peter was foreclosing because Whissel wasn't making the payments. Whissel argued he didn't get what he paid for. The dispute took at least 15 years to resolve and made several lawyers rich in the process.

"But in the middle of all this war mongering or whatever you want to call it, Peter is running for the leadership of the Conservatives," Kinasewich recalls, "and finances were a little tight. He was flying around the country on his jet, and it was always 'interesting' how he was going to pay for the gas, never mind anything else. But George Whissel came up with a whole pile of money for Peter, because he believed in what Peter was doing.

"And then they'd turn around the next day and fight with each other again over this property."

Peter remained undaunted, even if he wasn't so sure of his prospects. "I know I could do the job," he told Gzowski. "It's just getting there that poses a problem."

• • •

On the cusp of the second weekend in June, thousands of Canadians began to converge on Ottawa to decide who would be the next leader of the Progressive Conservative Party. Clearly, Peter was not among the favourites.

That distinction went to three of the candidates in the field of eight: Clark, as the incumbent; John Crosbie, who had been minister of finance in Clark's short-lived 1979–80 government; and Mulroney, who had lost to Clark in the 1976 leadership contest.

In his book, *Memoirs*, Mulroney wrote that he spent much of the campaign garnering support at the party's grassroots level, a strategy that would allow him to stay close to Clark in the early voting and, from there, build a coalition with the help of other candidates who had fallen off the ballot. If his candidacy could sustain itself long enough to get him to the final ballot with Clark, Mulroney was confident he could win.

Peter was prepared to provide that help if it came to that—and confessed as much to his friend Gretzky.

"Peter kept saying, 'I'm going to win,'" Gretzky recalls. "But he told me, 'If I don't win, I'm throwing all my votes to Brian Mulroney. I want him to win.'"

Gretzky agreed to go to Ottawa to lend Peter whatever moral support he could. It was one of only two things, Gretzky remembers, where he said, "I don't want to do this, but I'm doing it because of you." (The other was to fly to the Arctic to take part in one of Peter's fishing camps.)

Says Wayne: "I didn't want to be in politics and I didn't want to offend people and take a side, but I was there and as I said to those guys, 'I'm here supporting Peter Pocklington.'"

Unfortunately for Peter, not many other delegates shared the sentiment. One advisor, when asked for a prediction on how many votes Peter would get on the first ballot, replied, "99." He wouldn't be far off.

The night before the vote, Peter was in his hotel suite with two of his advisors—Paul Godfrey, then the regional chair for Metropolitan Toronto; and Ralph Lean, a Toronto lawyer and Tory bagman—when there was a knock on the door. It was Brian Mulroney.

Both men say they shared an affinity from the moment they met, and their friendship grew from there. In *Memoirs*, Mulroney wrote that, "While it is true I found some of [Peter's] positions too far right for my own liking, he was a delightful, intelligent and straightforward guy. I felt that his views deserved to be aired and that he had every right to contest the leadership."

Despite their differences, many of those views were the same. "Peter," says Mulroney, "long approved of free trade with the United States, getting rid of the National Energy Program, which I did, getting rid of the Foreign Investment Review Agency. He was strongly private-sector oriented, pro-American in terms of opposing the anti-Americanism of Trudeau, establishing a good reputation internationally, cutting down on government spending, which we did, and so on."

They were also outsiders. Both were criticized because, unlike the other major candidates, neither held a seat in the House of Commons. "We were both being attacked for the same reason—the same phony reason," says Mulroney, who would go on to become the longest serving Conservative prime minister of the twentieth century. "Peter would have made a fine leader if he had won."

But on the evening of June 10, in an Ottawa hotel room, both men knew Peter was not going to win. Brian Mulroney, however, just might.

"I told Peter that I'd be in a very strong second-place position after the first ballot, with Crosbie well behind," Mulroney wrote in his book. "That's where you'll have to make your move. . . . And you won't have much time. I've been around these conventions long enough to know that you'll only have about 10 minutes to make up your mind.

"Peter replied that his mind was indeed made up and that he knew what he'd be doing. I didn't press him further, and left his suite feeling confident."

Peter wanted only one thing if Brian Mulroney ever became prime minister: a royal commission on taxation to study the merits of a flat tax.

• • •

June 11, 1983: Inside the Ottawa Civic Centre—a 1960s-era hockey rink built under the football grandstands at Lansdowne Park—delegates began determining the candidates' fates.

The results of the first ballot held few surprises:

Joe Clark 1,091
Brian Mulroney 874
John Crosbie 639
Michael Wilson 144
David Crombie 116
Peter Pocklington 102
John Gamble 17
Neil Fraser 5

As the results were announced, Peter and Michael Wilson, the respected Bay Street banker and formerly Clark's international trade minister—nowadays the Canadian ambassador to the United States—met on the convention floor. Mulroney was convinced both men would soon be on their way to his section of the arena to give him their support.

Instead, they headed towards Crosbie.

Montreal Gazette writer L. Ian MacDonald described what happened next: "Brian Mulroney looked like someone who was witnessing a bank holdup or a shooting in the street," he wrote. "His face was frozen in helpless fascination. He was unable to stop it, unable to cry for help, unable to look but unable to look away."

Mulroney's wife Mila burst into tears. "In that moment, all our work together—the thousands of miles she logged, the countless notes she'd written, the hands she'd shaken and so much more—had apparently gone to waste," Mulroney wrote in his book. "Crosbie would now gain the momentum he needed to eventually place him alone against Joe Clark on the final ballot."

By all indications, Mulroney was finished, his dreams of ever becoming prime minister dead—only he wasn't, and they weren't.

> I dragged Wilson along with me, but strangely enough in that old coliseum, I missed the row to where Brian and Mila were—and we started heading towards Crosbie.
>
> Then I saw my mistake and we turned around and away we went, back to Brian. And Brian said, "My God, I thought you were going to Crosbie."

Mulroney remembers that moment as a pivotal one in his political career. "That decision by Peter and Michael at the convention was a seminal moment," Mulroney says. "Of course, had I not won the convention, I would never have been prime minister."

Mulroney finally caught Clark on the fourth and final ballot, and won the leadership with 54 per cent of the vote.

•   •   •

In time, many of the causes Peter championed did come to pass: free trade with the United States, the elimination of the NEP and FIRA, the privatization of Air Canada, Petro-Canada and CN, and significant reductions in government spending.

"The situation today—and by the end of my government, Jean Chrétien's government, and Paul Martin's government—reflect a lot of what Peter Pocklington advocated," says Mulroney. "Like Panasonic, he was a little ahead of his time."

. . .

A few weeks after the convention, Peter was in Montreal on business and met Mulroney over lunch. The topic: what role could Peter play in a future Progressive Conservative government.

Peter asked for his royal commission on taxation. He says Mulroney agreed. Mulroney doesn't say one way or the other, but it never did happen. Mulroney says the plan was rendered unnecessary because his finance minister, Michael Wilson, overhauled the taxation system with the introduction of the GST.

(At least the GST allowed for wealth creation, Peter says, because it took taxation off creating wealth and put it on spending, "where it should be.")

Peter didn't ask for anything else. "He was not interested in the board of the post office or something like that," Mulroney recalls, laughing. "Peter was a hugely successful entrepreneur. . . . He wasn't interested in appointments, he was interested in ideas."

Political office held no interest for Peter, either, not if he couldn't be in charge.

"Oh shit, could you believe that, to be a backbencher?" he asks. "The only way I could make change was to become prime minister. Otherwise you work for a hundred and a quarter a year and do nothing, and have no power. I had more power where I was."

Peter Pocklington had taken his best shot—and maybe done some good in the process. He wouldn't be contemplating the "what ifs" the rest of his life. But when he reviews his crack at politics, he can also be candid in his assessment:

"Me? Basically I was Don Quixote, tilting at windmills."

PART IX

'I'm going home. This deal is over'

Peter Pocklington's life and career have known only success and acclaim. Then, in the span of one year, his good fortune takes a turn for the worse. Peter's critics—with a measure of justification—say he is the one to blame. He begs to differ.

Nineteen eighty-three was a watershed year for Peter. By then he had been living in Edmonton 12 years and in that time had amassed much of his wealth. His companies—ranging from a Canadian professional hockey club to meat-packing company—were doing $2 billion worth of business a year.

On a personal level, Peter was fully recovered from the hostage-taking incident that nearly took his life. Moreover, he was embarking on a political career that would bring him a national profile and put him in the position to help determine who would ultimately become the country's prime minister.

But 1983 would also see Peter suffer his first serious financial setback—the failure of Fidelity Trust, the financial institution he had purchased a few years earlier. At the time, the Fidelity collapse was viewed in isolation, the result of a freak circumstance: the spectacular climb in interest rates. Retrospect, however, tells a far different story. From 1983 on, Peter's empire would never again be able to sustain the remarkable growth it had seemed to enjoy earlier. Within a few years, it would begin to shrink and 15 years later, it would be completely gone.

Up until Fidelity failed, I felt blessed. It had been one of those rocketship rides. What other young guy my age—I was 41—buys a hockey team and wins and wins and wins, and not just at hockey? Everything I touched seemed to turn to gold. But that's the way life is, sometimes.

The responsibility for Fidelity's failure is something he places squarely on the shoulders of the Liberal government in Ottawa he was so vigorously campaigning to replace.

Oh yeah, I was pretty browned off with the government. They made the mistake of printing too much money and spending it like drunken sailors. That caused inflation. Then, they tried to fix the problem by hiking the interest rates. All of a sudden, the prime rate was 18.5 per cent, but they accepted no responsibility at all for what they were doing to hard-working business people.

How the hell can any businessman survive when the prime rate is 18.5 per cent? If you owe a couple of hundred million dollars, all of a sudden it's costing you real money to pay the loan.

These idiots we elected had absolutely no idea what they were doing to the free-market economy, and that really upset me. I remember thinking it would get to the point where society was going to break down unless the government got its act together.

That's why it's so important to have a strong central bank, and not let governments print too much money or spend too much money. You have to run a balanced budget. To my mind, as a businessman, it seemed what they were doing was abusive to a system that created this great life we were all blessed to have.

So yeah, I wasn't very happy with government. That's why I ran for the leadership of the Conservative party.

• • •

Fidelity wasn't the only trust or mortgage company to wither and fail in the face of high interest rates. That same year, Crown Trust also went under, as did Greymac Trust, Seaway Trust and the AMIC Mortgage Investment Corporation.

According to the Canadian Deposit Insurance Corporation, a government-owned agency that insures depositors' money in case a bank, trust company or credit union shuts down, 43 financial institutions failed between 1967 and 1996. Among them were the Edmonton-based Canadian Commercial Bank in 1985 and the Allard family's North West Trust in 1987. In fact, during the 1980s, the CDIC paid out more than $1 billion in restitution to people who had accounts with failed Alberta-based financial institutions.

By 1996, almost all of Canada's trust companies had disappeared from the landscape, either through financial calamity or acquisition. One of the last to go was probably the most prominent, Canada Trust. It was taken over by the Toronto–Dominion Bank in 2000.

None of that was material in 1983, however. The CDIC paid $359 million of taxpayer money to Fidelity's depositors when it went down. And while Peter blamed the government, the public blamed Peter.

. . .

Peter had gone into the trust company business for the same reason many multimillion-dollar property developers did in those days—as a way to get ready access to financing for land deals.

According to *The Business of Professional Sports* by Paul D. Staudohar and J.A. Mangan, Fidelity was Canada's 12th-largest trust company when Peter bought a controlling interest in 1979 for $15 million. At the time, its assets totalled $1.6 billion. Peter later acquired the balance of the company for $10 million, then folded his property development company, Patrician Land Corporation, into it.

Yet according to the book *A Matter of Trust*, by Patricia Best and Ann Shortell, Peter acquired Fidelity at a time when it was struggling. It very well might have become the biggest bank failure in Canadian banking had he not stepped forward. That was one of the reasons the government allowed Peter to take it over in the manner he did.

But that didn't mean the government wasn't keeping an eye on

Fidelity. Quite the contrary. According to Best and Shortell, the government made it clear Peter was not to run the company himself. As was the case with all trust companies, a board of directors would be charged with ensuring operations were conducted responsibly. Simon Reisman, who negotiated the Canada–U.S. Free Trade Agreement on behalf of the Mulroney government and was, incidentally, the father of Chapters–Indigo book maven Heather Reisman, was named to the Fidelity board. So, too, was Douglas Fullerton, former chair of the National Capital Commission, and Byron J. Seaman, head of Calgary's Bow Valley Industries and one of the original owners of the Calgary Flames.

The company's president was the eminently qualified Brendan Calder. It was his job to keep Fidelity's nose clean. It was no easy task—even Peter recognizes that. "Fidelity was a source of money, like having your own bank," he says, "but you couldn't just write a cheque and do whatever the hell you wanted."

It was the heavily regulated nature of the business that helped keep Fidelity out of the disastrous American savings and loan sinkhole in the early 1980s—but it did result in Peter parting company with one of his most trusted advisors.

Harry Knutson was an investment banker who, from 1979 to 1982, was the senior vice-president for Peter's business operations. He and Peter were also friends. Bob Kinasewich, who was Peter's corporate counsel during that time, Knutson and Doug Horrey, Peter's chief financial officer, constituted the triumvirate that directed much of Peter's business interests.

In 1982, Peter was keen on gaining control of a U.S.-based savings and loan association in order to get a foothold in the American financial market. He and Knutson went after two, one in Texas, and when that didn't get anywhere, another in Utah. It was Peter's intent to use Fidelity assets as collateral, and it was Knutson's job to make it happen. Ultimately, Knutson ran up against Calder and the board, who took a dim view of his business approach.

Kinasewich and Bill O'Reilly—a lawyer who also did legal work for Peter—took it upon themselves to protect Peter and do their best to keep their boss out of the savings and loan business. "We couldn't kill the deal," Kinasewich remembers. "But we put enough conditions in there that eventually killed it. To this day Peter will still say to me, 'You know, you cost me a gazillion dollars.'"

Ultimately, "The savings and loans—they all blew up."

The widespread failure of savings and loan associations throughout the U.S. was one of the more significant financial scandals in American history—until, that is, the Wall Street meltdown in 2008.

When it was over, Knutson left the company. "They parted grounds on pretty nasty terms," says Kinasewich. "Harry and Doug and I were good friends as well as co-workers. Peter and Harry, as far as I knew, also got along very, very well until the end. I had to do the settlement with Harry, which I did, and away he went."

Since then, Knutson has done just fine for himself. He is a partner in the Vancouver investment firm Nova Bancorp. Horrey left the company, and the country, in the mid-'90s under somewhat more mysterious circumstances.

"We had a triumvirate in there that worked very well together; it was really enjoyable. And then it just all came apart, and with Harry it was primarily because of Fidelity Trust."

• • •

Owning a trust company can be a risky business, but it shouldn't be. I doubt that I'm a great lender. I'm a better borrower than a lender. I think people who lend money, they have to be very astute and probably think differently than I do. To me, every deal is a good deal. But as long as you didn't dip your fingers into the vault, you're fine. You have to have great fiduciary responsibility not to tamper with the vault.

You have to do more than that. Government regulations required that a portion of the company's assets, at least 5 per cent, had to be held in Canada Savings Bonds. Moreover, for every $20 the company loaned out, it had to have $1 in equity. "Also," says Peter, "if your trust company has $2 billion in gross assets, it has to have roughly 20 per cent of that in hard assets."

It is that requirement which would ultimately sink Fidelity Trust. As the Alberta economy sank under the weight of dropping oil prices and rising interest rates, the value of those assets—primarily the undeveloped real estate held by Patrician Land—simply disappeared.

As Kinasewich points out, it wasn't Fidelity that collapsed under the weight of a faltering economy, it was Patrician Land.

Land values fell dramatically in the early 1980s, and Peter owned a lot of land that did not produce any revenue. "It was either raw land or he had multiple-unit housing complexes—condominiums, townhouses—that he was in the process of building," Kinasewich says. But because of the high interest rates, Peter couldn't borrow the money to develop the land, or even finish projects that were underway. With no sales, little cash flow, and raw land not generating much in the way of revenue, Peter was vulnerable. "And the biggest real estate asset that he had?" Kinasewich asks. "Look at Canmore."

Kinasewich says the resemblence between Peter's vision for Canmore and what's there now, "is pretty close. He had that vision."

Yet with the exorbitant interest rates, the responsibility fell to Fidelity to keep financing Patrician Land—and just couldn't do it anymore. The losses mounted, totalling $17 million. Finally, the government told Peter he had to inject $20-million worth of equity into Fidelity. Otherwise it was game over.

Needless to say, Peter didn't have that kind of cash on hand. He sent Kinasewich and others on a mission throughout North America to see if they could scare up the money from just about anyone that had any, "including the people who owned the Grand Ole Opry," Kinasewich recalls.

"In any event, after spending I don't know how many months trying to find a buyer, Peter then decided, 'I'll buy it.'" In other words, Peter would personally buy Fidelity—on paper, anyway—for $20 million. His legal team went to work on doing the deal. "Bill O'Reilly acted for Fidelity and I acted for Peter, and we kept on going back and forth to Ottawa to get this transaction approved," Kinasewich remembers, "and they were approving it every step of the way."

The process was making Peter impatient, however. "Jesus, Bob, what are you doing?" he said. "Get the goddamn thing done. All it involves is transferring the title to me and bing, bing, bing, that's it."

"Peter, believe me, it's not that simple," Kinasewich responded. "We're doing you a favour. We think we can get it done. We're getting it, slowly but surely."

At the same time this was going on, the principals behind two other trust companies, Greymac Trust and Seaway Trust, were being investigated by federal regulators. Both would eventually go to jail, but the thrust of the Greymac investigation revolved around the owner seeking to inject equity into his trust company from third parties of suspect reputation. At that point, somebody blew the whistle and the government squashed the deal.

Even though Peter's plans did not involve a third party but, rather, himself, the guilt by coincident timing was enough to kill his plans as well. "We were doing a similar thing, only in-house, and we were consulting the government every step of the way," Kinasewich says. "Then suddenly we got a phone call one day that said, 'the deal's off.' They gave us just a few weeks to come up with the $20 million. I remember sitting there going, 'Holy shit.'"

• • •

Glen Sather says that sometimes his friend Peter Pocklington was often the captain of his own destiny—no matter how well or poorly that destiny played out—but that in the case of Fidelity Trust, Peter was a victim. "If the government hadn't screwed around with the interest rates, that whole chapter in his life would have been entirely different," Sather says. "A lot of outside influences affected his life."

• • •

Enter the Ghermezians.

Jacob Ghermezian was a rug merchant from Iran who parlayed the buying and selling of his wares into an Edmonton real estate empire. He and his sons, Bahman, Eskandar, Raphael and Nader Ghermezian, built West Edmonton Mall, the most popular tourist destination in Canada and at one time the largest shopping mall in the world.

Stories have circulated for years that the government offered the Ghermezian brothers money to step in and take over the bad real estate assets Fidelity owned through Patrician Land. Whatever the reason the Ghermezians became involved, Kinasewich says it was an opportunity that, in the end, they frittered away.

Kinasewich remembers the negotiations, though he was not allowed to take part—at least officially. Behind the scenes, he was doing his best to protect Peter's interests. "And there wasn't much hope of that," he adds. "I really didn't have that much to say because the government was dictating to Peter what was going to happen. Bill O'Reilly was acting for Fidelity."

He says the government brought a CDIC supervisor out of retirement to negotiate the deal with the Ghermezians, but the man soon grew weary of negotiating with them.

Finally, after a series of meetings with the brothers, the retired supervisor declared he would no longer negotiate directly with them. "I will talk to their lawyers, but not them," he said.

When it came down to the final weekend of negotiations in Toronto, the Ghermezians' lawyer insisted he needed them there so that he could consult with them more easily. The supervisor relented, but only slightly. "They can be in the building, but I will not talk to them," he said.

As the negotiations drew closer to a conclusion, the Ghermezians' lawyer would run down the hall to talk to the brothers, then come back and say, "OK, yup we can do this, we can do that." Finally, he came into the room and told the supervisor, "The brothers would like to just make one comment directly to you, and it's nothing of great import."

The supervisor rolled his eyes. "OK, but I'm warning you, if they start negotiating this thing, I'm outta here."

Once the Ghermezians were in the room, however, they began to raise some questions and asked for a few adjustments here and there. The supervisor—a stately looking gentleman, Kinasewich recalls—rose from his seat, looked at the brothers, looked at their lawyer, then said, "I told you not to bring them in here. That's it! I am not tolerating this, I am out of here." And with that, he slammed shut his book, closed his briefcase and headed for the elevator.

The brothers chased after him, pleading their case. "Leave me alone," the supervisor demanded. "I'm going home. This deal is over."

Kinasewich remembers he and O'Reilly just sat there, their mouths agape. "We had just spent three days of 15-hour days going through this thing, all the blood, sweat and tears, and at the end of the day, O'Reilly looked at me and said, 'Well, so much for that.'" The negotiations were over, and Kinasewich headed for home.

Eventually, Vancouver's First City Trust—which originated in Edmonton and was operated at the time by Peter's friend Sam Belzberg—stepped up and took over Fidelity. Ironically, nine years later, First City would also fail in the midst of the next great recession.

•   •   •

Fidelity wasn't the only company in Peter's stable to fall victim to the hard times in the early 1980s. So did his drilling firm.

In what was surely the most striking example of lousy timing, Peter paid $17 million for Capri Drilling in 1981 with the idea of leasing drilling rigs to oil companies that were in a rush to get their share of black gold out of Alberta's oil patch. Yet no sooner did he make his investment than the Alberta oil market collapsed. The oil companies stopped drilling and Peter's 13 rigs began to collect dust.

"Peter was a victim of circumstances," says Kinasewich. "I believe he paid around $1 million a rig, and the Laurentian Bank financed it. Of course, the transaction was 100 per cent leveraged. Within a few months of buying these rigs, oil prices cratered down to below $10 a barrel. You couldn't give away a drilling rig for leasing. Nobody was drilling for anything. And here Peter was with this debt."

Peter remembers he got into the drilling business because Paul Bowlen, the father of his friend Pat Bowlen, made a lot of money doing just that. "I decided I wasn't very smart in that business," Peter remembers. "Bowlen's dad wouldn't buy a rig until he had it contracted for three or four years. That's the smart way to do it.

"I bought it at a bit of a fire sale, but the fire still raged. It was tough drilling in those years."

Capri lost about $10 million by the time Peter gave up the fight.

Kinasewich remembers the day he and Peter met with the Laurentian bankers to resolve the debt. Many of them flew into town from Montreal for the meeting.

"I remember Peter saying, 'Come on, we've got to go to a meeting with the Laurentian Bank, we've got to figure it out there.' Peter looked them in the eye said, 'I don't know how I'm going to do it, gentlemen, but I guarantee you one thing. You'll get your money.'"

Kinasewich says the debt was rolled into Gainers and the bank was compensated. But there were oil barons in Calgary who weren't as fortunate.

"That was interesting, going to a creditors' meeting in Calgary, with all these Calgary oilmen, and offering them somewhere between 10 and 15 cents on the dollar. Oh, they were friendly and they were humorous. The really amazing thing, though, was that I didn't get shot."

. . .

Owing people money was something Peter did a lot. It was the nature of his business. Unfortunately, he developed a reputation for taking his time in making good on his debts, or for dodging them altogether.

Kinasewich says his creditors often misunderstood Peter and his determination to make good.

"Peter didn't voluntarily walk away from any debts," he says. Delays in paying bills were often a reflection of cash flow. If the money was there, the bills were paid promptly. If the money wasn't, he'd wait until it was.

• • •

Capri was not Peter's only venture in the oil patch. There was also Patrician Oil, a company that went around Alberta acquiring drilling leases. He never made much money from that, either, until he sold it. He made a few million off that deal. "It wasn't big on my plate," Peter admits.

• • •

By the time the dust settled from the Fidelity collapse, Peter was determined to rebuild his empire. After all, he did still have some winners in his stable: the Oilers, for one, were still profitable at that point; so was Gainers.

With that kind of leverage, Peter spent the next few years on a buying binge. Among the acquisitions:

- Palm Dairies, a producer of fresh and frozen dairy products, 1,200 employees and 22 plants in Western and Central Canada, for $52 million;
- Magic Pantry, a Hamilton-based producer of gourmet meals that require neither refrigeration nor freezing;
- Kretschmar Foods, a producer of beef, poultry and seafood for the specialty and deli markets in Canada and the U.S., which he bought from Loblaws;
- Cambra Foods, manufacturer of canola products, including vegetable oil, cooking oil, salad oil, margarine and shortening, for $13 million;
- Sodar Foods of Val-Belair, Quebec, producer of quality hams and pork shoulders;

- East Bay Packing, a California processor and marketer of pork and beef under the Farmers Hickory Brand and private labels for Albertsons, Safeway and other supermarket chains; and
- Green Acre Farms, producer of fresh and frozen chicken products, with plants in Texas and Mississippi.

There were also Z&W Foods, Marybank Foods and another oil and gas company, Cromwell Resources.

• • •

In the movie *Pretty Woman*, Richard Gere's character made his fortune buying companies, splitting them into their various components, then selling each part for considerably more than he paid for it.

Consider it a 1980s thing.

Peter had much the same idea when he bought Palm Dairies from Unicorp Canada. The ATB financed the entire $52-million purchase price for the chance of a quick profit on the turnaround. Unfortunately for Peter and the ATB, Palm Dairies wasn't broken up and sold as planned. The Mulroney government put a stop to that.

Peter's expectation was to sell parts of Palm to other dairy operations in British Columbia, Saskatchewan and Ontario for a combined $95 million—a profit of more than $40 million on his investment. His hope, once the ATB was paid off, was to reinvest the money in the Oilers to cover future losses. But before he could complete the deal, Peter was called to Ottawa to appear before the Competition Bureau.

The bureau's members took a dim view of Peter's plans. They said breaking up Palm Dairies would increase competition in the marketplace and make it harder for smaller dairy operations to keep up. In other words, the Competition Bureau was telling him more competition was a bad thing.

I could have made a fortune on that deal. But the Competition Bureau said, "Well, if you sell off this and this and this, you are going to impact this poor little guy and this poor little guy."

A deal like the one they killed is good for the economy. It's good for everybody. You create wealth. And if an old sleepy company isn't doing well, the folks come in and tear it apart and spin off the pieces and make the shareholders a fortune.

The guy who wins is the consumer. We live in a consumer-based economy. And the guy that sells the most is the guy who sells it the cheapest and the best.

Dealing with these little communist peckers at the Competition Bureau was awful, believe me. Talk about having to suffer fools, but they had me by the you-know-whats. So I ended up paying a lobbyist half a million dollars, too much money, to get the thing half-assed settled, to finally get some semblance of a deal approved. I ended up selling Palm Dairies for maybe what I paid for it.

In the end, Palm Dairies was sold for a profit of around $5 million, enough to pay off the ATB, but that's about all.

"It's unbelievable," Peter says. "I really ended up with a bad taste for most government regulation."

• • •

It was thanks to Ronnie Hawkins that Peter ended up in the chicken business.

Peter had caught up with his buddy, a Canadian rock 'n' roll legend, at a party Hawkins was hosting in Las Vegas, where he met Don Tyson—who, like Hawkins, is from Arkansas.

Tyson is also head of Tyson Foods, a *Fortune* 500 company that has carved its niche as the world's largest processor and marketer of chicken, beef and pork.

Tyson and I got to chatting about chickens. So I went down to visit Don, looked at his chicken operation, and I put my feelers out and ended up buying a chicken company.

Peter bought two companies actually. He purchased the first, based in Nacogdoches, Texas, from the Campbell Soup Company. It turns out Campbell's was happy to buy the chicken for their soup from someone else—they just didn't want to bother processing the chickens themselves.

The other company was in Sebastopol, Mississippi. Together, they became Green Acre Farms.

> There is more potential profit in the chicken business than in beef or pork. But it's feast or famine with chickens. It all depends on the price of corn, because that's what you feed them. Half the chicken is corn. So if the price of corn is $2.50 a bushel, you're making a fortune. If it's $5 a bushel, you're getting your ass kicked.
>
> Nowadays, of course, they're raising corn for ethanol and that's raised the bushel to about $7. So nobody in the chicken business is making any money right now.

Perhaps, but Peter did well by the chicken business, and it did well by him.

> I did enjoy it. It was great. You had to carve up the chicken and sell as much as you could. A lot of it went to rendering for dog food plants. Dark meat would go anywhere from 18 cents to 40 cents, depending on the market. And breasts were the premium. We also found a market for what they call paws in China. The paws are the feet. They got 19 cents a pound, I think, for paws.

Peter's chicken venture ended, however, when the ATB called his loan on the Oilers in 1997. Green Acres was among the companies sold to pay down the debt.

•   •   •

Peter takes particular pride in the accomplishments of Cambra Foods, the Lethbridge-based canola processor. The company was grossing about $70 million a year when he took it over, $220 million a year when it was taken away by the ATB as part of the Oilers' takeover and sold to James Richardson & Son from Winnipeg.

> It was a great little company. Richardson's destroyed it. There is no branding anymore, there is nothing, it's just a milling plant. The esprit de corps is gone, the workers are gone.

> Then there are Magic Pantry and Kretschmar.

> I really bought Magic Pantry for the tax loss. It came with a $30-million tax loss and I bought it for next to nothing. I built it up and sold a lot of Magic Pantry stuff to Jenny Craig, the weight-loss woman in San Diego.
> Kretschmar was originally from St. Louis. There were two branches, the Canadian and the American, and we sold top-end processed meat to restaurants and the deli markets.
> Both companies were Gainers' assets, so they were lost to the Alberta government as part of that whole devastating takeover.

● ● ●

In the midst of the Fidelity collapse, there was more trouble in store.

Peter owned the two largest-grossing Ford dealerships in Canada: Westown and Elgin Ford in Toronto. "I originally bought Elgin for the land it was on, seven to eight acres on Bay Street," Peter remembers. Yet he had long ago left both dealerships for others to operate, a decision that in one case he would come to rue.

Elgin was well-run; Westown, not so much. Kinasewich remembers Peter's manager at Elgin Ford as a straight shooter, but he suggests the guys who were running Westown owed Peter a lot of money.

"It was only because of Peter's goodwill that they didn't end up being sued," says Kinasewich who claims the money they owed Peter was in the hundreds of thousands of dollars.

Kinasewich argues Peter should never have given up active control of his car dealerships. "When Peter was in there running things, they made gobs of money, because Peter could sell the proverbial ice cubes to an Eskimo."

People took advantage of Peter in other ways, too, says Kinasewich. "He always paid top dollar for everything. Because it was Peter, people charged as much as they thought they could.

"There are a lot of people that hate him and think he is a real scoundrel. But you know, seeing the other side of him, if he liked a deal he would do it, be damned with the details and off he'd go. And people would take advantage of that."

• • •

Kinasewich remembers having a few heart-to-heart conversations with Peter around that time. "And they were thoughtful conversations on Peter's part. I always felt a little closer to him in just having those conversations because we didn't very often have things like that.

"One time, I can remember sitting there talking with Peter and asking, 'Peter, I hope to hell with all this money floating in and out and all over the place, that you're putting some of it away.' And he looked at me and he said, 'Bob, that's negative thinking. That means I'm planning for failure. It doesn't happen.'"

• • •

Such positive thinking, even in the face of adversity, was also part of Peter's approach in developing people.

It's like bringing up youngsters, when you can see they have been chastised so many times and swatted down and told, "Don't do that," and "You're no good." They are destroyed inside, but they can be saved.

You literally try and raise their self-concept, their self-esteem. You give them new goals and new ways to talk to themselves. The scars always remain, but at least you can pile on all the positives. Finally, when you put enough positives on top of these terribly negative things that happen to a lot of people, they can finally bridge the gap and get past the negatives.

And then they can tell themselves they can't keep suffering, to just get over it, to just say, "Too damn bad, life sucks, get on with it," and away they go.

Yet each one of the business setbacks Peter endured chipped away at his image as an Edmonton good guy. The Fidelity failure was particularly damaging, given the $359-million cost to the taxpayers' purse. Overall, however, Kinasewich doesn't think the damage done to Peter's reputation is a fair reflection of the man. "Fidelity Trust was doing fine, thank you very much. Was he a victim of circumstances? Well he certainly made his own bed, but if the market hadn't collapsed, he may still be doing it to this day."

Oilers' broadcaster Rod Phillips says the people around the hockey club were kept distant from Peter's ongoing business problems through 1983 and 1984. After all, they were in pursuit of their first Stanley Cup.

"Everything that was going on around him was obviously difficult for him, but it didn't affect the hockey team. The players and Glen and the coaching staff were all aware of what was going on, but it was business as usual for them.

"Peter's big phrase to me was, 'You've got to be positive with what you're doing, Rod. A lot of people listen to you and you've got to be positive.' And I said, 'Well I try to be as positive as I can.'"

• • •

If there are recurring themes to Peter's business failures during that time, and even the successes that weren't as successful as he had hoped, it would be bad timing and the injudicious involvement of government. Certainly all the other key ingredients for success were there: sufficient capital ("at least twice as much as you think you need," he says), surrounding yourself with good people, and an identifiable market ("be sure that what you're putting the money into is something people want").

Ah, but government—that's a different kettle of fish.

It's government that kills Canada, it's not the people. The people are hard-working, dedicated, smart—it's not the people. It's the damn system. The socialism.

I finally gave up. I couldn't stand the onslaught. You can't fight every corner. Fighting the government, fighting the ATB, fighting the socialist ideals and ideas.

There were times when I wished I'd sold the whole thing and moved to the States. The U.S. at least is a free market, much more so than Canada. In Canada, boy, it can be tough sledding.

The sledding was about to get a whole lot tougher. Within three years of the Fidelity failure, Peter and his workforce at Gainers Inc.— his meat-packing operation in Edmonton—would wage the most bitter, protracted labour dispute in Alberta history. The fallout from that strike would irretrievably alter Peter's life, and scar his reputation, forever.

PART X

'There is a difference between sports guys and other business guys'

If Peter Pocklington was living a charmed life, the charm is beginning to run out by 1986. He is beset with financial woes that, at first blush, are not of his making: a supplier governed more by ideology than economics, a hostile union and a duplicitous government.

Regrets. Peter Pocklington may have had a few, but then again, too few to mention. Perhaps there is really only one: the day he decided to go into the meat-packing business.

Peter had no burning desire to run an abattoir or, rather, several abattoirs. It was not his calling, the way becoming a doctor or a ballet dancer is a calling. Instead, he saw the business of slaughtering hogs and cows as an opportunity. After all, what he knew about meat-packing, he once told the *Edmonton Journal*, is "you put a cow in one end and get a steak out the other."

Going into meat-packing was just a deal, a good deal, but a deal. But then, all of a sudden, I was faced with the reality of owning a meat company. And I thought, "My God, maybe I should just sell the whole damn thing." That's because the guy I bought it from, Ben Torchinsky—well, it's no wonder he wanted out. It was a crazy business because the government had put in a hog marketing board that dictated how much you pay for hogs.

I guess Ben was smarter than I was.

The Alberta government established the Alberta Pork Producers Marketing Board in the late 1960s to market hogs on behalf of the farmers who raised them. It is a supplier-friendly approach to bringing a wide variety of commodities to market and is practised throughout Canada. But for Peter Pocklington, in Edmonton in the 1980s, a hog marketing board was the key ingredient in a recipe for financial disaster. Because of it, his company, Gainers Inc., would become synonymous with strife, conflict, failure and his ultimate ruin.

• • •

John Gainer founded his meat-packing business from the family home behind Edmonton's Strathcona Hotel in 1894—with only $250 in start-up capital. Nine years later, he built his first slaughter and packing house in the Mill Creek Ravine near Edmonton's legendary Whyte Avenue. Gainer died in 1937, but his family continued to run the business for another 35 years. It was then sold to Saskatoon's Agra Industries, of which Torchinsky was president. Six years later, in 1978, Agra sold to Peter Pocklington.

It was a non-cash deal. Instead, Torchinsky swapped Gainers for 300 apartments Peter owned in Calgary. Peter says construction wasn't even completed on some of the apartments, so once he paid off the mortgage, he was $3 million ahead.

Then Gainers made a profit of $2 million in its first year, so by then, Peter was $5 million to the good. That would get anybody's attention; it certainly had his.

By 1981, he was building quite a profitable business out of that 78-year-old building John Gainer had built by the ravine. But Peter had grander plans. He wasn't the biggest player in the meat-packing business in Western Canada. Hell, he wasn't even the biggest player in Edmonton. That role was filled by Swift Canadian, which operated a much larger operation on Yellowhead Trail at 66th Street. Years later, that site would become ground zero for one of the worst labour disputes in Canadian history.

• • •

Gainers was a little packing house. It did about $100 million in
business a year. Anyway, I saw that I had to do something on a
bigger scale if it was going to make any sense. Somebody came to
my office and said the Swift plant was available. We were doing a
lot of business and we needed a bigger plant and the place to do it
wasn't on Whyte Avenue.

So in 1982, Peter flew to Swift & Company's world headquarters
in Chicago to see about buying their Edmonton plant—but he knew
what he really wanted was the entire Canadian operation.

"Yeah, we'll sell you the plant," Swift's Chicago people said.

"I'm really not here to buy the plant," Peter replied. "Just buying
your old plant doesn't make much sense. It's a relic."

By the time Peter returned home, he had a deal to buy all of Swift of
Canada for $45 million—a deal that included not only Swift's Edmonton
plant but another in Toronto, several facilities for edible oil production
(they are made from animal renderings), Butterball turkeys, and about
a billion dollars in annual sales. But he also inherited Swift's testy
union—a circumstance that was destined to lead him to ruination.

It was at that point Peter made a critical mistake.

I knew I could merge Gainers into Swift and add another $100
million in sales. Then I started selling off the pieces I didn't want,
and ended up selling about three pieces for close to the price I paid
for the whole thing. So that worked pretty well. Unfortunately I
kept the wrong parts.

I should have sold off the Edmonton meat-packing business—
because of that damn union.

Instead, Peter sold the Butterball turkey operation, the edible oil
plants and the associated real estate for about $43 million. Had he
flipped the entire operation, he says, it probably would have fetched
at least $85 million.

Instead, he kept the beef-and pork-packing operations. It was a decision that has influenced his life's course to this day—though he has no quarrel with beef producers.

"Cattle people are very independent and they try to live on the market. If the market for beef is high, they get rich; if it isn't, they lose. It's simple," Peter says. "They are wonderful people to deal with. During the mad cow crisis, they hunkered down and rode 'er out."

The pork producers, on the other hand, had their marketing board to protect them—and they didn't have to tough anything out if they could set a price that bore no relation to the market value of their commodity. The price meat-packers could afford to pay, or the price pork would fetch in the supermarket, mattered not a whit.

•   •   •

By the mid-1980s, Gainers was Canada's second-largest meat-processing company. The company boasted six plants and 17 sales, distribution and warehouse facilities in Canada and the western United States. Its brands—Swifts Premium, Lazy Maple, Superior, Light & Flaky, Eversweet and others—were supermarket staples. Yet all of it was about to go into the crapper.

There is no real trick to making money in the meat-packing business. When Swift first started in the 1800s, they made a fortune, 15 to 20 per cent. Then everybody got into the business. It didn't take a rocket scientist to build a meat plant, hang up a cow, kill it and cut it. At that time, they were mainly butchers, small-town butchers who did the job, and then they mechanized it and made some cost-savings and, of course, then everybody did it. Cattle and hogs became commodities.

As a businessman, you've got to stay away from commodities. You've got to get into something with higher margins, like this guy Jim Balsillie with BlackBerry. Like Google or Yahoo. Look at poor General Motors, they were going down the pipe. They ended up in bankruptcy protection because they could not compete with such low margins. They were paying $77 US, all in, per employee per hour. In China, they're getting 60 cents an hour. How can you compete with that?

With the slim margins and volatile price fluctuations that come with the commodity business, you have to have high volumes. As long as the commodity pricing is on the right side of the ledger, you can still make a lot of money. But it also means you can lose a lot of money with even a minor change in fortunes.

With the hog marketing board throwing market pricing out the window, Peter was facing a change in fortunes that was more than minor.

• • •

The Alberta Pork Producers Marketing Board was a strange beast to enjoy the benevolence of an ideologically conservative government. But for the Progressive Conservatives that ruled Alberta in the '80s, the only ideology was to pragmatically preserve their grip on power. Currying the favour of the province's pork producers was evidently sounder political strategy than worrying about the welfare of a billion-dollar meat packer. After all, there were 7,000 pork producers in Alberta, with 7,000 votes. Peter Pocklington had just one.

Why a so-called free-market government would get into collectivism is beyond me. I don't think they understood the economics of it. Obviously they didn't, it was all about vote-getting. Go to the farmers and say, "We'll make sure you get so much for your hogs, regardless of the market." It wiped out the packing business in Alberta. The province went from 10 packers to one by the time they dismantled the hog marketing board. And the one plant that was left was owned by the pork producers themselves.

If that's capitalism, that's ridiculous.

Peter has always been the poster child for free-market capitalism, but his sentiments are particularly strong on the topic of the meat-packing business. It's ironic, because it is Peter's experience with Gainers that his critics point to when arguing he was a corporate freeloader, a rich man who would ultimately live off the multi-million dollar largesse of the provincial government.

In fact, he argues just the opposite. Had the government not interfered with market forces, Gainers would have been profitable—and its workers would have prospered, too. The provincial bailout that would come to haunt him would never have been necessary.

In the States, if you create too many hogs, the price goes down, and when there are not enough hogs, the price goes up. The gestation period for a hog is three months, three weeks and three days. It's just bing, bing, bing, pop out. Pigs are a dime a dozen.

So the free market in the States works and it's the only thing that does. I can expound forever on markets and capitalism, but that government in Alberta was not a free-market government.

For Gainers, and for Peter, the problems began when the hog marketing board hiked the price of a hog an average of $20 a head. Peter will point to that moment as the beginning of the end for the meat-packing industry in Alberta. Even when meat-packers were paying a competitive price to get a hog to the killing floor, they were lucky to make 20 per cent after cutting it up and sending it to market—and from that 20 per cent they had to pay for their labour, overhead and other expenses. The extra $20 a head the marketing board was charging was more than a meat-packer could pay and still earn a profit. After all, super-markets weren't about to pay more just because the hog marketing board wanted more. Supply and demand dictated the price they paid.

The basis of the hog business is you buy a hog, and you pay for it based on what you can sell the parts for. But the government said, "No, no, you've got to pay the farmer, say, $140 because he needs $140." So I said, "If he needs $140, tell him not to raise hogs. Let me buy it from someone who will sell them to me for $100." It's as simple as that. If you're paying $140 for a hog, and after everything you've done, you're selling it for $140, you're just losing your ass.

England tried a hog marketing board in the 1930s and it almost destroyed the hog business there. You can't regulate price. As soon as you interfere with the marketplace, you are causing great havoc and pain to everybody.

In a free market, if the price is where the farmers aren't making any money, they quit producing hogs. But if a marketing board sets an artificially high price, the farmers turn out more hogs. Now if there are more hogs than the market needs, the retail price drops even more, yet the packers are still stuck paying the higher price. So there is no margin. You can't make any money.

Then on top of that, along came the union and said, "We want a 27-per-cent wage increase."

• • •

The first signs of labour strife came in 1984, when the United Food & Commercial Workers union threatened strike action. Peter had no appetite for a strike.

> We had a good run to about '84. We had been making good money because we were the only game in town and the hogs were at a price we could afford to pay. But that was beginning to change, so when the union raised its head, I put up a tent and said, "I'll hire all new workers if you're going to strike," and they backed down.

According to a report produced by the Edmonton Public Library, Gainers won a wage freeze for existing employees, a wage cut for new employees, from $12 to $7 an hour, a reduction in benefits and mandatory overtime.

In return, Peter promised profit-sharing for employees. But with the hog marketing board beginning to flex its muscle, profits would soon be hard to find—and hard feelings began to fester.

Peter's corporate lawyer, Bob Kinasewich, remembers that time.

"There were years that Gainers did make a ton of money," Kinasewich says. "But you could go from making $12 million to losing $12 million in the span of one year."

So after the 1984 strike was averted, Peter and his advisors decided to try to improve the relationship with their disenchanted workforce.

"Sure, Peter was tough on the workers, but at that point the company wasn't making money," Kinasewich recalls. "I remember Peter turning around and saying, 'OK, we're gonna try and get the workers onside. I'm going to throw a big party for them.' So he threw this big party at the Northlands Sportex, and brought in Tanya Tucker to perform."

All 1,100 workers were there and everything was free—everything. "It wasn't cheap," Kinasewich says. He remembers something else, too, a disturbing incident that was in some ways a portent of things to come:

"There was this one guy—I was on the fringe, watching—and this guy was stalking Eva Pocklington. Then he walked up to her and asked her to dance. And Eva said, 'Sure.' So I went over to the security guy and I said, 'I think we may be having a little issue here. As soon as this guy is finished dancing with Mrs. Pocklington, let's not make a scene, but hopefully he'll move when we tell him.' So the security people walked up to this guy and they just picked him up by his arms and walked him out. And he was armed. He was a disgruntled employee."

Two years later, Peter's labour problems would be more widespread.

. . .

In 1986, the Alberta economy was flat on its back. Oil prices had nosedived and 50,000 Albertans had lost their jobs. Meanwhile, 1,100 workers at the Gainers plant in Edmonton were determined to make up the concessions they had yielded two years earlier and gain wage parity with other meat-packing plants in Canada.

On June 1, they struck the 66th Street plant. It grew into one of the most bitter labour disputes in Alberta history. Violence on the picket lines was commonplace. As many as 300 police were called in on a daily basis to enforce the peace. More than 400 union members and their supporters were arrested. Workers went more than six months without a paycheque. A boycott of Gainers products was organized that crippled the company and undermined its market share. And Peter Pocklington's reputation with organized labour was shredded.

Nobody won.

The union entered the fray demanding a 27-per-cent raise for workers. Peter argued that would make the ancient Gainers' plant even less competitive than it already was. "In Taiwan, workers get $300 a month for the same jobs," he famously announced.

Instead, the company offered 5 per cent. I must admit I am not a fan of unions, for many reasons, mainly the libertarian one: they don't work. They're like a convoy in time of war. They travel at the speed of the slowest.

But this union was pretty militant and they thought they could control me. Obviously, they didn't. I like running things. I like paying people to do a job they want to do and pay them more if they do more, produce more—not base it on, "This is what you get if you're here 30 years."

So it was a collision of my libertarian beliefs and the union's collective, communist beliefs. It had nothing to do with whether I liked or disliked the people, it was the philosophy. I knew all kinds of people at the plant who I liked a lot. They were wonderful people, they just got caught up in this crazy unionism.

Once he knew a strike was inevitable, Peter had three options: he could negotiate a settlement his company could not afford; he could close the plant and salvage what he could from the company; or he could take the most problematic course—hire replacement workers. He chose the latter, and hired 1,000 of them to take the place of his strike-bound workforce. "I had to compete in the marketplace—and with the government controlling the hog prices, I had no alternative," Peter said at the time.

> When you mix a union telling you they want a 27-per-cent raise
> and a government telling you that you have to pay more than a hog
> is worth, it's all over! You cannot make money.

The fallout was immediate. On June 1, the first day of the strike, picketers prevented the buses filled with replacement workers from entering the plant. The same went for the farm trucks delivering hogs.

On the second day, the company was granted an injunction to limit the number of pickets at the plant, with the intent of allowing the replacements and the hogs to get through. The strikers defied the court order and the police intervened, outfitted in full riot gear. The strike turned really nasty, really fast.

Peter responded in kind. Some of the strikers were "terrorists" and "former employees," he indelicately declared, adding he would never sign a collective agreement. He even threatened to terminate the company pension plan, which at that time was valued at about $50 million.

Alberta's labour leaders were outraged over Peter's sabre-rattling. On June 13, a rally at the Alberta Legislature drew an estimated 10,000 people, protesting for better labour-relations laws for the province.

> Sure, I hired what I called free-market labour. The union called
> them scabs, but to me they were people who wanted a job and
> would work for a wage that was a good wage. We hired people
> from Quebec, who would break the strike lines. And of course,
> every morning, the city had to bring in probably 200 or 300
> policemen. It was madness. It was chaos. Anyway, I ran the
> company for about six months with this free-market labour.

● ● ●

As the strike continued and Peter took more and more of a thrashing in the media and with the public, his friends recall he held his head high throughout.

Glen Sather remembers when he, Peter and several of their friends were returning from one of their fishing trips to the Arctic. When they arrived at the airport in Edmonton, the Gainers' strikers were waiting for them.

"There were 400 or 500 picketers at the airport," Sather recalls. "The security people came on and said, 'Listen, we'll take you guys out the back way.' Most of them went the back way, too, but four or five of us marched right through the crowd. Peter was in front. He marched right through them all. They were all yelling, but nobody did anything."

"I remember the strikers saying, 'You can pay Gretzky, why can't you pay us,'" Peter remembers with a laugh.

Sather argues that owners of sports clubs are treated differently than other business people when there are disputes such as the Gainers' strike.

In 1997, when the same workforce and the same union struck the same plant—by this time operated by Maple Leaf Foods—over the same issue of wage parity, Maple Leaf closed the plant, laid off the employees, and moved the work to a new plant in Brandon, Manitoba.

Yet Maple Leaf's president, Michael McCain, was not demonized the way Peter had been, though it could be argued his "crime" was far worse. Sather says it's because McCain did not own a hockey club.

"There's a difference between sports guys and other business guys," Sather says. To his mind, people in those circumstances do wonder why they can't get their raise if Wayne Gretzky is being paid millions.

"I think that's got a lot to do with it. And they don't resent Wayne. They just resent the guy who doesn't pay it on the other side. They all figure, 'That guy's got a ton of money, because look what he can do here. He's gotta be able to afford us.'"

•   •   •

The most effective tool in the union's strategy to hurt the company was a co-ordinated boycott of Gainers product that not only discouraged consumers from buying their products, but supermarkets from stocking them.

At the time, it was reported the boycott was the most successful ever organized in Canada. The fact the same union was also active in Safeway, the largest supermarket chain in Western Canada, was the key to helping the boycott flourish.

"Safeway and the various big stores, they all buckled," Peter remembers. "They had no balls. I was shocked."

One striker, quoted at the time in the *Journal*, boasted how 20 union members had fanned out across Canada to promote the boycott. It was so successful, some Gainers' brands disappeared forever. "We did a good number on them," said the striker, whose livelihood ironically depended on the company he was helping to cripple. "They never got half their contracts back."

By December, as the strike entered its sixth month, it was estimated the cost to the local economy had exceeded $100 million. The pressure on Peter to settle was getting more difficult to ignore— and he was losing the public relations war.

I didn't have a printing press. I didn't have an army. I was one guy—and especially one guy they're not very happy with. There were 1,100 people on the street demanding a 27-per-cent pay increase and because of the hog marketing board, I couldn't afford to give them that. I couldn't afford anything.

The government destroys you with their policies and then expects you to deal with a union wanting a big raise. It's just beyond comprehension. As a free person in a free society, how do you deal with that?

Being a sane individual, you have to deal with it the best you can.

Finally, in early December, Peter took a call from Don Getty, the premier of Alberta. "Peter," said Getty, "I'd like to have a chat."

• • •

To say each side in this dispute had underestimated the resolve of the other is simply stating the obvious. Yet for months, no resolution seemed forthcoming. The union, emboldened by its successful boycott of Gainers' products and swelling public support, decided bringing Peter Pocklington to his knees was only a matter of time. Yet all Peter needed was time for his replacement workers to get up to speed.

> We were just gradually training them, and getting efficient again, when Getty phoned me. He said, "What's it going to take to settle this strike?" And I said, "Don, we have a real problem. You have a hog marketing board, which means I'm paying too much for hogs. I can't make ends meet this way. This is ridiculous."

Moreover, Peter told the premier, he was having difficulty getting financing from his bank because they wouldn't accept Gainers' $40 million in inventory receivables as collateral because the wholesale price for hogs was too high and the retail price for pork products was too low.

"If you want me to settle this strike, I will. I'll hold my nose and settle it, and take back most of the union workers," Peter told the premier. But he also said he was going to keep at least half of his replacement workers because "they're good guys and gals who are working hard and now they are trained."

Then Peter laid out his terms to settle: a $50-million interest-free loan. In return, Gainers would pay the province 10 per cent of its operating profit every year for the first four years in lieu of a fixed interest rate. "So if the company makes $10 million a year, you get $1 million in interest," Peter told Getty.

After four years, the company would assume a regular mortgage to pay off the balance.

Peter also offered more than 100-per-cent collateral in return for a long-term repayment: the inventory receivables, as well as the plant, the property and the equipment, valued at $25 million, for a total of $65 million in security.

But, Peter emphasized, the hog marketing board had to go.

"All right, you've got a deal," Getty told Peter and they shook hands. It was the last time the two sides would agree on anything.

. . .

The first sign the deal was headed south came from Getty: "Now you'll have to deal with Johnston," he told Peter.

Dick Johnston was an MLA from Lethbridge and the provincial treasurer. That gave him responsibility for the province's finances. It also put him in charge of the Alberta Treasury Branches (ATB) which, according to testimony Johnston would later give in court, the Tory government treated as a slush fund through which public funds could be directed without legislative scrutiny.

Dick Johnston was no fan of Peter Pocklington. The feeling was mutual.

From the outset, Peter says, Johnston began to change the terms of the deal. "Well, no, we can't do an interest-free loan," Johnston told him. Instead, the province would guarantee a $2-million loan to Gainers every six months at a floating interest rate starting at 10.5 per cent, and "we'll stamp it with a government guarantee, so you take that to whichever bank you want." That meant Gainers could borrow the money at the prime rate, the same rate the government received. And because the terms were changed, the value of the loan was bumped from $50 million to $55 million.

But it also meant the loan was incurring interest, plus a 0.5-per-cent "stamping fee," irrespective of how much money Gainers was making or losing. What was intended as a loan where interest was tied to profit would, within two years, turn into a $6-million drain, says Peter. Oh, and "they wouldn't get rid of the hog marketing board, either."

By the time the deal was ready for signing, it bore no relation to the agreement Peter had with Getty. So, why sign it? "They said, 'Take it or leave it,'" Peter remembers.

Unfortunately, I had already done my part. I brought back the union within a week. There was no raise. I think everybody was worn out. But a lot of the workers had quit by this time and gone elsewhere, so I was able to keep half of my non-union replacement employees, even though they had to join the union.

I was in business again, trying to rebuild again after the trauma of the strike. Only this time we were also under the debt load the government had put on the company and we still had the hog marketing board, despite their promises to the contrary. "You guys speak with forked tongues," I told them. "That wasn't the deal. What goes on here?" They said, "Well, we had to get it approved by cabinet and cabinet wouldn't approve it." What a load of horseshit.

But by this time, I had no choice. The bank that I had been dealing with, the Continental Bank, they were happy to get repaid and get out of a losing situation. So away we went.

Crippled with a debt load that had been forced upon it, and handicapped by inflated production costs, the company began hemorrhaging money—at least $1 million a month.

This went on for two years, Gainers losing $1 million a month, the province "loaning" its $2 million every six months. It was almost a foregone conclusion Gainers would miss its first $400,000 loan payment.

On top of that was a $67-million aid package the province had promised provided the money was used for upgrading Gainers' Edmonton plant and to help build a $25-million meat-packing operation in Picture Butte, a small town north of Lethbridge.

Gainers failed to start construction on the new plant, even after the province gave it a three-month extension. "Why should I build another plant?" asks Peter. "So I could lose another million a month?"

By October of 1989, the government decided it was putting Peter Pocklington out of the meat-packing business.

The government brought me in to a meeting around a big round table and said, "Well, we're pulling the plug." And I said, "Oh really? Nice of you to let me know. Here are the keys."

I said, "Good luck. If you think you can run it better than I can, be my guest."

The Alberta government assumed control of Gainers, Kretschmar Foods and Magic Pantry, a move that, four years later, then provincial treasurer Jim Dinning would term "a mistake."

It was an expensive mistake, too. By the time the province sold Gainers to Burns Foods of Calgary in 1993, Gainers had lost $80 million as a government-owned business. That rate of loss, an average $20 million a year, was almost twice what Peter was sustaining in his final two years at the helm. In addition, the province was forced that same year to kick in an additional $9.25 million or the Banque de Paris would have foreclosed on a $27 million line of credit.

In the end, Burns paid $3 million for Gainers, about 1/20th of the price Peter paid for it 11 years earlier.

"They just destroyed the business," says Peter of the government. "They didn't know what the hell they were doing. They destroyed everything."

After that, the chastened Tories pledged to "get out of the business of business."

Meanwhile, the Alberta Pork Producers Marketing Board continued its price-fixing until 1996, when it lost its monopoly with hog producers. In 2001, the board's role became solely a marketing one.

· · ·

In 1996, three years after Burns bought Gainers from the Alberta government, both companies were purchased by Maple Leaf Foods, a company operated by Wallace and Michael McCain, whose family had made their fortune in New Brunswick as purveyors of frozen pizzas and French fries.

The very next year, the UFCW went back on strike. Edmontonians feared there would be a repeat of the bitter labour dispute on the same site that 11 years earlier had demonized Peter Pocklington.

This time, the province declared it would not get involved in helping settle the strike. "We will be staying out of the labour situation. Let them make their decisions," declared Agriculture Minister Ed Stelmach, who in 2006 would become premier himself.

While Michael McCain responded by closing the plant, he was not, unlike Peter, hung in effigy.

A few years after that, the 80-year-old Gainers' plant was torn down. A warehouse now stands on the site.

· · ·

Whatever regrets Peter harbours in his heart of hearts, he does not dwell on them.

> You can't turn the clock back. You've got to deal with what's on the table. I can have all kinds of regrets that I should have done this, this or this differently. Hindsight is 20/20, but you can't re-spin the tapestry of your life.
>
> You know, I've got 20 or 30 years left, and I'm sure as hell not going to worry about what I did wrong in those days. I'm just not going to repeat the mistakes—and keep moving.

That said, this chapter in Peter's life took a financial toll from which he would never recover. Prior to 1986, Peter always seemed to have enough money to do what he wanted. Afterwards, he never seemed to have enough.

To this day, some of Peter's friends won't speak at length about the Gainers' strike. "That was pretty ugly," says Kevin Lowe.

But if Peter's public standing sustained a serious blow during that six-month strike in 1986, it would suffer an even worse one two years later. Moreover, there can be little doubt that what happened on a summer day in 1988 would be attributed, at least in part, to Peter's suddenly precarious finances.

"Maybe it's unfair because Peter did so many other things. He was a generous guy with charities and everything," says Oilers broadcaster Rod Phillips. "But his legacy is going to be as the guy who traded Wayne Gretzky. And there is nothing anyone can do about it."

PART XI

'I was captured by bandidos for three days. That was fun'

*Peter Pocklington makes a name for himself as the owner of a
professional hockey team, but he is also the proprietor of one of the
most successful franchises in the history of minor-league baseball.
Then there is his love of speed.*

Given the success Peter Pocklington would find in the world of minor-
league baseball, he was surprisingly reluctant to get into the business.
But never before had he encountered a man with the persistence of
Mel Kowalchuk.

For 18 years, Kowalchuk was for the Edmonton Trappers what
Glen Sather was for the Oilers—the man who ran the club on Peter's
behalf, and did so successfully. And from day one, it was Mel
Kowalchuk who was the inspiration behind the Trappers.

Peter first met him at an Oilers' game in the fall of 1980.

> Mel just bugged the piss out of me. "Look, I found a triple-A team
> that's available," he said to me. "Please, you've got to help me buy
> this team." After four or five times, I gave up telling him to go away,
> so I said, "Well, come and see me in my office." Sure enough, the
> next day, he was there. His persistence paid off.

The triple-A team Kowalchuk was so keen on buying had been
playing out of Ogden, Utah, for the previous three years. But the
Ogden A's were in fact one of the more storied teams in the Pacific

Coast League. They were born in 1919 as the Seattle Rainiers, and played there for the next 50 years. In 1969, Major League Baseball awarded a franchise to Seattle, the Pilots—now the Milwaukee Brewers—so the Rainiers moved to Eugene, Oregon. After five seasons, they moved on to Sacramento for four seasons, followed by two years in San Jose and then to Ogden.

The team's owner was a local trucking magnate named Dennis Job. Peter suggested they go to Ogden to meet with him.

I told Job, "Look, I'll give you $100,000 a year for three years, no interest. Take it or leave it." He took it, so I moved the team to Edmonton. Then I went down to Scottsdale—where I think the PCL had its headquarters—and they approved the move. It was a helluva little organization.

According to one published report, the PCL executives wanted to know if Peter had the financial wherewithal to take on a team. His response: he had lost millions on his sports ventures in the past and a few hundred thousand more wouldn't hurt. But as it turned out, the Trappers turned a tidy profit every year, anywhere from $200,000 to $400,000 a season.

Kowalchuk took over as club president and the Trappers snared a major-league affiliation with the Chicago White Sox. Over the years, they would also work with the Florida Marlins, Oakland Athletics and California Angels. They played out of Renfrew Park, a 6,500-seat stadium built in 1935 in Edmonton's river valley. It was creaky, the roof leaked, and so did the plumbing, but the Trappers filled it most every night.

In 1995, Peter contributed $4 million towards a $9-million renovation that rebuilt the stadium from the ground up and expanded the seating to 10,000. The City of Edmonton kicked in the rest in return for the Trappers signing a lease that was supposed to keep them in Edmonton until 2019. A 14-year deal on the naming rights for another $2 million followed with the telecommunications giant Telus.

One of the unique features at Telus Field were the field-level luxury boxes behind home plate and along the baselines. "We had those boxes sold in a matter of weeks," Peter remembers. "You know, they were cheap, $15,000 or so a season."

He credits Kowalchuk for the success of that venture, and for most every other success the Trappers enjoyed.

> Mel was perfect. I could stay in the background and watch him work. He did everything, even got out and sold tickets. He's got more balls than a canal horse, you know. He steps right up and is a hard-working guy. He certainly knows his business.

The Trappers were a success at the gate and on the field. They won the league championship three times during Peter's tenure as owner, and added another divisional championship. They were also among the league leaders in attendance, averaging over a half-million fans a season, and over time became the most successful triple-A team in Canada.

That didn't stop offers to buy the team from several U.S. cities. Kowalchuk admitted once to CFRN's John Short he would often counsel Peter to sell.

"Peter always refused," said Kowalchuk. "I told him the deals would be good financially, but he thought the franchise was good for Edmonton and he liked going to the park on a warm night."

One of those offers came from Dan Orlich, the controversial Florida businessman who would later own the Edmonton Cracker-Cats, the independent baseball team that would take over Telus Field in 2005 after the Trappers were moved to Texas. Orlich, too, hired Mel Kowalchuk to run his team, but fired him halfway through their first season.

> As I said when I was in the car business, if you find them too tough to deal with, you don't. I kicked his ass out. I said, "Go away, I wouldn't want you to own the team. You'd ruin it." And away he went. Of course, then he came back and did his thing with this other team and almost ruined baseball in Edmonton.

. . .

That the Trappers no longer play in Edmonton, despite the team's obvious success, is a sore point for Peter.

In 1999, after the Alberta Treasury Branches had taken control of the Trappers, the Edmonton Eskimos of the Canadian Football League bought them out of receivership for $5 million US, or around $8 million CDN.

Five years later, the Eskimos sold the team for $13 million CDN to a group that moved them to a suburb of Austin, Texas. The reason? The Eskimos claimed the Pacific Coast League no longer wanted a team in Edmonton. At that time, the Trappers were the only Canadian franchise left in the PCL; the Vancouver Canadians had moved to Sacramento in 2000, the Calgary Cannons went to Albuquerque in 2002. The U.S.-based teams grew tired of the travel costs to Edmonton, the constant rescheduling of games because of inclement weather, and the hassles at customs. There was even a prevalent pro-American, anti-foreigner jingoism in the wake of 9/11.

Moreover, there was nothing in the Trappers' lease on Telus Field to keep them there, particularly when the league did not want them in Edmonton.

Peter says as long as the team was viable, he would not have caved to the pressure to move.

If the league wanted the team moved, there was not a hell of a lot they could do about it. The Trappers were in Edmonton, they couldn't cancel the franchise.

What the Eskimos said about the league making it pretty difficult for them was bullshit, and it was wrong. If the people in Edmonton are bitter about the team leaving, they should be. The Trappers outdrew most of the other teams in the league.

. . .

If Peter harbours hard feelings about the Eskimos, it's more than something personal. He cannot fathom the appeal of football in general, and of the Canadian Football League in particular.

In 1981, when Peter heard his friend Nelson Skalbania had bought the Montreal Alouettes, he famously declared: "The CFL has a future as long as my dong." Physical attributes aside, he's been more right than wrong, given the checkered history of the Canadian league.

He is kinder in his assessment of the National Football League, especially since one of his buddies from Edmonton's heady boom days, Pat Bowlen, owns the Denver Broncos. Nevertheless, the sport leaves him cold.

"Football is three hours' worth of watching for 12 minutes of actual playing time," he says.

Now soccer, says Peter, that's a game that's worth watching. "I'd rather go watch a good soccer game than a football game any day. It's constant excitement."

All of which goes a long way towards explaining Peter's passion for the Edmonton Drillers.

The original Drillers were born as the Hartford Bicentennials in 1975 as part of the North American Soccer League. It was a time when the league was aggressively marketing itself to North American audiences with such teams as the New York Cosmos, Chicago Sting and Toronto Blizzard, and featured Pelé, Franz Beckenbauer and other prominent players.

After three years in Hartford, the team moved to Oakland to become the Stompers and that's where Peter found them at the end of the 1978 season. The next year, the Drillers were playing out of Commonwealth Stadium.

Before he brought the Stompers to town, Peter spoke with several of the ethnic communities in Edmonton, trying to gauge how supportive they'd be.

When I checked it out, they were all supportive like mad. Every ethnic group in the city was just excited as hell about the idea of the team, and said they'd sell, you know, 20,000 season tickets.

But it didn't turn out that way. It ended up if the star wasn't a German or from one of the other groups, they would be pissed with you. And if the star was from one of the other ethnic groups, they would all be pissed at you, big time. Oh, it was crazy.

Despite the challenges that came with finding harmony among the Italian, Croatian and Ukrainian communities, the Drillers were a success, on the field and at the gate.

Oh hell, the Drillers were great. They actually did pretty well. We got great crowds. And the soccer was really, really good.

Peter brought in soccer legends Timo Liekoski as coach and Graham Leggat as general manager. Liekoski was named the NASL's coach of the year in the Drillers' first season, and took the team to the division championship in their second.

The team averaged 10,000 fans that first year, 11,000 the next. Then the NASL decided to add an indoor soccer season to its schedule. Peter thinks that was a mistake.

"The NASL could have been great, but they pushed into indoor soccer at the same time," he remembers.

Nevertheless, the Drillers were a hit indoors, too, attracting up to 7,000 fans to Northlands Coliseum over their two seasons. Moreover, the indoor Drillers won the league championship over the Chicago Sting in their first indoor season, 1980–81. "It was a great team," says Peter.

Unfortunately, it was also an expensive one. Most of the Drillers' players for both the indoor and outdoor teams were imported from Europe and South America, and insisted on being paid "*Neto*"—that is, without any taxes deducted. It was the club's responsibility to not only pay the players, but pay their taxes, too.

The only way you could get the great players was to pay them tax-free dollars, which obviously I had to do. And then, of course,

if you didn't get an Englishman on the team, the English fans
wouldn't come. If you didn't get an Italian, the Italians wouldn't
come. It was never easy.

Unfortunately the league grew too much, too fast and began to
implode. For 1982, the Drillers' last season, the NASL shrank from 21
teams to 14. The Drillers moved from Commonwealth to the much
smaller Clarke Stadium, a strategy that cut their costs but also cut
their attendance in half. When the season ended, so did the Drillers.
The NASL continued to shrink to 12 teams, then nine, and disappeared
two years later.

Bob Kinasewich estimates Peter lost between $10 million and
$12 million on the Drillers. "People can crap over Peter all they want,
but who else would put up that kind of money to try and bring that
sport to this city?" he asks.

· · ·

It was Kinasewich's job to keep Peter out of trouble whenever he
could, and the business of professional soccer gave Peter ample
opportunities for getting into trouble.

One of those times was when he decided to buy the Calgary
Boomers from his buddy Skalbania.

"Peter goes to a soccer league meeting in Toronto, and he comes
back and he's got this crumpled up napkin and he says, 'I just bought
the Calgary franchise from Skalbania. There it is. Call the lawyer, do
the deal,'" Kinasewich recalls.

The fact the deal was scribbled out on a napkin was only the first
sign of trouble. The Boomers carried a lot of player contracts that
Kinasewich considered excessive—"absolutely ludicrous," he says—
and it was his opinion the organization was not well run. "Jesus, Peter,
this franchise is so far upside down," Kinasewich told him. Peter
wouldn't budge.

"It will be the most powerful franchise in the league," Peter
responded. "We'll win everything. See what you can do."

But Kinasewich wasn't sure Peter could even do the deal. "I don't know where you are going to get the money from because I don't know who is going to lend you money for this," he told Peter.

Then Skalbania's lawyer called. "OK, I want documents," the lawyer said.

"Hold on, I'm not doing anything," replied Kinasewich. "I'm doing some due diligence first."

"You've got a binding agreement," Skalbania's lawyer said, "and we'll sue Peter Pocklington so fast it will make your head swim."

Kinasewich laughed. "Give me a break, I got a napkin in front of me. Get lost."

It wasn't long after that, Kinasewich remembers, that the Drillers, the Boomers and the North American Soccer League all closed up shop.

. . .

Peter wasn't done with soccer, though, nor with the Drillers. Fourteen years later, he was running the Coliseum and was casting about for a tenant to help keep the place full. Enter Mel Kowalchuk with another idea—a second go-round with an indoor soccer team.

"Again, I got talked into it by Mel Kowalchuk, believe it or not," says Peter. The idea was to create some synergy between the Trappers and the Drillers, using the same office and administrative staff for both—Trappers in the summer, Drillers in the winter.

So Peter bought the Chicago Power of the National Professional Soccer League and revived the Drillers for the 1996–97 season. Kowalchuk was the first general manager, followed by Peter's son Zach a year later.

In their home opener, the Drillers attracted 9,000 fans. A first-round playoff game against the Milwaukee Wave attracted 10,000 fans. They averaged 7,200 for the season—and lost $300,000 rather than the projected $500,000.

The Drillers' second season, however, started the same year Peter was forced to sell the Oilers and his other assets under threat of receivership. The uncertainty over Peter's finances had its effect on attendance, and the average fell to 5,200. By season's end, the club was sold to advertising executive Wojtek Wojcicki. He would run the club for two-and-a-half seasons more before it folded. The NPSL folded a year later.

> Soccer is a great sport, but I don't know if it will ever work in North America as a game people will watch. It works with kids, where you can put on a pair of runners and a pair of shorts and a shirt and away you go, you're playing soccer. It's a very healthy sport for youngsters to play.
>
> But soccer just will not go as a paying proposition. You just can't get enough folks in the seats.

• • •

One sport that does put folks in the seats is junior hockey, but it's been largely forgotten that Peter Pocklington once had a franchise in the Western Hockey League—and he is one of the reasons the city of Kamloops has a team today.

In 1981, the Oilers bought the New Westminster Bruins from Skalbania, moved them to Kamloops, and renamed them the Junior Oilers. They operated the team for three seasons before selling to local owners, who retitled them the Blazers.

While the Blazers have become one of the most successful junior teams in Canada, they might never have had the chance. "We put that team in Kamloops when nobody wanted them," recalls Glen Sather, "and they've been a huge success."

They also gave Sather an appetite for junior hockey. These days, he and his partner, Toronto Maple Leafs' general manager Brian Burke, own the WHL team in Chilliwack.

• • •

Peter didn't concern himself with only the business side of sport, however. He was, after all, a doer, not just a watcher. So he was a sportsman, too—a sportsman who was able to indulge his love of speed for fun and competitive accomplishment.

From Alberta to Mexico, Peter Pocklington was a powerboat racer.

> Because I view speed in slow motion, I looked at racing differently. The faster I went, the slower I thought I was going. I got pretty good at boat racing. It's a strange feeling when you're going 100 miles an hour in a boat on a river—everything slows down for me. Others are terrified. I am frozen in time. To me, it's just a dream. It was like—"Wow, how can I make this thing go faster?"
>
> I ended up with a boat with two turbocharged 850-horsepower engines, two of them in one boat. And this sucker would go! I was always looking for ways to make it go faster.

The boat, through its various incarnations and power outputs, was christened, appropriately enough, Free Enterprise. ("I remember putting up a billboard during an election," says Peter. "It read: 'Free Enterprise, Free People. Westown Ford.'")

One of Peter's more memorable races came in 1978 on the Smoky River between the towns of Grande Cache and Peace River in northern Alberta, a distance of about 300 kilometres.

Riding with Peter was Sather, his best friend.

"Peter got into the Smoky River race—the world championship—and he asked me if I wanted to go. So I said sure, why not?" Sather remembers. "We had a kind of trial run on the North Saskatchewan. It was fun."

Once they got up to Grand Cache, however, it was even more memorable. In fact, a photo of what transpired still graces the office walls of both Peter's home in Palm Desert and Sather's place in Banff.

Sather was Peter's navigator. "I was supposed to tell Peter where to go on the river. And, of course, Peter wouldn't listen to anybody when it came to that stuff, and we just went right into a huge trough."

God, we hit the rapids too fast, going about 90 miles an hour, and
the boat went up then crashed down through a big wave, and
almost broke my neck. The wave hit my helmet and knocked
Sather right out of the boat.

"I was sitting in the back of the seat, telling him to go right and
he just went straight," Sather recalls. "We were lucky the boat didn't
go right over backwards. We went straight up and then, when we
came down, a wave caught me and pulled me out of the boat. That
was exciting, I had whiplash for four or five days after that."

Though he never felt his life was in danger, Sather's adventure on
the Smoky River was over. "I couldn't move the next day," he says.
"But I didn't mind. That was Peter."

I had to get a new partner, so I ended up with an English
photographer named Nigel Ash. He was a real character. Nothing
bothered him. We had to have three in the boat though, so my wife
actually went the last leg because the other guy we had cracked his
ribs too hard on something and he wasn't going any further.

So it was Eva, Nigel and I who came steaming across in Peace
River. I think we came in second. It was just great. We came in
flying about 110 miles an hour, with a big roostertail you know,
coming out the back of the boat.

• • •

For a sport, powerboat racing is serious business. Sather recalls a
couple of Mexican racers who were killed on the Smoky course. "If
you lose power, you can't turn the boat," he says. The Mexicans lost
power and went into a rock wall. "Yeah, it can be dangerous."

Peter would face a different kind of risk the next year when he
decided to race the Rio Balsas in Mexico—roving bandidos. As it
turned out, however, Peter and these "desperados" grew to know each
other pretty well.

The Rio Balsas is one of Mexico's largest rivers, flowing downstream from the country's central region towards the Pacific Ocean near Acapulco. But farther upstream, past the plantations, are plenty of rapids and eddies, rocky terrain, and regions of the countryside that are largely ungovernable. It is there you will find the roving bands of gun-toting bandits.

Picture the pod races in *Star Wars Episode I (The Phantom Menace)*, and add water.

It was a 500-mile race, from a spot about 100 miles outside of Mexico City, down the Rio Balsas to the ocean, then down the coast for 100 miles to Acapulco. The bandidos literally controlled a lot of that area.

Guerrero province, at that time, wasn't what they might call civilized under the rule of law. The army went along with the race to make sure nobody was captured. They were flying overhead in helicopters. A lot of good that did.

My wife thought I was nuts for going on that river, so she decided to wait for me at the Acapulco Princess Resort.

Like the Mexican army, Peter flew over the course in a helicopter a few times to check out what to expect in the way of rapids and other obstacles. In the end, however, the reconnaissance mission didn't have the desired effect. He set off, with his friend Pat Bowlen riding shotgun, along with another friend. Again, Peter admits he was going too fast.

We went flying along this river at 70 or 80 miles an hour when we came around a corner and suddenly went into these rapids. They bubbled up to six, seven feet high. We banged way up, and went down and, unfortunately, I slammed the boat into reverse. Big mistake.

Now if you go into reverse on a jet boat, the cups go over the jets and that shoots the water forward. It lifts the back end up, the front goes down and the water pours in. We sank in the middle of this gawdamn river. I couldn't stop it.

The boat went straight down in about eight feet of water and the three of us—and, of course, all you have on are a pair of sneakers, shorts, a heavy-duty life jacket with steel mesh inside so you don't crush your chest, and a helmet—started swimming to shore.

Waiting on the embankment was a band of 20 or so bandidos, all of them armed.

Old army carbines, mostly—I think they were to shoot rabbits more than anything. They were simple backwoods people, villagers from a small town along the river that was totally isolated. It's just that they made their living, a lot of them, as bandidos. They were like Robin Hood and his band.

These Merry Men may have made their livings robbing anyone who came along, but they struck out with Peter and his compatriots.

I had nothing, just runners and shorts, and my boat, of course. Sure, they're outlaws, but outlaws are good people, too if you, know, you're not threatening them. And they certainly weren't going to threaten me or shoot me. It was like, "Go ahead, but what's that going to get you?" So they all kind of laughed, and began the job of getting me out.

Bowlen and Peter's other teammate—Peter doesn't remember who it was—decided they weren't going to stick around for any salvage operation, and the bandidos had no problem letting them go. Another boat picked them up and they headed off for Acapulco. Not Peter. "I wanted my boat," he says.

The army was too afraid to come after me. Great army. Most people would be frightened out of their minds, I suppose, but I enjoyed it. I got to know them all and they treated me well. I didn't find them anything but very hospitable.

One of the bandits, thank goodness, spoke a little English and I got along with him pretty well.

The leader was in his early 30s, and [he was] obviously the gang leader. He had the gift of the gab, so the others followed him easily. His sidekick was a tubbier guy and could speak fairly good English, so he helped me with communication. He was kind of a charming character.

Luckily, they ended up treating me like a good guy. And over the next three or four days, they helped me get the boat out.

The powerboat sat at the bottom of the Rio Balsas in eight feet of water. Its two 400-horsepower turbo-charged engines had been fried and the gas tanks were full.

The boat weighed at least a ton, 2,000 pounds of moulded aluminum, motors and gas. They had to dive down and put lines on it. It took a lot of work to get it out. Each engine would be worth at least $20,000 in today's money. They were engineered engines, balanced and turbo-charged and all the nonsense.

So we would work during the day, and then party every night. We had a helluva time. We finally got my boat out, and we floated it down the river and they helped me get it on a trailer and away I went. It was great fun. I have great, very fond memories of that.

. . .

And how exactly did Peter get into the powerboat business? "I bought the damn company—I don't know why," he says. He owned three boats in total, all built in Edmonton by a guy named Norman Deitch. "He got me into this crazy river racing. Buying that company was a complete waste of time, but I enjoyed it. Eventually we just closed it."

PART XII

'George Bush fished here with his pal, Peter Pocklington'

Peter makes many friends in Edmonton, but he also makes them easily in places that are, figuratively if not literally, a world away. These friendships become not only the stuff of memories, they afford Peter the luxury of being a benefactor for the city he loves to calls home.

A peek inside Peter Pocklington's Rolodex will yield several well-known names—not just hockey players but movie stars, recording artists, world leaders.

His critics would say that's only because Peter was the owner of a professional hockey club—in fact, one pundit posed the question whether Peter would even travel in such circles if he was solely the proprietor of a meat-packing business.

But does owning a hockey team bring with it that kind of currency? After all, Harold Ballard did not have the ear of presidents and prime ministers. No, if Peter held the respect of respected people, it may be because he earned it. And to hear him tell it, that's a two-way street. Much of what his friends find in him, he seeks out in others.

> Good friends have to have integrity. It takes a while for me to be sure that what you say is what you do, so I watch behaviour, and then what someone has to say, to see if the two match. If they do, then you have a trustworthy person. I also watch how people treat others, especially people in the service industry. If you are rude to a

clerk in a store, who else do you treat that way?

If you do find a trustworthy person, then you know if you need advice, you can phone them and ask, "What do you think?" and know you'll get a straight answer.

Peter's friends also speak to a generosity of spirit that belies his image.

Bob Kinasewich recalls a time in 1983 when Peter bought a condo on the Hawaiian island of Maui from Hy Aisenstat, the founder of the Hy's Steakhouse chain. "Bob, you've got to go over there and close this deal," Peter told him. Kinasewich replied that he was about to take some time off. "Well, then take your family over there and stay in the place," Peter responded.

"So I stayed in the condo before he did," recalls Kinasewich. "He's very generous that way."

Oilers' radio announcer Rod Phillips remembers staying at the same condo. "Yeah, I was telling Peter we were going to Hawaii on vacation. He asked, 'Where are you going?' I said, 'We're going to rent a place in Maui,' and he said, 'No you're not. You're going to use my place.' And I told him, 'Well I've got to pay you for it, Peter.' 'Are you kidding me?' he said. 'Don't be silly.' So, we were there for a month— right on the beach. It was just a fabulous place and he wouldn't think about taking a nickel. He's just a good guy."

Kinasewich says it was not unusual for Peter to show that kind of generosity. "I won't mention names but I ended up doing legal work for Peter's people, house deals and so on," he remembers. "There was one person, I had to go out East at Peter's expense and negotiate this person out of a horrendous deal they were just getting hosed on. I did a few others like that, too.

"I would say there were, during my three years working for Peter, maybe $75,000 worth of what would have been normal legal bills; Peter would cover them. Somebody would come in with a legal problem and Peter would say: 'Kinas, c'mon in.' Then we'd talk, and he'd say, 'Okay. Bob will solve it for you.' I did a lot of that. Peter was very generous that way."

If such sentiments were rarely expressed, they could be readily dismissed as an aberration, since they obviously don't mesh with the more commonly held perception of Peter as a self-absorbed welcher, mooch and scoundrel. But they're not rare—particularly as they relate to Peter's charitable efforts.

There was the $1.5 million he helped raise for the Canadian Cystic Fibrosis Association in the fall of 1986. It stands to this day as the single most successful fundraiser in the association's history.

The organizer was Mila Mulroney, who at the time was the chair of the Canadian Cystic Fibrosis Foundation; the event was a charity hockey game at the Ottawa Civic Centre between Peter's Oilers and the Montreal Canadiens. Mila Mulroney's husband, Brian Mulroney, speaks of the event with pride.

The former prime minister recalls a visit by Canadiens' owner Ronald Corey to 24 Sussex Drive inspired the game, but "it wouldn't have happened without Peter," he says.

Peter remembers he and Eva were visiting the Mulroneys when Mila asked for ideas for a fundraiser. "Have a hockey game," Peter responded.

Brian Mulroney says that, "without hesitation, Peter brought the Oilers down to Ottawa. There was a huge crowd—it was totally sold out—and a lot of money was made. In those days, as you know, the Oilers were the biggest thing in town. It was a great thing, just a wonderful evening."

Capping the night was the entertainment: Dinah Shore, a friend of Peter's from Palm Springs; and a young singer Mila had discovered in Montreal—Céline Dion.

Peter was also a long-time supporter of the $1,000 Henry Singer memorial bursaries awarded annually for many years to members of the University of Alberta Golden Bears hockey teams. Among the recipients was Cory Cross, who would later play 113 games for the Oilers in the mid-2000s.

As an active supporter of the University of Alberta, Peter's most notable contributions were with the faculties of physical education and business.

Peter gave the university $300,000 to help establish a clinic for the diagnosis, treatment and rehabilitation of sports-related injuries. The province matched Peter's contribution, and another $400,000 came from public fundraising. However, it was Peter who was granted the privilege of giving the facility its name. He chose the Glen Sather Sports Medicine Clinic.

In 1987, Peter also gave the university $250,000 to establish a chair at the School of Business. The Pocklington Professor of Private Enterprise is Mark Huson, who oversees a select group of finance students who manage a fund worth more than $1.2 million. Today, the Pocklington Chair in Free Enterprise has a book value in excess of $2.7 million and generates $108,000 in spending income each year.

There were times when Peter would financially support a cause even when he wasn't particularly enthusiastic about it. Kinasewich remembers such a time. In the mid-1990s, a new concert hall was being built in downtown Edmonton—a facility that came to be known as the Francis Winspear Centre for Music—and Kinasewich was helping with the fundraising. He agreed to see Peter for a donation.

At the time, Peter was running the Coliseum, Edmonton was going through a rough patch economically, and Peter saw the concert hall as competition for a shrinking entertainment dollar.

"Bob, why would I give money to my competitor?" Peter asked.

Kinasewich knew Peter loved both the opera and the symphony, each of which would call the concert hall home. "Forget the competition," he replied.

"No, I've got to fill in my dates at the Coliseum," Peter said. By that point, the Oilers weren't doing quite so well at the gate. "These guys at the opera, if the symphony is on that night, I lose those customers, or I might."

Kinasewich was unmoved. "Get over it, Peter," he said. "You know you love music."

And he did make a donation, too, says Kinasewich—around $25,000. "It wasn't a large amount of money—well, large for me, but not for him," laughs Kinasewich.

• • •

One of Peter's most significant philanthropic gestures, however, is also probably his least known—though no one would even know if the YMCA had not insisted on going public with the news. That would be the $1 million he gave in 1989 to build the Jamie Platz YMCA in Edmonton's west end.

At first, Peter insisted the donation be anonymous. "It was only with some convincing that he agreed to be known," YMCA president Wylie Stratford told the *Journal*'s Jim Farrell at the time.

Peter's donation gave him the naming rights to the $4.8-million facility. But, as was the case with the Sather clinic, he declined to put his own name to the building. He chose instead to name it in the memory of Jamie Platz, a young cancer patient. Peter credits the boy with helping inspire the Oilers to their Stanley Cup victory in 1985.

He remembers how he and the Oilers' players came to meet young Jamie.

> After every game, I took a bunch of kids into the dressing room to meet the players. And he was one of the youngsters that showed up. I took him inside and he became kind of an instant hit.
>
> I remember Jamie made a speech to the players. It was a short, boyish speech obviously, but he was a real inspiration to the guys. He was so rock solid, even in the face of what he was going through. He obviously knew what was happening to him, but I think deep down he really thought he was going to make the cut.
>
> He reminded the players that if they work hard, they can beat the challenges they face. And he said, "I've got a bit of a challenge, and I think I'm going to beat it." That did great things to a bunch of grown men, listening to this kid.

> Jamie Platz died of cancer in 1987. He was 12.

• • •

Then there were Peter's efforts on behalf of the students at McCauley School, located in Edmonton's rough-edged inner city.

In 1995, Peter made a pledge: if a McCauley student achieved an average over 80 per cent in Grade 9, and maintained grades throughout high school to get into a university or college, Peter would pay the tuition. He says he was helping students this way on an ad hoc basis for years but formalized it with this offer.

"A lot of the people I knew in Edmonton went to that school; like Joe Shoctor. Joe was a good friend of mine," Peter recalls of the Edmonton lawyer and civic booster.

It was Peter's intent to run the program for 10 years but, three years later, his battle with the ATB left him without the financial wherewithal to continue.

In 2001, Peter estimated he'd spent about $120,000 on the program. He does, however, assert he left additional funds, between $50,000 and $100,000, in an account with the ATB, with instructions it be used to continue to fund the scholarships. But the money disappeared, Peter says, and he has no idea what happened to it.

That said, many of Peter's other charitable efforts were directed at kids, particularly those from underprivileged backgrounds. And it wasn't just Oilers' games in Calgary and Winnipeg they were treated to—CFRN's John Short learned Peter once took a bunch of inner-city kids to Denver on a private jet for a Broncos' NFL game. Peter's good friend Pat Bowlen, the Broncos' owner, played host. "How did you find out we were there? Is nothing secret from you guys?" Peter asked Short afterwards. "I do a lot of things for kids—they're special to me. Don't tell anybody."

• • •

If Peter had a favourite charity, then it was the one that benefited most from his efforts: Junior Achievement.

A sort of chamber of commerce for kids, Junior Achievement fits nicely with Peter's own free enterprise beliefs. It focuses on providing young people with a business education, entrepreneurial skills and a workplace ethic to help them succeed.

Over the 20 years Peter was involved, he helped raise as much as $2 million for the Edmonton chapter, which Junior Achievement's local CEO Justin Dahlen said helped 100,000 kids take the program. When Peter left Edmonton in 1998, Dahlen told the *Journal's* Farrell it was "a terrible day for Junior Achievement."

> Because I'm a libertarian and don't like government interference in society—let alone business—I could work through Junior Achievement to open the door for youngsters, so they can learn how to create wealth rather than get on welfare. It makes people feel so much better about themselves if they can create something themselves and get a kick out of doing it and doing it well. So that's why I do it, for no other reason—and I brought in people of stature so I could get into the pockets of wealthy people to pay for Junior Achievement.

It was those "people of stature" who provided Peter with his primary fundraising vehicle. People would pay to meet world leaders and to hear them speak.

Among those Peter brought to Edmonton for this ongoing series: former U.S. presidents Gerald Ford and the elder George Bush, presidential advisors Alexander Haig and Henry Kissinger, former British prime ministers Margaret Thatcher and James Callaghan, and the late Israeli leader Menachem Begin. Peter was able to connect with them through his work with the Fraser Institute, the Canadian conservative think-tank.

"It would take a lot of phone calls and I was the main arm twister," Peter says of his ticket-selling prowess. "But I'm good at that."

• • •

Thatcher's visit in 1997 left a particularly big impression on Peter. Attendees were charged $225 for dinner at the Coliseum, $775 if they wished to also attend a pre-dinner reception outside the Oilers' dressing room. Then there was the dinner Peter and Eva hosted in honour of Lady Thatcher the night before, at their home on St. George's Crescent in Edmonton's exclusive Glenora neighbourhood. Peter charged five couples $5,000 each for attending.

Peter estimates the event raised half a million dollars for Junior Achievement.

After the speech, we drove Lady Thatcher back to the Macdonald Hotel—well, actually her plainclothesman did—and she leaned over and said to Eva and me, "Would you like to come up for a wee noggin?"

Eva looked at me and whispered, "What the hell is a noggin?" She knew that if Maggie so much as winked at me, I'd probably have run away with her. To me, she was one of the greatest women in the world. She was a real heroine of mine.

So I said, "Sure, we would love to." We went up to her suite and we quaffed a whole bottle of single malt scotch, chatted for about three hours, and got absolutely, um, shiny.

She and Eva talked about her family and her husband Dennis and the problems all women have with kids and so on. It was delightful.

Then the next morning, I flew her out to Vancouver for a meeting with the Fraser Institute, so I really got to know her well—as well as you can get to know somebody in three days. Lady Thatcher was probably the greatest woman of the twentieth century, she and Golda Meir. She transformed Britain, brought it from the struggling, socialist-dominated country having serious problems to the great country it is now. She lifted it right up.

She took on the unions and whipped them; she drew the line in the sand and won. And the other controversial thing was, she went to the Falklands and said to the Argentines, "To hell with you guys, you're not going to take my little piece of dirt," and sent the Royal Navy 7,000 miles to take them on. People thought she was mad, but, quite frankly, nobody screwed with Maggie. She was a tough gal.

. . .

Peter fancies himself a singer, though these days he rarely shows off his voice outside the shower. That wasn't always the case.

About a year after the Thatcher visit—and while the Alberta Treasury Branches was tightening its grip around his throat—Peter wowed a crowd of 400 at a fundraiser for the Cross Cancer Clinic with an impressive operatic aria.

"Not only was he the chief fundraiser, but he could sing," the institute's Jane Weller told the *Journal*'s Farrell. The event raised $43,000, but Peter garnered most of the attention. He "was a virtual Pavarotti," said Weller.

Peter's friend Don Berry says he's to blame for convincing Peter to get up and sing. "I think we made a bet or something: 'You get up and do this and I'll do something,'" Berry laughs. "I forget exactly how it worked."

But Berry does remember how well Peter sang. "He was outstanding. He could have been a professional. And he loves to get up and do that sort of thing."

If Peter did indeed sound like Pavarotti, he was no doubt inspired by the real thing.

When he took over management of the Coliseum in 1995, Peter decided the first big act he wanted to bring to Edmonton was the great Italian tenor.

I thought, "I'm going to get Luciano Pavarotti here. Let's see, who would know him." So I phoned his general manager, this guy named Herbert Breslin, who lived in Carmel, California, and he said, "I don't know. Who are you?" And I said, "Well . . ."

So I made a call to George Bush, Sr., and I said, "George, you want to phone this guy and tell him it's time he brought a concert to Edmonton?" So President Bush did. That impressed Breslin all to hell, and he flew up to Edmonton. He played this little game of clap, clap, clap in the middle of the Coliseum, and I guess the place had good noise, because he signed the deal that day. That's how it happened.

Pavarotti's Edmonton concert, his first in Canada in more than a decade, was an enormous critical and financial success. Moreover, Peter and Pavarotti remained friends up until the great tenor's death. The Pocklingtons were invited to Pavarotti shows in London and New York; the latter they attended with George and Barbara Bush. Fourteen months later, Peter staged a concert by the Three Tenors—Placido Domingo and José Carreras were the others—at the SkyDome in Toronto. Peter remembers fondly travelling with Pavarotti:

I got to sing with Luciano, to practise with him, and I got such a kick out of it. I certainly can't hold a hair to anything he did, but I did enjoy it.

It's fun to be with people like Luciano. People like him walk with the Great Spirit and they use that great creative energy they are blessed with. If you can find where your energy and creative thoughts are, and you zero in on that place, you, too, can become the best in the world.

That's why I like to be with young people. I tell them about the gift we've all been given, that they can do these great things, to discover what it is they're good at, and be passionate about whatever their talent may be. I enjoy hanging out with people like that.

• • •

Peter credits the discovery of his singing voice to Ronnie Hawkins, the legendary rockabilly star from Arkansas. Hawkins emigrated to Canada in 1958 and his band, the Hawks—who would later find fame of their own as Bob Dylan's backup band and most notably as the iconic rock ensemble known as The Band—frequently played dates in the London area. Hawkins would occasionally invite Peter to join him on stage and sing along with Rick Danko and Levon Helm.

In a *Toronto Star* story about Hawkins published in 2007, writer Ellen Moorhouse described the teenaged Peter as "Hawkins's roadie."

"I learned how to drink beer with Ronnie," laughs Peter. "We have a long-time friendship. When the Oilers would go to Palm Springs for their golf tournament, we'd stop in Vegas and catch up with him there. He'd have these wild parties."

The friendship with Hawkins has endured over the years. Peter was among the guests invited to a celebratory dinner for Hawkins in Toronto in 2002. Among the other attendees: Paul Anka, Whoopi Goldberg, Paul Simon, David Foster and Hawkins's fellow Arkansan, former U.S. president Bill Clinton.

• • •

One of Peter's most enduring friendships, though, was with the late Gerald Ford. They first met in 1977, when Peter brought the former U.S. president to Edmonton to speak at one of his Junior Achievement fundraisers. The two men quickly became fast friends.

"I honestly don't know why we hit it off," Peter recalls. "We just seemed to really get along well; he was one of my mentors."

During that visit, Peter invited Alberta's then premier, Peter Lougheed, to join them for dinner at the Pocklingtons' Saskatchewan Drive home. "They talked politics non-stop during dinner. I enjoyed Peter Lougheed. He was a good guy. He's a good politician, not a lot of wind." (Peter is not as flattering in his assessment of Lougheed's successors, Don Getty and Ralph Klein.)

Jerry Ford was one of my special friends. He had integrity; he was just so straight line. When he said something, he meant it. It was his word, his bond, his honour.

I asked him once why he pardoned Richard Nixon, knowing full well it would hurt his re-election chances, and he said it was just the right thing to do. "The country had to heal. Obviously the country's a lot bigger than I am," he told me.

He was also on the Warren Commission that investigated John F. Kennedy's assassination, and I asked him, "Do you really believe Lee Harvey Oswald acted alone?" He said, "With the information we were given, that was my conclusion."

He wouldn't go beyond that, wouldn't veer from that story. He couldn't.

There are so many conspiracy theories that have been presented over the years, but more and more, it appears Oswald in fact did do it. I know I've come to that conclusion. Obviously he was a patsy for somebody, whether it was the mob or Castro or whoever. Oswald knew too much so they got him out of the way in a hell of a hurry. I doubt we will ever know the whole story.

Peter serves on the board of the Gerald R. Ford Presidential Library and Museum on the campus of the University of Michigan in Ann Arbor. President Ford, conversely, was on the board of Peter's Gainers meat-packing operation. But it was on the golf course where their friendship was forged.

Every hockey season, during a break in the Oilers' schedule, Peter would organize a golf tournament for the players, as well as a group of his business associates, in California—first in the Coachella Valley, later at the famed Pebble Beach course south of San Francisco. Ford always served as host.

We would spend a couple of days there, with golf and dinner and a speech from Jerry. It was the kind of relationship where the guys thought, "God, if we can hang out with former presidents of the United States, we're all right." It really lifted them all up, in my opinion. And I think it was something they all looked forward to every year. I know I sure did.

Wayne Gretzky fondly remembers the golf tourneys as a welcome respite from the grind of the hockey season. "That was a big thing for us because in those days, road trips were long and the year was long and Peter would always make it so that we had four days in Palm Springs in February or early March," Gretzky says. "It would give us a break, and mentally get away from the game.

"We would always play golf with the president. Peter was very close to Gerald Ford. I remember the first time I heard Peter call the president of the United States 'Jerry.' I went over to him and I said, 'You're that close?' Peter said, 'Wayne, protocol.' 'Protocol?' I asked. He said, 'You either call him Mr. President or you call him Jerry if you're his friend.'

"Of course, I called him 'Mr. President.'"

Gretzky remembers the golf outings as not being particularly successful, for any of them.

"Of course, in late February, we hadn't played any golf all year long. We had the rented clubs and all that.

"For me, it was nerve-wracking, because I had to play in that group—Peter, myself and the president—and I'm not a very good golfer. At the time, none of us were very good.

"It was a really intriguing time though, to walk around with the president. He had a true friendship with Peter. I would listen to him asking Peter for advice on business. That was really interesting."

During the Palm Springs days, before the tournament moved to Pebble Beach, Ford and his wife Betty would invite the players over to their home in Palm Desert before they would all go for dinner at an exclusive desert eatery called Wally's Turtle. Former Oiler Dave Hunter remembers a particularly embarrassing incident while visiting the Fords.

Hunter had excused himself to use the bathroom, then was mortified when the toilet overflowed. "I looked around and said, 'Geez, they must have a plunger somewhere,' but they didn't. There was water everywhere," Hunter told the *Journal's* Jim Matheson. "The guys were hanging around outside the bathroom and who started coming down the hall? Mrs. Ford. I don't think I've ever been so embarrassed."

Sather says those trips were not only memorable and enjoyable for the players, but for any others who made the trip.

"There were probably 50 to 75 business guys who would come for those three days," Sather remembers.

There was, however, another more memorable annual function that involved Peter's friends, business associates, hockey people and world leaders—his annual fishing trip to the Canadian Arctic.

. . .

Peter does remember trying his hand at hunting geese, but it didn't stick.

"We used to go shooting up by Viking, [Alberta,] but I gave that up," he recalls. On his last trip, "hundreds of geese came in, we all jumped up, and I shot one. But when it came down, it hit me on the chest. I could have shot the guy next to me. I thought, 'Enough of this crap, let the birds live. I'll eat chicken.'"

But Peter does love to fish.

. . .

In the high Arctic, in what is now the territory of Nunavut, the Tree River flows north toward Coronation Gulf. It is there, about 150 kilometres east of Coppermine and not far from a fishing resort known as Plummer's Lodge, where there is perhaps the greatest fishing in the world for 30-pound Arctic char.

Every year for more than 20 years, Peter and Glen Sather would take 20 to 25 men to the lodge for five or six days of fishing.

"They were great trips. We had a lot of fun, caught a lot of fish," says Sather.

Included on the guest list were people "I enjoyed being around," says Peter: Michael Walker, executive director of the Fraser Institute; former Ontario premier and close Pocklington friend Mike Harris ("a good pal and a great guy"); Peter Cole, a senior vice-president at the Canadian Imperial Bank of Commerce; Simon Reisman, who negotiated the Free Trade Agreement with the United States for Brian Mulroney; Bill Comrie, founder of The Brick furniture chain; Bill Wilson, a senior vice-president with the Ford Motor Company of Canada, who granted Peter his first Ford dealership in Tilbury; Canada's former ambassador to Iran, Ken Taylor (who spirited 12 Americans out of Iran during the 1979–80 hostage crisis); Boston Bruins president Harry Sinden; and, on three or four trips, former president of the United States, George H.W. Bush (the elder).

Always joining them would be a number of Peter's executives from Cambra Foods, Pocklington Financial and his other companies. One of them was Bob Kinasewich.

"I asked Peter, 'Why do you do this? These trips are not cheap. They're expensive.' And he said, 'Bob, it's tough for friends to say no to friends.' I've always remembered that.

"There was nothing sinister about the trips," Kinasewich adds. "They were a lot of fun, there was a lot of camaraderie."

As a business expense, Sather says the trips weren't that expensive. "In relation to what a lot of people do now for team building, the money you spend on those things isn't that great," he says. "I read about a company that took 400 guys to New Zealand, took them on a huge trail that was like an endurance test. The people in the company, you know, would fight to go on this thing every year.

"It was a pretty good deal for Peter. I think the bank at some point didn't think it was a great deal, but that's the way you've got to do business today."

Sather remembers that preparations for the trip grew more complex with each passing year. "We started off with Oiler hats. Somebody else would bring something else along, so then the gifts became more elaborate. The next thing you knew, the guests were getting fishing apparatus or jackets. We gave them all leather jackets one year: 'Pocklington's Tree River Annual Fishing Trip,' stitched on them. And we'd give them a brochure that outlined what would happen on the trip, and the number of days they'd be there, and what to bring, what not to bring. It was like an itinerary for everybody. It was a regular printed brochure, that we'd do out of the office."

The group would fly up to Great Slave Lake in the Northwest Territories for a few days, then make the trek to the Tree River on an old DC-3 prop plane.

Throughout, says Sather, Peter was the perfect host. In turn, says Kinasewich, Sather was the ringleader, leading everybody on their fly-fishing routines. But as much as most of their friends and acquaintances clamoured to tag along, there was one who didn't—Wayne Gretzky.

"Oh yeah, Wayne's a real mountain man," laughs Peter.

There are two things, says Wayne, that Peter convinced him to do that he didn't want to. One was going to Ottawa with Peter for the 1983 Progressive Conservative leadership convention. The other was fishing with him on the Tree River.

"The biggest reason I didn't want to go was because I didn't like flying and Peter used to fly a DC-3 into the Arctic and land on a dirt runway, you know? And the pilot had long hair and one tooth and I hate fishing," Wayne says laughing. "So, I did that, I went along, and I said, 'Peter, I'm never going again.' But we ended up having a lot of fun there."

We'd leave Yellowknife in that DC-3 and there was a clay landing strip right there beside the river. Eustace P. Bohay was the name of the pilot. A big Texan, he was about six-foot-five and rougher than a—well, you wouldn't want to tangle with him. He could eat a tractor, that guy. And he's long since dead, but he was a folk hero up there. Great pilot, too.

Kinasewich vividly remembers Gretzky's experience with Bohay.

"Poor Wayne," Kinasewich recalls. "He was just scared shitless. This guy is flying the old DC-3 and he's about 200 feet above the water. It felt like you could touch the water, and Gretzky was going nuts."

Kinasewich says it helped that Bohay sat Gretzky in the co-pilot's seat. "He was sitting beside the pilot and the pilot kept saying, 'Wayne, relax. This is the safest place we can be.'"

Once there, Wayne settled into a routine of fishing during the day, and sitting around the fire at night, chewing the fat and having a few drinks. But that flight stayed with him as a white-knuckle experience that did nothing to ease his fear of flying.

There was one fellow who did enjoy sitting in the co-pilot's seat, though: the roughly 70-year-old George Bush.

Bush was a torpedo pilot in the United States Navy during the Second World War. His TBM Avenger was shot down over the Pacific in 1944, and his two crewmates were killed. Bush was rescued by a nearby submarine.

"George got a real kick out of sitting in the right seat next to Bohay on the way up to the Tree and back," remembers Peter. "Everybody got great pictures of the president sitting up in the cockpit."

Peter met the elder George Bush, the 41st president, while golfing with Ford, the 38th president, in Palm Springs in 1994. The following year, Bush agreed to come to Edmonton as one of Peter's guest speakers at a Junior Achievement fundraiser.

Among the guests who had dinner with Bush and the Pocklingtons the night before the speech: Bill Comrie, Don Stanley, Bruce Sanson, Angus Watt and their spouses.

George Bush is just a sweet, sweet, sweet man. I remember he had his picture taken with all the folks in the kitchen and the servers the night of the Junior Achievement dinner. And anything you do for him, you get an immediate letter. He really follows up with letters, with best wishes for everybody.

One year when we took him up to the Arctic fishing, there was a pool that he really loved, and to this day it is known as the Presidential Pool on the Tree River. He sent me a bronze plaque that I had embedded in the stone on the side of the presidential pool. It reads: "George Bush, 41st president of the United States, fished here with his pal, Peter Pocklington . . ." and the date.

The Tree was one of his favourite fishing spots; now with his bad hips he can't make the walk. After you get to the camp, you have to walk about three miles up. It's a tough walk, but at that time, God, he could almost run it. He was in really good shape.

Of course, the U.S. Secret Service came along, plus a few Canadian Mounties. They didn't want anything tragic to happen to a U.S. president on Canadian soil. Well, one afternoon after we were done fishing, we went back to the camp around 5 o'clock— and we were whipped. We went in the tent for a half-hour laydown—just as a grizzly came running through the area. And of course the Secret Service didn't want a grizzly going after the prez. I think the first time the bear came around, they just shot over his head to scare him away.

"They didn't shoot the grizzly. They wanted to," remembers Sather. Nevertheless, because Bush was there, as well as Ontario premier Mike Harris, the Secret Service and the RCMP were getting antsy.

"They all had guns, I mean big guns, and they were just waiting for this bear to come closer," Sather recalls. "Harry Sinden and I were there watching him, and we said, 'If you guys shoot that bear, you'll have every person in Canada who is concerned about protecting animal rights up here the next day.' The bear was maybe 150 yards away, and after we said that, he turned around and left. He was a big beautiful grizzly, too. You could see the hair on his back move as he walked."

Sather figures he knows what lured the bear to the camp. "Harry had brought a bunch of lobster from Boston, and of course we cooked it the night before and the Inuit guys hadn't cleaned it up. So the smell was wafting all over the area. I'm sure the bear could smell it from 10 miles away. No wonder he came around."

Peter has fond memories of the fishing camp regulars sitting around a fire at the end of day, having drinks, smoking cigars "and telling some lies about the day." But for many of them, there was more to these trips than that.

"We'd always have these contests, who could bag the biggest char," recalls Kinasewich. "I don't know how much money was there but it was a fair chunk. But no trolling was allowed. You had to be on the riverbank. They'd drop you off and you fish from the bank. Invariably, halfway through the thing, here comes this boat, and here's this guy in the boat, trolling and laughing.

"It was Peter. But he never did win."

The only one in the group Kinasewich ever saw win was Comrie. "We were getting ready to leave the camp and Comrie says, 'Aw shit, I'm damn near skunked and we've got to leave.' And right outside the camp, swish, he reels in this 25-pound char just like that.

"Of course, everybody booed and hissed."

. . .

Probably Peter's favourite fishing companion, though, was his father, Basil. Their relationship strengthened as the years passed, as evidenced by Peter's decision in 1984 to have his dad's name engraved on the Stanley Cup alongside his own. The NHL had the inscription, "Basil Pocklington," crossed off.

"Dad was quite annoyed," Peter remembers. "He couldn't understand why they'd do that. I said, 'Dad, those are the rules. You know the bureaucracies of this world.'"

• • •

Peter continues to be in regular contact with the elder George Bush. "He is one of my heroes," Peter says of the former president. Peter and Eva were among the VIPs invited to the launch of the aircraft carrier *USS George H.W. Bush* at Newport News, Virginia, in October 2006. To commemorate the occasion, Peter presented the former president a model of the ship that is on display at the George Bush Presidential Library and Museum, which is located on the campus of Texas A&M University in College Station, Texas.

They were also together at the state funeral of Gerald R. Ford in Washington, D.C. Ford died at the age of 93 in December 2006.

Ford arranged for Peter to be given one of the 75-mm gun casings from the funeral's 21-gun salute. Afterwards, the *St. Louis Post-Dispatch* and the *Detroit News* were among the newspapers whose columnists reflected on the special relationship Peter shared with the president.

• • •

Peter did invite Ford's predecessor, Richard Nixon, to speak at a Junior Achievement fundraiser, but it couldn't be arranged before Nixon died in 1994.

I asked Jerry to write—in fact, I still have a copy of the letter he sent to Nixon—to see if he'd mind coming to Edmonton. I thought he would certainly be of high interest, if anything. Nixon was

actually not a bad president, he was just a very strange guy.
According to Jerry, he had a really dark side to him.

Peter also had occasion to meet briefly with Bush's predecessor as president, Ronald Reagan. That opportunity came when the 1981 NHL All-Star Game was played in Washington, D.C. Peter used the occasion to ensure Gretzky also had the chance to meet Reagan.

"President Reagan hosted a luncheon for all the players," Gretzky recalls, "and Peter and Bill Wirtz (the owner of the Chicago Blackhawks) insisted I sit at the same table as the president. Here I was, 19 years old and sitting with President Reagan! That was pretty overpowering. At the time, there was this whole Cold War thing with Russia and, you know, Canada hated Russia in hockey, so it was pretty intriguing."

• • •

Surprisingly, one of Peter's dearest friends was a man with whom, on the surface, he shared little in common: Admiral Elmo R. (Bud) Zumwalt, Jr., of the United States Navy.

A Vietnam veteran, Adm. Zumwalt was the youngest man to become chief of Naval Operations when Nixon named him to the Pentagon post in 1970. He was 50. After he left the navy, Zumwalt retired to the Washington suburb of Arlington, Virginia.

But retired didn't mean he was done working. President Ford introduced Peter and Bud Zumwalt and, despite the fact Peter was not an American, had never served a day in the military, and Zumwalt was a decorated war veteran, they became close friends.

Later, Zumwalt would serve on the board of Peter's U.S.-based chicken-processing company, Green Acre Farms, which had plants in Texas and Mississippi. He would also stage an unsuccessful run for the U.S. Senate as a Democratic candidate for Virginia.

"Bud Zumwalt was a good friend, just a great character," says Peter. The admiral died in 2000 at the age of 79, the victim of a lung cancer caused by his exposure to asbestos while in the navy.

• • •

Peter's circle of friends have extended to the likes of actor and one-time mayor of Carmel-by-the-Sea, California, Clint Eastwood, and the late astronaut Alan Shepard, Jr., with whom Peter shared a birthday.

There can be no doubt, however, that Peter's most renowned celebrity friendship was with the late actor Paul Newman.

A friendship that endured for more than 30 years—Newman died in 2008—began in, of all places, Mexico, the result of their mutual love of motorsports.

Newman got hooked on racing in 1968 while making the movie *Winning*. By the late '70s, that love had taken him to the Rio Balsas, where Peter Pocklington happened to be racing powerboats.

It was Peter's second trip to the Rio Balsas—this time, he brought a lighter boat that hopefully wouldn't sink—but it was Newman's first. According to Peter, the actor was there with a son of the owner of the Bank of Mexico—someone who fit the stereotype of the spoiled rich kid. The Mexican heir brought with him a five-ton stake struck that ferried a hot-air balloon, a two-person submarine, his speedboat and, in Peter's words, "three of the sexiest-looking broads you have ever seen."

> That guy was a real character. Paul and I agreed to go up in his hot-air balloon, but flames scorched the side and the thing caught on fire. We came down rather quickly. I can't remember the guy's name, but he ended up in jail, and the Mexican government nationalized the bank.
>
> But Paul and I became pretty good pals, and we stayed in touch after that. I really enjoyed Paul.

When the Champ Car circuit first came to Edmonton in 2005, among the celebrities in attendance was Paul Newman, one of the leaders of the legendary racing team Newman-Haas-Lanigan. It wasn't his first visit to Edmonton, however.

In the late 1970s and early '80s, Edmonton was on the Can-Am Challenge Cup circuit. Among the famed drivers who in those days raced at Edmonton International Speedway were Denny Hulme, Peter Revson and Jackie Stewart. In 1981, Paul Newman's racing team had two drivers in the $85,000 race, Teo Fabi and Al Unser. Fabi, the pacesetter, was forced out by a blown rear tire, reported the *New York Times*. Unser, did not finish either, thanks to a blown engine.

Peter was the sponsor so, not surprisingly, he and Eva threw a party for all the drivers at their Saskatchewan Drive home after the race. It was a chance for Peter to reconnect with Newman, but the party was memorable for other reasons, too.

I met a lot of the drivers. There was one in particular, Danny Sullivan, who later drove in Formula One. I remember he took a shine to our daughter Jill, and I had to keep them apart. She was too young for that. But that party lasted all night, it was crazy.

Danny was a good friend. In fact, when I was racing boats, I raced one time at Lake Havasu in Arizona, a marathon thing of seven or eight hours, and he came down to help me out. I'd go an hour, then he'd go an hour. We had a lot of fun.

When Sullivan retired to the south of France, he and Peter lost touch. Newman, though, kept in contact.

I talked to Paul a few times in New York, and I met him here in California at Ontario Raceway. He was a diehard racer.

He was very liberal in his political beliefs. He and I would have some great political discussions. Finally, I had to quit. I'm a libertarian; I don't much like government, so I found it's unwise to talk politics. There are other things we could talk about.

Hockey, for instance.

Paul Newman is probably best known in Canada for his role as Reg Dunlop in the 1977 hockey movie *Slap Shot*. In 1998, *Maxim* magazine rated it one of "the greatest 'guy' movies of all time."

After Newman made the movie, the *Journal*'s Jim Matheson remembers seeing him with Peter in the press box in Quebec City, watching a Nordiques game. He was yelling, "Where's the fights?" Matheson recalls.

•　•　•

After an association that goes back more than 25 years, Peter is now retired from his post on the board of the Betty Ford Center. Betty Ford, now in her nineties, is no longer involved, either. Her daughter, Susan Ford Bales, is the current chair of the centre. "She is a very skilled young woman," Peter says of Ford Bales. "She has many of Jerry's characteristics. You can tell she is his daughter."

Peter is especially admiring of Betty:

> She's a very feisty, strong woman. I mean, she's been through a lot: breast cancer to drug addiction to alcoholism. She came back from it all and she's sure done a great job of building the pre-eminent drug- and alcohol-treatment centre in the world.

•　•　•

Over the past few years, Peter has spent his free time golfing, fly fishing and making the occasional gambling trip to Las Vegas.

> I love to play 21 for a few hours. I get a kick out of that, but I've never been much of a gambler. If I lose, I'm pissed off at myself and if I win, it doesn't matter. But it's relaxing. So is fishing.

•　•　•

Sather looks back fondly on the time he spent fishing with Peter. "We fished around the world, fished in Iceland, went to the Arctic 20 years in a row," he says. So in the spring of 2008, he invited many of the regulars from those fishing trips to New York for a reunion.

"We had a cocktail party at my place, we took them all to the Rangers' game, we had dinner at the 21 Club," Sather remembers. "It was great. Peter seemed to have mellowed a bit. He was gracious to everybody, appreciated everybody's friendship."

•   •   •

Peter's friends may be scattered around the world, but there is no doubt the vast majority of them are in Edmonton. He also makes it quite clear his affection for Edmonton has not waned over the years. If anything, it's stronger.

> When I came in '71, Edmonton was a bustling little prairie city. And I loved it, fell in love with the place, because I was very successful there. If not for my quarrel with the government and Alberta Treasury Branches, I would still be there.
>
> But it wasn't just because I was successful in Edmonton. I loved the people. I related well to the people, I thought I was part of the community. I brought a Can-Am race and Paul Newman to town, and all those speakers and the NHL, and triple-A baseball and soccer. I brought Gretzky to Edmonton—and because of him, Edmonton became a well-known city around the world. Nobody ever heard of it before then, except for maybe during the Second World War when the Americans were building the Alaska Highway.
>
> I'd like to think I was an integral part of the community. I get a real kick out of that.

PART XIII

'How could you turn down $18.5 million?'

The trade. The sale. The sellout. The deal to move Wayne Gretzky to sunny California is viewed many different ways by Canadian hockey fans—few of them positive. So why do it? What's to be gained? To hear Peter Pocklington tell it, a lot. Peter is anxious to move his prized asset while Wayne's skills are at their peak—and before he is lost to free agency. In return, the Oilers stand to profit mightily, in terms of players and cash, but also in getting the bank off their backs. In the end, Peter feels it's a deal that is just too good to refuse.

It was a warm spring night in Edmonton when the Oilers defeated the Boston Bruins 6–3 at Northlands Coliseum to win their fourth Stanley Cup in five years. At the time, the date—May 26, 1988—should have been remembered for that singular and rather significant achievement. But it would soon take on an even greater meaning. As the players and fans celebrated, none of them knew—though Peter Pocklington certainly had his suspicions—that May 26, 1988, was also the final time Wayne Gretzky would don an Oilers' uniform.

At 7:00 the next morning, Wayne—who'd been partying late into the night with teammates, friends, his parents and fiancée Janet Jones—was awakened by a phone call. It was his old boss, Nelson Skalbania, calling from Vancouver. Skalbania had an offer he didn't think could wait. Wayne didn't agree, and was in no mood to hear it.

"We really didn't get much sleep. We were pretty much enjoying winning the Cup," recalls Wayne.

But Skalbania pressed his case, relating how he and some partners were trying to buy the Canucks and were offering Wayne part ownership in the club to clinch the deal. "We're going to give you 20 per cent of the team," Skalbania excitedly said. "You want to play in Vancouver?"

"Whoa, whoa, whoa, we've just won the Stanley Cup," Wayne replied. Finally, he told a persistent Skalbania the answer was no. A move to Vancouver was not in the cards. It was a step sideways, a prospect that did not interest him in the least. Wayne hung up the phone.

But a few weeks later, Wayne began to hear rumours. As unthinkable as it seemed, some sort of deal to move him was indeed in the works—if not to Vancouver, then to somewhere else. He admits to being disturbed by the prospect but, at the same time, he wasn't surprised.

For about three months, Wayne had been in the midst of contract negotiations with his boss, Peter Pocklington, and they weren't making much headway.

"They were very cordial," Wayne remembers of the talks to extend his contract. "Peter was always the kind of guy who'd just say, 'Hey Wayne, let's go for dinner.' We would go for dinner with Peter and Eva and it was always nothing but positive. And he'd say, 'Don't worry, I'll take care of you.' So at the time, I never really put much stock into not being in Edmonton."

But Wayne's existing five-year contract, which by that point paid the star $850,000 a season ("I was handsomely paid; a huge amount of money," he says), was due to expire after the 1989 season. It was the hope on both sides to keep him in Edmonton for at least three more years—provided, of course, it was at a price Peter could afford. "Peter wanted to negotiate a new deal with me," Wayne says, "and I wasn't thinking about leaving. But my theory was I owed it to myself to at least wait until the end of the next year to see what my value was on the open market."

And so, with that decision, the stage was set for a clash of interests—and what would eventually become one of the biggest trades in North American sport. Wayne wanted to find out what other teams might offer for his services. Peter wasn't prepared to let that happen and risk losing his franchise player without getting anything in return. The Oilers' owner was faced with a decision: if there was even a possibility Wayne Gretzky was going to take his leave, Peter Pocklington wanted to be sure it would be on his terms.

Peter made one last effort to sign his young star to an extension, but when Gretzky said no, "that's when, I think in Peter's mind, he made the decision, 'I've got to do this now,'" says Wayne.

More than anyone who was in Edmonton at the time, Wayne understands that. "Peter had to do it," he says.

There were other influences at play, as well. Wayne not only wanted to determine his value, but he says he also felt he owed it to the other players in the league to raise the bar on salaries. "I wasn't the highest-paid player," he admits. "Marcel Dionne was the highest-paid player at that time—or Charlie Simmer, one of those guys." Wayne, on the other hand, had been playing for what would today be termed a hometown discount—not that he was complaining. "With the bonuses I had—Peter was always very fair to me about bonuses, and what with winning the Cup—I did make over a million dollars, so in a way I was the highest paid.

"If I had a good year, he'd bring me in and say, 'I know you're not the highest paid,' and then one year he bought me a Ferrari. I was never worried about Peter taking care of me as sort of a business partner. But I felt like I owed it to myself for some reason. I wanted to be able to sign a deal with a salary based strictly on my performance. I mean, he could understand that."

Peter did understand, but he also had to face some hard financial facts. Players' salaries had been escalating. By the 1987–88 season, the Oilers were no longer profitable. Peter had begun to fund the club's operations from a line of credit he carried with the Alberta Treasury Branches—a line of credit the ATB was already demanding be paid down. If he was going to do that, one way would be to do what Nelson Skalbania did 10 years earlier: sell Wayne Gretzky. "God, I should really blame it on the ATB," Peter says.

During Klondike Days in July 1995, Ronnie Hawkins welcomes his old roadie Peter Pocklington to the stage where they croon "Mary Lou" and "Ruby." When there is a time delay before a subsequent appearance by Jerry Lee Lewis, Peter offers the crowd free beer.
— Rick MacWilliam, *Edmonton Journal*

A distraught Eva Pocklington explains to a police detective what is happening inside her Edmonton home after she escapes the clutches of a kidnapper on April 20, 1982.   — Jon Murray, *Edmonton Journal*

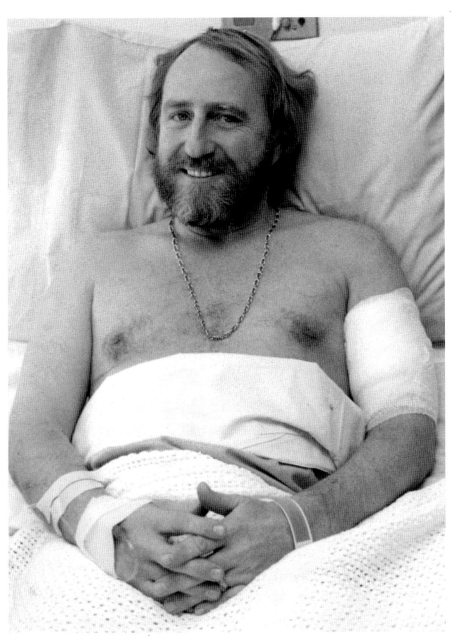

The day after a hostage-taking incident that almost takes his life, Peter Pocklington is all smiles in his bed at Edmonton's University Hospital. He says he didn't make a good patient.

— Dean Bicknell, *Edmonton Journal*

Internationally syndicated Edmonton cartoonists Gary Delainey and Gerry Rasmussen (*Betty*), who gain fame locally with a comic strip called *Bub Slug*, turn their satirical attention on Peter Pocklington, particularly in the aftermath of the Gretzky trade.

— Courtesy Gary Delainey & Gerry Rasmussen

Kevin Lowe, Mark Messier and Jari Kurri parade the Stanley Cup around Edmonton's Commonwealth Stadium after the Oilers' 1990 Cup win. It is a time of mixed emotions for the Oilers' stalwarts. They dedicate their victory to the departed Wayne Gretzky but, at the same time, they're eager to prove they can win without him. — Don Metz, Aquila Productions

Peter and Eva Pocklington enter Edmonton's St. Joseph's Basilica for the wedding of Wayne Gretzky and Janet Jones on July 16, 1988. Glen Sather can be seen behind them. — Brian Gavriloff, *Edmonton Journal*

It's trade day, August 9, 1988, and, in Edmonton, smiles are in short supply. Peter Pocklington and Los Angeles Kings owner Bruce McNall (far right) listen as Glen Sather addresses the news conference held to announce Wayne Gretzky's departure for the Kings. Gretzky struggles to compose himself.

— Brian Gavriloff, *Edmonton Journal*

Racing buddies Peter Pocklington and Paul Newman exchange war stories at the 1981 Can-Am Challenge Cup race at Edmonton International Speedway.

— Courtesy Peter Pocklington

Every summer over a 20-year period, Peter organizes a fishing trip to the Arctic and invites many of his closest friends. In the mid-1990s, those guests included then Ontario Premier Mike Harris, left, and former U.S. president George Bush.

— Courtesy Peter Pocklington

Certainly, he knew Gretzky would command a high price—Peter had been offered as much as $15 million US for his star player. If that kind of money was still out there, and he paid all of it to the ATB, it was certainly enough to get the bankers off his back.

It was business. I think Wayne understands that. If he didn't then, he probably does now. He is certainly bright, he's quite capable, and now that he's running his own club in Phoenix, he is facing the reality of hockey. Even with a Gretzky on your team and a lot of skilled folks with you, it's a tough business to make money in.

• • •

The NHL awards ceremony would be held in Toronto on June 8, 13 days after the Oilers' Stanley Cup victory. Peter resolved to keep his eye out for Bruce McNall, the new owner of the Los Angeles Kings. Maybe, just maybe, if the price was right, Peter could be persuaded to part with Wayne Gretzky.

Jerry Buss, who owned the Kings before Bruce McNall, was the first guy to offer me $15 million for Wayne. That was, I think, in 1985. I told him then I wouldn't do it. It was just too early—I knew we'd win more Cups with Wayne. After all, Wayne made the whole team. Why, without him in the early days, the Oilers would have been nothing.

But then McNall came along a few years later and told me he'd match Jerry's offer. So when I saw McNall at Massey Hall, where the NHL awards were being held, I told him, "If you still want to do Jerry's deal for $15 million, and throw in some players and draft choices, I might consider it." Sure enough, he phoned me later and said yeah, he wanted to do it. So I said, "Fine, let's explore it some more." It took about a month to do the deal, and then McNall asked for permission to talk to Wayne. I gave it to him.

I think Wayne was shocked as hell, quite frankly, when Bruce called him. I don't know if there were any rumours before then, but

I suspect Bruce might have been spreading them once we started talking.

If Wayne was shocked when McNall called him, he would eventually get over it. He married actor and dancer Janet Jones on July 16 in a lavish ceremony in Edmonton's largest cathedral. By then, he and his bride were starting to consider the possibilities—and the opportunities—that California presented. Certainly Los Angeles was a better choice for his family than, say, Detroit. And so, for the second time in his career, Wayne Gretzky—perhaps the greatest player the game has ever known—found himself faced with the realization of getting traded. But this time, it was so much bigger, the ramifications so much greater. Not since the Red Sox sent Babe Ruth to the Yankees before the 1920 baseball season had a trade of this magnitude been engineered.

. . .

Towards the end of July, Peter Pocklington and Glen Sather packed up for their annual week-long fishing trip to the Arctic. Joining them was the customary assemblage of friends, co-workers, business associates, bankers, politicians and hockey people.

During their time on the Tree River, Peter began to confide to his fishing mates that a deal to sell Gretzky to the Los Angeles Kings was in the works. He says the initial reaction from his compatriots was shock, but that was soon replaced with support for his reasoning. Nevertheless, his friends warned him what such a move would mean for Peter. "They all thought it would be pretty tough," he says.

Sather maintains he had no part in those discussions. Peter insists that's not the case. But even if Peter was yet to take Sather into his confidence, the Oilers' GM began hearing about it from others in the camp.

"Peter talked to a lot of guys on this trip and they would come to me and I'd say 'No, he hasn't traded him. He would have told me,'" recalls Sather.

One of the people who approached him was Boston Bruins'

general manager Harry Sinden—a regular on these fishing trips for the better part of 15 years.

"Harry mentioned to me that Peter sounded him out about this deal," Sather recalls. Sinden warned Sather that if Peter did indeed sell Gretzky, it could have serious repercussions for the Oilers, and for Peter's stake in the franchise.

"Harry said the same thing happened in Boston when Bobby Orr was sold to Chicago," recalls Sather. "He said the season-ticket holders left that place like rats from a ship." The reputation of Weston Adams, Jr., whose family had owned the Bruins through three generations and for more than 50 years, was so badly shredded, he was left with little choice but to sell the team, said Sinden. "Well," Sather responded, "if Peter is seriously thinking about this, he never told me. But you should be sure to tell him that story."

• • •

A few days later, Peter, Sather and a friend of Peter's from Italy, Falicci Garducci—who had also accompanied them on their fishing trip— flew to Colorado to participate in a golf tournament organized by Peter's friend, President Ford.

After a day of golfing, they returned to Peter's condo in Beaver Creek. By then, Sather was expecting to hear the worst. "Peter had to tell me sooner or later," Sather recalls. "He was nervous about it."

Peter opened one of his expensive bottles of wine. "Peter in those days used to buy the most expensive wine, thinking it was always going to taste good," Sather recalls. "But sometimes it doesn't taste so good." That day was one of those times. "It was pretty sour, actually."

Peter finally broke the news to his best friend: he was selling Gretzky to the Kings for $15 million US, about $18.5 million CDN. It was a good deal, Peter told him, and besides, he needed the money— the ATB was tightening the screws.

Sather's response? "I told him he was out of his fucking mind." Sather thought fleetingly about giving his boss a punch in the nose, but it's not an idea he entertained for long. After all, "it's his team. He has the right to do what he wants."

Sather knew Peter was trying to get Gretzky to sign a contract extension to keep him in Edmonton for at least a few more years, but this? This he never expected. "I figured at some point we'd get this new deal put together, or something would happen.

"But I never thought we'd ever sell the guy. I was angry—and disappointed."

To Sather's way of thinking, Wayne Gretzky was the best player in the league, playing on the best team in the league. He was an icon, and you don't trade an icon. Do this deal, he told Peter, and "you go from being a hero in Canada to a schmuck"—overnight.

"I think this is the biggest mistake you'll make in your life, selling this guy."

• • •

I had to do it. It was a good business deal. How could you turn down $18.5 million—plus the players and draft choices we'd get?

To my mind, Wayne had 9 per cent, maybe 10 per cent, left in him. Economist Joseph Schumpeter, in his theory of "Creative Destruction," said you have to sell assets at their peak. And one of the reasons the most successful business people in the world are successful is because they believe that.

• • •

There is some legitimacy to Peter's assertion that Gretzky's best days were behind him. His top-producing years were the five seasons between 1981 and 1986, when he averaged a phenomenal 2.5 points a game. His best season in terms of pure production was 1983–84, the year the Oilers won their first Stanley Cup, when he averaged close to 2.8 points a game. It was a scoring pace that had been unheard of before, and that no one has come even close to matching since. He was only 22 years old.

Even four years later, in his final season with the Oilers, Wayne was still clicking along at 2.3 points a game, yet he never came close to that pace again—not in Los Angeles, St. Louis or New York.

That said, Peter's critics can find justification in suggesting he underestimated his superstar's staying power as a bona fide NHL phenomenon. After completing his nine NHL seasons in Edmonton, Wayne would play for 11 more; he recorded 1,188 more points, 41 per cent of his career total. That's significantly greater than Peter's estimate that Wayne had "maybe 10 per cent left in him." Moreover, Gretzky would continue to record, on average, more than a point a game until his very last season, when the scars and wounds of a 21-year career finally began to take their toll.

And there are other considerations—ones that can't be measured by statistics alone—that critics can say Peter either failed to take into account or chose to ignore. Gretzky was, without dispute, the best player in the NHL at the time. With Gordie Howe and Bobby Orr, he is widely considered among the best of all time. Paul Coffey, who was traded to Pittsburgh in 1987 after a contract dispute with Sather, said in the *New York Times* that Peter had treated Wayne like a "piece of meat." That may have been harsh and said more about Coffey's own relationship with the Oilers than Gretzky's. Still, wouldn't the game's best player merit consideration that transcended the boundaries of being just another one of Peter's business deals?

Would Joe Montana have been treated that way? Would Michael Jordan?

Evidently, they would, if they worked for Peter Pocklington—and for that, the late Chicago Blackhawks owner Bill Wirtz derided the Oilers' owner. "Peter never changes," said Wirtz in an interview with the *Edmonton Journal*. "Everybody is for sale, from Wayne Gretzky down to the team trainer."

• • •

Glen Sather had grown accustomed to Peter's musings over the years about Gretzky's worth—"Maybe I could get $50 million for him"—but sloughed it off as idle speculation. Plus he thought no one would ever be crazy enough to pay the kind of money Peter would expect.

But then, Sather didn't know Bruce McNall. He was about to find out. The deal to sell Gretzky may have been put together, but the corresponding negotiations to arrange an exchange of players and draft choices had yet to be undertaken. Peter left that job to Sather. It was a less than desirable negotiating position for any general manager to find himself in, even one as skilled as Glen Sather. After all, the deal was done, Peter needed the money, and Gretzky was already packing his bags. Moreover, the Great One had asked that teammates Mike Krushelnyski and Marty McSorley come with him to L.A. "I don't blame him for that," says Sather. McSorley would protect Gretzky; Krushelnyski would ensure he had someone to pass the puck to.

"I said, 'Well, if you've decided this is it, let's see what else we can get out of this deal,'" Sather finally told Peter.

Peter would be quite enamoured with the end result of those negotiations: "What people forget," says Peter, "is that the trade retooled the team for another crack at the Stanley Cup, and of course we won it again in 1990."

Sather isn't so convinced. "If you're going to make a trade, you're going to make a lot better deal than the one we made by selling Wayne," he says.

Sather wanted Luc Robitaille. "They wouldn't give me Robitaille." Sather threatened to kill the deal. McNall threatened to sue if he did. "Go ahead and sue us," Sather responded. McNall relented and offered Jimmy Carson.

When the dust settled, Sather and McNall settled on Carson, Martin Gelinas and three draft choices.

> Oh, I really liked Gelinas. Why Glen would trade him [to Quebec in 1993 for Scott Pearson] I'll never know.
>
> On the other hand, Carson turned out to be horseshit. But then we traded him to Detroit for Joe Murphy, Adam Graves and Petr Klima. Murphy was great; Graves was great; even Klima was great.
>
> That whole line—Gelinas, Murphy, Graves—was just

unbelievable. Those guys were one of the main reasons we won the Stanley Cup in 1990. And they were all the result of the Gretzky deal.

That Carson was, in Peter's words, "horseshit" remains a curiosity for Oilers' fans to debate to this day. In his one and only season in Edmonton, he scored 49 goals. Yet even Kevin Lowe says of the U.S.-born Carson, "he was never an Oiler."

"The wrong personality," says Sather. "He just didn't fit for the team."

Early the following season, Carson requested the trade that would bring them Murphy, Graves, Klima and their fifth Stanley Cup.

• • •

After their trip to Colorado, Peter Pocklington and Glen Sather returned to Edmonton to put the final touches on the Gretzky deal and prepare for the maelstrom that was sure to follow. But the rumours already circulating in Edmonton were beginning to spread, forcing them to confront the fact that sooner rather than later, the truth would have to be told.

One of those to hear the whispers was Oilers' broadcaster Rod Phillips. He and his wife Debbie had just returned with their kids from a Florida holiday when he received a 7 a.m. phone call from Al McCann, a fellow sportscaster at CFRN Television. The date was August 9, 1988.

"Al said there is something going on, that the wire services were full of stories about Gretzky going to Los Angeles. I said, 'Aw, not a chance.'

"He said, 'Rod, something's going on, honest to God.' So I said, 'OK I'll call Slats.'"

Sather was at his home in Banff that morning and took Phillips's call around 7:10. "Did I get you up?" Phillips asked, but Sather sounded like he had been up all night. "Slats, what's going on here? The wire services are going nuts."

"Well, I can't say anything officially," Sather replied.

"Well all right, don't tell me anything officially, but are you coming up to Edmonton today?"

"Yeah, I'll be up to Edmonton."

"I think that tells me all I need to know."

And with that, Phillips phoned McCann back and broke the news. "Yeah, they're going to do the deal today."

The word was out. A news conference was being called at Molson House in downtown Edmonton that afternoon. Soon, the whole nation would hear the shocking news.

Rod Phillips was at that news conference. As he watched events unfold, he said to himself, "Peter, what have you done?"

PART XIV

'All good things have to come to an end, I guess'

Wayne Gretzky may lose his composure when it's announced he is leaving Edmonton for the Los Angeles Kings but, in the end, he is the only one who keeps his head. As Peter Pocklington gets cold feet and Glen Sather offers to throw himself on his sword, it is Gretzky who stays true to a course that ultimately changes the face of hockey in North America.

Molson House is a reception centre built by the Molson brewery in the 1960s as a place where company officials could entertain their customers. It's not a particularly historic building, despite its appearance—it resembles an old fort from Edmonton's fur-trading days—but it is famous nonetheless.

It was at Molson House on August 9, 1988, a little more than 10 weeks after the Oilers won their fourth Stanley Cup, that Edmonton ceased to be home for the greatest hockey player Canada has ever produced. And, for the first time, many Edmontonians began to entertain the thought that maybe their town was no longer a special place in the hockey firmament.

The moment has been exhaustively documented, and millions of Canadians over the age of 30 remember it well. Who among them doesn't remember watching Wayne Gretzky dabbing his teary eyes with a tissue and saying, "I promised Mess I wouldn't do this"?

What he almost didn't do is go through with it.

As Gretzky writes in the preceding foreword, "I was this close, this close, to killing the deal."

It was an emotional time, "for all of us," he recalls.

"I got to Edmonton that day and I started remembering how great it was, and I began to ask myself, 'What are you thinking?' The reality was that had I killed the deal, had I remained an Oiler, I would probably have signed the contract extension Peter wanted me to sign, that afternoon.

"Peter would have said, 'What do you want? I'll give it to you,' because that's the kid of guy he was, that's the kind of guy he is."

But Gretzky didn't change his mind, despite the last-minute entreaties of one former boss and the last-second change of heart of the other.

Before the news conference began, Glen Sather sat Wayne down in a meeting room at the Molson House, and for the next hour tried to convince him to change his mind. "If you want me to kill this deal, I'll tell Peter I'll quit," Sather told his protege.

But Gretzky held fast. "No," he said, "it's gone too far."

By the time Peter also pulled Wayne aside and offered to cancel the deal, No. 99's resolve had been further steeled.

"It was emotional, yeah" says Wayne. "It was one of the worst days of my life. I'm sure it was one of the worst days in Peter's life, too."

But as Peter wavered, ultimately Wayne did not. Then and there, he definitively decided his future wasn't in Edmonton. Instead, he was going to step out front of all those cameras and announce he was beginning a new life and a new career in Los Angeles.

"All good things have to come to an end, I guess," he says with the benefit of 20 years of hindsight, though he might well have thought the same thing that day.

Says Wayne's buddy, Kevin Lowe, "Yeah, once you get that whole thing moving, it's pretty hard to turn back."

"By this time, Wayne really wanted to go," Peter remembers. "I don't think his wife looked forward to another winter in Edmonton, and quite frankly, I don't blame her; an American girl, an actress and so on. And it was kind of a moon shot for Wayne."

Sather agrees. "He just got married, he's got a chance to go to L.A.

I'm sure he was excited about the idea."

Then there was the question of money. More than one pundit has suggested Wayne's Alberta-based investments, caught in the grip of a recession-wracked Alberta oil patch, had been seriously depleted. McNall is said to have offered Wayne a salary in the range of $3 million a year, a significant jump from the $850,000 he was making in Edmonton. A multimillion-dollar signing bonus and a percentage of the Kings' ballooning gate receipts have also been floated.

"I'm not sure there had been discussions with McNall about a new salary at that stage, but I'm pretty positive there were," says Sather. "At that point, a lot of things were changing in Wayne's life that I don't think he could have changed his mind and stayed."

Gretzky did ask one favour of Peter before the news conference began. He wanted help paying for his moving expenses.

"Five minutes before we went out on stage, Wayne hit me up for another 100 grand for moving," Peter says with a laugh.

"Well," says Wayne, chuckling at the memory, "I figured if he got $15 million, I deserved at least 100 grand. That was my theory. But you know what's amazing? Peter didn't bat an eyelash. 'Okay,' he said."

. . .

And with that, the news conference began:

"It is with mixed emotions, a heavy heart for our community and our hockey club, but I guess with delight and sincere best wishes for Wayne Gretzky that I announce, and I guess more important confirm, that the Edmonton Oilers have agreed to trade Wayne Gretzky to Los Angeles," Peter announced, his voice showing only a hint of a quiver.

Gretzky said little. He couldn't as he struggled to contain his emotions, and failed. His discomfort ended only after he was helped from his chair and led to a seat at the back of the stage by his agent, Michael Barnett. It could almost be considered an example of life imitating art, Barnett playing the role of supportive band member to Gretzky's sobbing James Brown.

But then Sather stepped into the breach, took his seat in Gretzky's chair, and eloquently expressed his thoughts. "I don't want to try and philosophize on what's happened—because I don't think we can justify the reasons why this has happened—but we're all trying to do something that's good for Wayne, for the Edmonton Oilers, for the National Hockey League," the GM said. "We all would like to be proud of what we do to make a living, and I think you can see here today that the reason we've won four Stanley Cups is because of the emotion we display for each other. It's genuine and in a couple of days I know that we'll adjust to it—and I'm going to work my hardest to try and find a way to kick the hell out of the Los Angeles Kings.

"But right now I really feel a lot of empathy for Wayne and for what he's going through."

And that was that. Gretzky and McNall returned to Los Angeles for another news conference later in the day—one with more smiles, fewer tears—while Edmontonians and Canadians were left to ponder what only days before had been the imponderable.

As the media and hockey people filed out of the hall, Rod Phillips filed a report for CFRN Television. "I remember saying it will be hard for a lot of people to believe in Edmonton that the next time we see Wayne Gretzky in a hockey uniform, he will be the enemy," Phillips recalls, still choking up at the memory. "It took a couple of years to get our heads around that one. I mean, it was just something that happened that nobody thought could happen."

• • •

For the fans, hell for all of us, my God, it was like a death in the family. But the folks in L.A. were sure excited as hell. I can remember in one of the L.A. papers, somebody wrote that Gretzky was from a one-horse town and the horse had just left. I admit that one hurt a bit, even if there was some truth to it.

Los Angeles was excited, all right. According to Jim Matheson in the *Edmonton Journal*, the Kings sold 2,000 new season tickets in the first 36 hours after the trade was announced. Peter says the Kings' annual gate went from $4 million to $21.5 million in Gretzky's first year alone. Jim Fox, a former Kings' player and now the colour commentator on their broadcasts, told ESPN that while he was injured during Gretzky's first season, he invested his time in the team's community-relations department, helping process the demands for No. 99's time. Before 1988, the Kings never had a community-relations department. They never needed one.

Then there were the millions of dollars in endorsement deals that awaited Gretzky in L.A. His face appeared in pizza commercials and on soup labels. He was in a TV commercial broadcast during the Super Bowl. He was even featured in a kids' Saturday morning cartoon.

Never before did hockey enjoy such a profile in southern California. Before the trade, the Kings averaged only about 10,000 fans a game. By the time Gretzky led them to the Stanley Cup finals in 1993, they were selling out every home date. By 1999, the Kings had built themselves a new arena, the Staples Center, in downtown Los Angeles.

. . .

After their business was concluded and the Oilers were enriched with an $18.5-million CDN cash infusion from Bruce McNall, speculation was rampant as to what happened with the money. To hear the rumours tell it, the money went to prop up other businesses in the Pocklington financial empire, or it simply disappeared into one of his offshore bank accounts. In actual fact, says Peter, the money went to the Alberta Treasury Branches to pay down the Oilers' line of credit.

"If Peter says that's where it went, that's where it went," says Sather. "Think about it. If Peter put the money someplace else, the tax people would be all over him. After all, everybody in the world knew about that deal."

I can remember when the deal was done, McNall delivered me a cheque from Credit Lyonnais, the French bank where he borrowed the money. I think he stiffed them on it, though; didn't pay them back a dime. Bruce was quite the character. I hear he got the Bank of America, too—false records, false books. That's why he ended up going to the hoosegow.

In 1993, McNall pleaded guilty to five counts of conspiracy and fraud, and admitted bilking six banks out of $236 million over a 10-year period. He was sentenced to 70 months in prison, and was released in 2001.

Irrespective of McNall's suspect business practices, many business people at the time lauded the trade as a sound business move for both sides. At least one hockey person agreed. "I think it may have been the best business decision two sports franchises ever made," said then–New York Rangers general manager Phil Esposito.

Yet the fallout in Canada, and particularly in Edmonton, was anything but positive.

• • •

"Gretzky Gone!" read the banner headline in the *Edmonton Journal* on August 10, over a photo of Gretzky wiping his eyes. "99 Tears" wailed the unforgettable headline on the front page of the *Edmonton Sun*.

Yet if Peter has ever paused to second-guess himself, if he's had any regrets about what has become known without further elaboration as "The Trade"—a transaction that defined his own career in sports as much as it did Gretzky's—he will not admit to it.

"Hell, I'd trade him again!" he defiantly proclaims. "That deal was good for everybody. It was good for the league, good for Wayne, good for Los Angeles, good for me and I think it was good for the Oilers, too."

This is a critical point in understanding Peter's thinking. To his mind, the Gretzky deal was, quite simply, too good an offer to refuse. And with Peter, business is about crafting deals in which everyone wins something.

Oh, I knew the reaction to the news that we traded Wayne Gretzky was going to be bad—because I knew how I felt, when I stopped to think about it. It took me nine weeks to kind of get over the emotional shock of "Do I really want to do this?" I knew the backlash was going to be huge.

But I really felt I didn't have a helluva lot of choice.

•   •   •

There are critics who argue that Peter Pocklington did have a choice, that he didn't have to trade Gretzky. Under the terms of the collective bargaining agreement that was in place at the time, if Wayne had received an offer from another team after the 1988–89 season, as he hoped would happen, the Oilers would have had the right to match— which was also Gretzky's hope.

But to Peter's mind, that was no choice at all.

"We knew if Wayne became a free agent after '89, he could get as much as $5 million to $6 million," says Peter. "That would have been three-quarters of Edmonton's payroll."

Moreover, says Peter, if he decided to sign Gretzky to a matching offer, then trade him, there would have been players coming back, but there would be nothing resembling the money Peter got from McNall to get the ATB off his back and financially stabilize the Oilers.

"I would rather do the deal in '88 and get the $18.5 million, the two players and the three draft choices, and reseed the team."

•   •   •

To be sure, Peter always points to the Stanley Cup victory in 1990 as proof the Gretzky deal was a good one for the Oilers and, by extension, for their fans. But without Wayne—and soon many of the other stars that constituted the Oiler dynasty—the club would, within three seasons, slip from playoff contention. They would not return to the Stanley Cup finals for another 16 years.

There can also be no doubt that telling the people of Edmonton the trade was good for them was bitter medicine indeed after they'd grown accustomed to watching the best player in hockey for a decade—even if fans in other cities would say they'd become complacent, even spoiled.

Former Oilers assistant coach Charlie Huddy gets that. "As a hockey fan, if you're coming to Oilers games and you're watching Wayne Gretzky play every night, that's pretty exciting," notes the one-time defensive stalwart. "But then, all of a sudden, the person who's running the team says that 'we're moving him.' As a fan, you can't quite understand why that's happening."

Huddy remembers he didn't get it then, either—and he freely admits he still doesn't. "When you've got the best player in the game, it's tough," he says. "It would be different if Wayne was near the end of his career, and you figure, 'I can make a deal that will improve the team down the road.' But at the age Wayne was at—I mean, I played with him in L.A. and he was still at the top of his game.

"I guess Peter had his reasons."

So if there were players who didn't get it, how were the fans supposed to react?

"It's hard for fans to drill down into the whole thing," explains Kevin Lowe who, as the Oilers' president of hockey operations, knows a few things about fan expectations. "Their perception is just to keep shovelling out the money. But at some point, somebody has to pay for it."

Lowe does get the trade—sort of. He is quick to admit he does not know what the Oilers' revenue stream was like in 1988, nor does he know what sort of money Wayne was looking for. "I suspect he and his agent wanted to go to a level that was never heard of in this town before," Lowe says.

"I don't know whether Peter felt he could still make money at that level, or if it was a case of, 'Hey, I'm going to make less money, here's a diminishing asset, let's just move it.' I mean, you've got to have the big picture."

But he does know he didn't take news of the trade as hard as others did, particularly teammate Mark Messier. "Mess took it a lot harder than I did. Many of the guys did. I was like, 'Hey, get over it. It's a business, let's move on and play the game. We've got a job to do.'"

Ironically, Lowe was with Marty McSorley, one of the Oilers who went to Los Angeles with Gretzky, at Bob Cole's golf tournament in Newfoundland when he heard the news. "It was pretty shocking," Lowe recalls. "But my favourite expression in life and business is to expect the unexpected."

Huddy was at home when Oilers' trainer Barrie Stafford called to tell him. "I kind of went, 'Yeah, right,'" he remembers. "'C'mon, Barrie. It wouldn't happen.'"

. . .

The next day I saw Jim Matheson from the *Edmonton Journal*, who I always liked. So I said, "Well Jimmy, you really didn't get to ask a question at the press conference. Come on in and we'll chat about it."

So we're talking, and I said, "You know, I really admire this guy Gretzky. I'm really sorry to lose him. I'm as big a fan as anybody."

But then I shared an opinion about Wayne I wish I hadn't. I said, "You know, his ego is almost *as big as mine*, and that's what I like about him."

But the next day, Matheson wrote that "Pocklington says Gretzky's ego is *as big as Manhattan*."

And everybody turned against me.

Matheson has a different recollection of events. He insists Peter did say what he was quoted as saying. In any event, the hostility that resulted has hardly diminished over time—yet Peter remains unbowed by it.

"You know, I don't care what people think," he says. "There is nothing I can do about it anyway. Besides," he adds, referring to the Oilers' five Stanley Cup championships, "the achievement speaks for itself."

It is an impressive achievement, but one many Oilers fans look beyond in their withering assessment of the Pocklington legacy. For that, Lowe thinks more than the Gretzky trade is to blame. He attributes the lingering enmity to the way Peter did business. "If he was disliked, it was for a lot of things he did. The Gretzky thing was sort of the crème de la crème, but there was Gainers and there was all the other stuff and it was just his own private life."

It's an opinion Huddy doesn't share. For him, it's the trade that has Edmontonians bugged to this day. "If he doesn't trade Wayne Gretzky, what do people think of him then?" Huddy wonders. Just as Glen Sather had forecast, Peter Pocklington went from national hero to schmuck. Says Charlie: "As it is, 15 years from now, people will still be spittin' bullets."

Gretzky blames the backlash against Peter on the fact there was cash involved in the transaction—"blood money," as the *Journal*'s Cam Cole referred to it at the time.

"It probably wouldn't have been such a media frenzy had there not been the money involved," Gretzky says. "Had it been a straight hockey trade, people would have said, 'Well, Peter had to make the deal. Wayne Gretzky wouldn't sign.'

"Ultimately, it came down to the fact that I didn't want to sign an extension and Peter didn't want me to play without one, and so he traded me. It's pretty simple when you cut through all the B.S., you know?"

Nevertheless, in Edmonton, the hate-on for Peter Pocklington was on.

PART XV

'Wayne Gretzky is a national symbol—like the beaver'

When Peter Pocklington first pondered the idea of selling Wayne Gretzky, his friends told him he'd be in for a rough ride. He quickly discovers they didn't know the half of it. Meanwhile, Wayne Gretzky begins to second-guess himself, while Glen Sather is faced with the task of rebuilding a championship team.

In the aftermath of Wayne Gretzky's move to Los Angeles, his decade-long bond with the man he had come to trust as a father, Peter Pocklington, came unglued. In its place was something that more resembled an ugly family spat.

Both men were sustaining serious blows to their public images, their reputations, and to their egos. Wayne was being cast as a traitor to his country. Even more unfairly, he was being portrayed as a cowed husband, browbeaten by his beautiful Hollywood wife into abandoning Edmonton in favour of the sunnier climes of California.

Ironically, it would not be the last time an Oiler fan favourite would be accused of deserting the city at the supposed behest of a Missouri-born spouse. Eighteen years later, the villain was Lauren Pronger.

But while Pronger was probably guilty as charged, Janet Jones Gretzky was getting a bum rap. And for that, she blamed Peter Pocklington. Two days after the trade, she called *Edmonton Sun* sports columnist Terry Jones.

In a column published the next day, Jones wrote that Janet told him, "Peter Pocklington is the reason Wayne Gretzky is no longer an Edmonton Oiler."

She confirmed that Wayne first heard of the trade from Bruce McNall, then told the columnist, "There was no call from Pocklington. You play for a man 10 years and he doesn't even have the courtesy to call you and tell you what is happening."

She had been quite prepared to live in Edmonton, said Janet, and now she was being made the scapegoat—hockey's Yoko Ono as it were. "It gets to your heart."

Peter has since admitted that linking Gretzky's wife to the trade might have been more wishful thinking on his part than actual fact. But at the time, he, too, was being excoriated.

"I was mad at him," recalls Oilers' broadcaster Rod Phillips. "I felt betrayed. The city felt betrayed and anybody who was involved with the organization felt the same way. It was a bad time."

Then there were Glen Sather's thoughts on the trade: "It destroyed a great team."

And this was just what Peter was hearing from his friends. Whatever merits there may have been to shipping Wayne Gretzky to California, the public in Edmonton and the rest of Canada was not taking the news well.

There were death threats and public demonstrations. Effigies of Peter were being hung and torched. Nelson Riis, an NDP MP, called on Parliament to block the trade. "Wayne Gretzky is a national symbol," said Riis, "like the beaver." It was a comment that provided momentary comic relief to what was otherwise a grim time.

Peter was under relentless attack and he responded in textbook fashion: by lashing out, not just at Janet but at her husband. Just as quickly, Gretzky responded in kind.

"We all got mad when it happened. We got into this whole thing of who's to blame, whose fault it was, you know, all that kind of stuff—which is all so ludicrous," recalls Wayne. "We were all just trying to protect ourselves.

"Had we both to do it over again, we would have stood up and said, 'Look, this is a business deal.'

"We kind of laugh about it now. It's too bad it unfolded the way it did because deep down, Peter is a good man. I truly enjoyed our friendship."

*   *   *

So, how many more Stanley Cups would the Oilers have won if Gretzky had remained with the team?

Peter figures they might have won one more, if you don't count the Cup they won without Gretzky in 1990.

"Maybe," Gretzky says.

But had the Oilers advanced to the Cup finals in '91 or '92—instead, they were eliminated in the semi-finals by Minnesota and Chicago respectively—they would have been matched against a Pittsburgh Penguins team that had Coffey, Jaromir Jagr, Ron Francis and Mario Lemieux, all in their prime.

Charlie Huddy won't even hazard an educated guess on how that would have turned out.

"In hockey, you can never know from one year to another what's going to happen," he says. Huddy helped coach the Oilers to the Stanley Cup final in 2006, when they lost to the Hurricanes in seven games, so he knows a few things about the experience.

"To be able to win Stanley Cups, a lot of things have to fall into place. You can have 20 of the greatest players in the league but if certain things don't fall into place, then—wham!—one bump in the road and you're out of the playoffs pretty damn fast.

"You can't predict it. Gretz could have been hurt; Messier could have been hurt. Or maybe both of them. Then, all of a sudden, you're going, 'Holy shit!' Now you've hit that bump in the road, right?"

Sather, on the other hand, is not convinced that Pittsburgh—or any other team, for that matter—could have beaten his Oilers with Gretzky in the lineup.

To his mind, the Oilers would have continued winning, and posting many more Stanley Cup championships, had the core of the team been kept intact.

"You look back on what happened and how everything changed, and how that team was built," says Sather. "We were a team that could have done that for a long time.

"It was young, strong, it was tough. Good at everything."

Sather says a review of the personnel on the Oilers' five Stanley Cup–winners will reveal a nucleus of seven or eight guys, around whom was a constantly changing supporting cast. That core—Gretzky, Messier, Kurri, Coffey, Fuhr, Anderson and Lowe—"were the ones who drove the bus," remembers Sather. "They made things work because they knew how it worked, and they expected everyone else to do their part."

Sather figures that team, built around that nucleus, would have held their own against the Penguins—and any other team that rose to challenge them in the 1990s. "They might not have won the Stanley Cup every year," he says, "but that team was in a position to be a winner for a long time."

A lot longer, evidently, than Peter Pocklington had anticipated. But how long the Edmonton market could have continued to financially support such a team—in Sather's words, each one of them was getting older, better and more expensive—is a question that remains unanswered. It was, however, at the core of Peter's dilemma.

•   •   •

My hands were tied. I had no choice, and everybody in the organization knew that. Of course, Glen was very upset about it all. So, because I sold off Gretzky, I gave Glen 5 per cent of the team. That paid off nicely for him when the club was sold 10 years later for $80 million US.

Sather acknowledges Peter gave him a piece of the team. But, notes Gretzky, "Glen earned that 5 per cent."

•   •   •

At the time, Sather had a more pressing priority than dwelling on the departure of his superstar: getting his team to start believing in itself again, without Gretzky.

Coffey had left after a protracted contract dispute following the 1987 Cup win, and Gretzky a year later. But the Oilers were still a team with an embarrassment of riches and an abundance of leadership. The trick was in getting the players to see it.

It was that fact which ultimately persuaded Sather to stick with the team rather than quit as he had contemplated. "If I tell Peter to stuff it at that point, that place is going to blow right up. I really couldn't leave the rest of the guys in the lurch."

But what do you say to a team that has lost its best player, someone who is arguably the best player in the world? "There is not a whole lot to say," remembers Sather. "Everyone knew the team was weaker."

Ultimately, Sather and his head coach John Muckler would stitch that team together again, and they did win another Cup two seasons later. But that would only come, he says, after everybody began to think positively, to think about winning and to stop worrying about themselves.

It was no easy task, convincing the post-Gretzky Oilers to believe in themselves and believe they could win. "They were all thinking in their own minds 'Are you crazy?'" Sather says. "You could see it in their eyes. No, it was kind of gloomy for a while."

* * *

Today, Wayne Gretzky finds himself in the same position Peter Pocklington was in 20 years ago—as owner of an NHL franchise with salary issues. Gretzky is part owner and coach of the recently bankrupt Phoenix Coyotes.

So, would he trade a Wayne Gretzky in his prime?

Well, for one thing, you can't sell a player for cash any more. And since there is a salary cap, teams can only trade for a player if they can afford to pay him and remain under the cap.

"But if it was under the same rules and everything, I would

probably have done what Peter did, sit down and try to negotiate a deal," says Wayne. "I might have waited a little bit longer before I made a move but, you know . . . you've got to get that asset back. It's as simple as that."

. . .

The years since 1988 have not diminished Kevin Lowe's assessment of the enormity of what transpired that summer. "Let's get one thing straight," he says, "nothing can be compared to the Gretzky trade. Nothing. I don't think you can compare any trade in sports, and certainly not, with all due respect, the Ryan Smyth deal in 2007. You know, Gretz is in his prime, the team just wins its fourth Stanley Cup in five years—he's just won the Conn Smythe Trophy."

And Gretzky would need all that going for him if he was to succeed in establishing a beachhead for hockey in southern California. "He needed to be in his prime to do what he did in L.A.," says Lowe.

He may have been in his prime but, early on, Wayne still had his doubts about the wisdom of his move to Los Angeles. "I remember my first exhibition game in front of 10,000 people in L.A., and I'm thinking, 'What am I doing here? This might have been the biggest mistake of my life.'"

The problem wasn't just the support for hockey in California—or the lack of support at that time would be more accurate—it was the calibre of the players around him.

"Listen, nothing personal or an attack on any player I played with or was around, but I just came from the best team in hockey. And that first day in training camp, I got off the ice and I thought, 'What did I do?' I looked over at the right side and there was no Jari Kurri. I looked in the net and there was no Grant Fuhr. So, trust me, it wasn't all gravy when I first got there.

"Fortunately, I produced and I was still young. I was in the prime of my career, so I wasn't worried about my ability. Had I gotten there at 33 or 34, it would have been a really bad thing. It would not have been the right thing to do. But going to L.A. at 28, it was the right thing."

• • •

If going to Los Angeles was the right thing for Wayne Gretzky, letting him go didn't turn out so well for Peter Pocklington.

"Let's face it, that was the beginning of the end for Peter in Edmonton—certainly in the fans' minds that was the beginning of the end," Rod Phillips surmises. "And you know what? I don't think a lot of fans really give a damn about what the reasons were. They don't care that Peter wasn't going to be able to sign Wayne. Fans don't care about that kind of stuff. They just felt betrayed. Gretzky was their guy and that's the way they looked at it. He was the best player in the world and he should have been in Edmonton. Find a way to make it happen, that's all they care about.

"I suppose in the year 2030, they'll probably still be talking about the trade. I don't know how many people who were involved in it will still be alive, but it's always going to be a part of the team's history. A hundred years from now, it's going to be a part of the team. It's like Babe Ruth, you know. They still talk about the Babe Ruth trade in Boston."

Crazy as it may sound to some, Phillips's assertions are probably closer to the truth than the casual observer might suspect. If hockey fans—particularly Edmonton hockey fans—failed to understand in 1988 why the trade happened, their understanding hasn't improved over time.

In a poll taken by the *Edmonton Journal* on the trade's 20th anniversary in 2008, one-third of the respondents admitted they were still bitter about Peter selling Gretzky to L.A. It was the single largest response for any category (though another 9 per cent admitted they were "almost over it.")

"What do you mean, 20 years ago?" asked one reader. "Last night, the boys and I were so upset by this trade, we went down to the bar to really tie one on."

• • •

Oilers fans may persist in being cranky, but not so the two principals involved. Their long-standing friendship survived the turmoil of August 9, 1988, and it endures to this day.

> I actually don't remember the next time I saw Wayne after August 9. Probably when he played in Edmonton again on October 19. He was on the ice. I said, "Hi"; he said, "Hi." And that was it.
>
> One door closes, another one opens. But, you know, I love him dearly. I hope he is successful in everything he does.

The feeling is mutual. "I consider Peter a friend," says Wayne.

Four months after the trade, Wayne and Janet Gretzky gave birth to their first child, daughter Paulina. For a present, the man Wayne had come to think of as a father figure gave the newborn a $25,000 savings bond.

PART XVI

'Hey, we contributed quite a bit to this whole thing'

Wayne Gretzky has been traded to Los Angeles and the Oilers face the task of winning without him. Competitive fires ensure other leaders step to the fore, yet even so, the owner soon recognizes he cannot keep hockey's best team together.

In Boston, Massachusetts, on May 24, 1990, the Oilers beat the Bruins 4–1 to win their fifth Stanley Cup—their first without Wayne Gretzky. That night, their former star performer was 5,500 kilometres away, in Paris, watching the game on Europe's Sky TV.

Gretzky was in France for a horse race. He and his new boss, Bruce McNall, owned a horse that would be competing in the Prix de l'Arc de Triomphe later that year. "It was good for the Oilers when they won the Cup after trading me," says Wayne. "I think it relieved a lot of the pressure on Peter and Glen."

Well, it might have taken some pressure off Glen Sather. But Peter Pocklington? Not so much. The Oilers' owner was getting a rough ride in the media, even as his team was clinching another championship.

Five days before the Oilers won the Cup, Norm Ovenden wrote in the *Edmonton Journal* of the mixed emotions entertained by many Oilers' fans. "They'd dearly love their team to cage the Boston Bruins," he wrote. "But the vision of vilified owner Peter Pocklington slurping champagne from the Stanley Cup and self-righteously gloating that he was right all along to sell Wayne Gretzky is almost too much to stomach."

The ongoing scorn directed at Peter while his team marched towards another title did not escape his attention. "I know pretty well how you can go from a hero to a zero real quick," he told one reporter.

The *Hartford Courant*, in describing the split-personality disorder exhibited by many Edmonton hockey fans, noted that Peter was risking life and limb by even going out in public.

"Everybody jumped on me after the Gretzky trade as if the end of the world had come," Peter told the *Courant*. "People boycotted my dairy and threw eggs at my house. . . . I had over 100 death threats. . . . Wayne was an icon. Not a hockey player or even a hero, but an icon. When you trade an icon in a city that loves its sports, you are literally taking your life in your hands."

At the heart of this contradiction was the notion that even if the Oilers did deserve to win the Stanley Cup, their owner did not. *Journal* sports columnist Cam Cole gave voice to those sentiments. The Oilers, he wrote, should be also-rans forever after the Gretzky trade, "because justice would not let a man sell the world's greatest hockey player and have his team blithely carry on winning."

But win they did, and Peter's critics were choked about it.

"For Oiler owner Peter Pocklington, Thursday night's Stanley Cup victory may have been bittersweet: vindication will never truly be his in Edmonton, yet his hockey team won again, just as he said it would," wrote Cole.

On the evening of the 24th, as the Oilers' celebrated in their Boston Garden dressing room, an impartial observer, and certainly a partisan one, would have understood if Peter Pocklington emerged from the champagne spray to do a bit of crowing. But Peter would have none of it. He didn't claim vindication. He didn't rub his critics' noses in the bubbly that was spilling out of Lord Stanley's mug.

He told reporters it didn't matter if the fans liked him, as long as they loved their Oilers. "Edmonton's a city that demands winners, and sometimes the owner has to put up with some nonsense to see it happen," said Peter, his hair soaked in champagne. "But I don't look at it as personal vindication. I did what I had to do."

As for the victory, no matter how improbable, "when you have a GM like Glen Sather, all things are possible."

Indeed. "Peter maybe saw the big picture better than any of us," Sather said after the win, but he was being generous. Peter was right. It was Sather, after all, who turned the sale of Gretzky into a trade, who engineered the deal that sent the disenchanted Jimmy Carson to Detroit and secured the players that would help the Oilers win another Stanley Cup.

Peter also acknowledged that even though Wayne Gretzky was absent, his influence was still fashioning championships. Gretzky "affected so many players on this team, and made them become like him," Peter told the assembled reporters. "And you saw that in this series.

"The fifth [Cup], objectively, is very satisfying, just as the first one was satisfying emotionally. I was especially happy for Mark Messier, who was hurt very deeply by the Gretzky trade, and grew up a whole ton in the past two years and really led this team to the Cup."

Only a very few could be heard above the din of condemnation and coming to Peter's defence. Sather was one of them. CFRN Radio's John Short noted Peter was keeping his head down in the wake of the Oilers' Stanley Cup win, to which Sather replied, "It's too bad Peter has to do that. The media isn't fair to him.

"Peter has his critics and he has made mistakes—everybody does—but he's a total positive for this hockey team," said Sather.

. . .

Cam Cole was just one of a host of critics ready to write the Oilers' obituary in the wake of Peter's decision to trade Wayne Gretzky two years earlier. The *Journal* columnist would have plenty more opportunities to do just that before he himself left Edmonton in 1998. One of the first times Cole prepared a eulogy though was in the summer of 1989, after the Oilers had been eliminated from the playoffs by Gretzky's Kings.

"It seems the players who were conned into thinking there was something sacred about playing for the Oilers, largely on the strength of Gretzky's presence, won't be fooled again," he wrote.

What the columnist didn't count on—what no one who wasn't a part of that dressing room could have counted on—was that the Oilers did think they were special, though perhaps they needed a championship in 1990 to remind them.

"Wayne didn't win this Cup, the guys who are here right now won it," said Jari Kurri during the post-Cup celebrations. "Those are the guys we should be happy for. The young guys and the veterans."

In time, Kurri—like Gretzky—would leave the Oilers. So, too, would Messier, Kevin Lowe, Glenn Anderson, Grant Fuhr, Craig MacTavish and Charlie Huddy.

But Huddy says the veterans were diligent in imparting their values and beliefs about the Oilers to the newcomers in their midst. It's the conviction that being an Oiler is "special," something that has been passed on to each and every Oiler, and it continues to this day.

They didn't need Wayne Gretzky to show them how to do that.

"The team was always known as a tight-knit group that spent a lot of time together," says Huddy, "and it still is to this day. That's one of the things that continues. Hanging around with each other, and spending time together, and going into battle with each other.

"The guys who were playing back then passed it on to other guys that came in and it kind of keeps going down the road, you know."

It's a tradition that comes with a legacy of winning. "You look at other teams, like Montreal. They have a lot of tradition there because of the Cups they've won. It's the same feeling here. It continued on from when we played, right to now."

The Montreal Canadiens were an inspiration in more ways than one. "Glen went into training camp saying, 'I want to win the Stanley Cup, the MVP, the scoring race, the best defenceman, the goals against,'" recalls Gretzky. "He'd kept that Montreal mentality that we are going to win every award. That was his theory. And you can do that without taking anything away from the team philosophy.

"So, when they won in 1990, I was part of that. I understood. I know what those guys went through, and the pressure and the microscope they were under. I was probably more relieved and happy for them than they were."

. . .

Unlike the players still with the Oilers in 1990, Wayne Gretzky never won another Stanley Cup in his career. He came close only once, in 1993 when the Kings lost to the Canadiens in a five-game final.

"That was the most crushing one for me, the saddest moment in my career, losing to Montreal," Gretzky remembers. "We were so close."

The Kings advanced to the Stanley Cup final by beating the Toronto Maple Leafs in a memorable seven-game semi-final. Gretzky was the pivotal player in the deciding game—one that some hockey observers have called the last great showcase for old-time hockey. The Kings won 5–4, with Gretzky scoring three goals and assisting on another.

"It was so emotional to win Game 7 when the whole country wanted to see a Montreal–Toronto final," Gretzky recalls.

In the final, the Kings won the first game in Montreal, and were leading the second with 30 seconds to play, before the Canadiens tied the score and won in overtime. The Kings went quietly after that. "Had we won Game 2, I really believe we would have won the Stanley Cup. And nothing against Montreal, they deserved to win, but that was heart-wrenching for me. That was my biggest disappointment, the biggest letdown in my life."

Because he won in Edmonton, Gretzky knew he wanted to experience winning again, and again. "Part of the reason I'm back in the NHL now, in ownership and coaching, is I want the opportunity again to win a championship."

His experiences in Phoenix have given Gretzky a renewed perspective on his playing career, and the chain of events that took him away from Edmonton and from a team that was at its peak and destined to win many more championships.

"At the time, there were a lot of things I didn't understand, a lot of things about the business of sports I didn't grasp because I was a young kid," admits Gretzky. "And now, on the other side of it, I totally understand. And I'm at peace with it. I have no hard feelings towards Peter whatsoever."

• • •

Yet even if Gretzky was able to come to terms with his abrupt departure from Edmonton, some of his teammates were not. Nor could they reconcile why Peter had done it.

Three weeks before the Oilers won that fifth Stanley Cup, Glenn Anderson was telling the *Journal*'s Curtis Stock he had difficulties dealing with the trade for quite a while afterwards.

"I lost part of my heart. That's what the bottom line was," said Anderson. "I've always been a very positive person but two years ago my thoughts were all negative.

"When Gretzky got traded I couldn't understand how anyone could trade someone we were so close to. It was like another death. When people leave who you are close to, it's upsetting and it took me longer to recover than somebody who maybe wasn't as close.

"It was a good business deal for Peter, but from a personal end of it, I couldn't see it and it took me that much longer to bounce back. The unity wasn't there. Some guys came together; others fell further apart, that's what it was all about. We had lost the heart and soul and a big part of our hockey team."

• • •

The emotionally spent post-Gretzky Oilers hit rock bottom in the spring of '89 when they were eliminated by the Kings.

It was Gretzky himself who put them away, fighting off a check from Kurri and scoring into an empty Edmonton net. And as the last seconds ticked away, Kevin Lowe sat on the bench, tears in his eyes.

"I just hated to lose," says Lowe. "Wayne is one of my dearest friends to this day, but I have a lot of pride as an athlete and to me, losing it just said, well, 'Wayne was the Oilers and the Oilers weren't the Oilers. Wayne clearly proved that he is what made that team.'

"And in some respects, that's what motivated us in 1990. And there again, it's just us, just me, trying to prop up my place in life as an athlete, and saying 'Hey, we contributed quite a bit to this whole thing.'"

That contribution was the stuff of championships, all right. Yet, a year later, even though the triumph was theirs, it was Gretzky they saluted.

"Mess and I looked at each other, and said: 'This one's for the G-man because he's still such a big part of our team,'" Lowe told Curtis Stock during the post-Cup celebration.

"Kevin and I talked about the game this afternoon," Messier added. "And I said, 'What do you think?' He said, 'I think we should go out and win it for Gretz. It's the perfect way to show how big a part of this team he's been, and how he's still with us, really.'"

Well no, not really.

Gretzky never did think the Oilers were all about him, and the 1990 Stanley Cup was proof of that. There were other leaders—Lowe, Messier, Kurri and Anderson—who were the measure of a true champion. Of that, Peter Pocklington was convinced.

* * *

Lowe was always a leader in the dressing room, but Messier blossomed as a leader in Wayne's absence. Sather thinks he became more assertive, "because he had to be."

Sather says Messier had a different attitude towards leadership than did Gretzky, but the dynamic they shared was always healthy because their leadership styles complemented each other. They never seemed to clash.

"Mark was very careful in how he handled Wayne," Sather remembers. "He would never kind of get in his way. He was never the kind of guy who wanted to jump over the boards when there was an empty net.

"If Wayne had five points, I'd like to see him get seven, so I put him in a position where he could get to seven points. Whereas Mark could care less about that. He just wanted to win. But those guys shared everything, they got along well, they functioned well together. It was the team first."

Lowe was assertive from the moment he arrived in Edmonton. Sather could see it when he and Peter scouted him in Quebec, where Lowe played his junior hockey.

"He was head and shoulders, I thought, above everybody else," Sather recalls. He also remembers fining Lowe a few times for his show of temper—breaking light fixtures in the hallway to the dressing room, or flipping over the Ping-Pong table.

Yet even then, with those displays of passion, Sather could see the potential for leadership in Kevin Lowe. "I liked the way he worked. He understands the game," says Sather. "You know, it's too bad he quit coaching when he did. He was a good coach."

Lowe coached with the Oilers for two years—1998–99 as an assistant and the following season as the head coach—before becoming general manager when Sather left for the Rangers. Craig MacTavish, an assistant coach under Lowe, took over as the head coach.

It was a development that eight years earlier, Peter Pocklington had forecast.

"I wish some of our young guys had the heart of MacT and Kevin Lowe," Peter told the *Journal* in 1991. "In my opinion, both are great management material."

He saw leadership potential in others as well, as Peter mentioned in an interview with John Short after the '89 season.

"Mark Messier is getting older; some say Glenn Anderson is finished. Charlie Huddy and Kevin Lowe are getting up there in age." But, said Peter, they were all playing so incredibly well—"especially Charlie. It doesn't matter what goes on, he just goes out and he works harder."

• • •

In the two seasons that followed the 1990 Stanley Cup win, the Oilers advanced to the conference finals. They lost both series, to Minnesota in '91 and Chicago in '92. But after that, the champions who had led the Oilers to success drifted away, piece by valuable piece. Kurri left after the Stanley Cup victory to play in Italy. Messier, Fuhr, Anderson, Huddy, Adam Graves and Steve Smith all left after 1990–91. Lowe departed after '92, as did Joe Murphy and Jeff Beukeboom. The slow slide into mediocrity was on.

In almost every circumstance, players left or were moved because the Oilers simply could not afford to keep them. Trades were no more than ill-disguised salary dumps. Glen Sather's prophesy that money that would tear his team apart had come to pass.

"When the salaries started to become so huge, that's when you saw guys saying, well, 'You know, I'm going to go someplace else and play,'" recalls Rod Phillips, the Oilers' broadcaster. "They could make three times as much money in New York or wherever."

New York was a favoured destination. When the Rangers won the Stanley Cup in 1994, seven former Oilers were in their lineup: Messier, Lowe, Anderson, MacTavish, Graves, Beukeboom and Esa Tikkanen; a quarter of their roster. By comparison, the Oilers had only two players from their 1990 Cup-winning lineup still on the team: Kelly Buchberger and Bill Ranford.

Sather's handling of the Lowe trade was the boilerplate for a pattern that was repeated over and over by the Oilers.

"You know he was underpaid for the ability he had," Sather says of Lowe. "He was still a good player and, yeah, a great leader, but we couldn't afford to pay him, so he held out. Eventually, I let New York take him so they could have a chance to win the Stanley Cup, because Messier was there, and the others. I wanted to give those guys another opportunity to win. We weren't going to win it in Edmonton."

• • •

While Anderson, too, would end up with the Rangers in time to win another Stanley Cup, he and Fuhr were first traded to the Maple

Leafs, in exchange for a lot of young talent that didn't stick around Edmonton for long. Peter remembers that, earlier, he could have fetched a better price for Fuhr.

> I had an offer from the pizza king in Detroit, Mike Ilitch—$5 million for Fuhr. I should have taken that.
>
> I said to Glen, "I think we should dump Fuhr for five million," but Glen was against it. He said, "You can't do that." I said, "Glen, it's six and a half million CDN and the guy is at the end of his rope." I should have just done it. I kick myself now.
>
> Of course, Glen would go crazy because he said, "Well, I can't win any games if I don't have these players," but it was always a constant battle between salaries and losing money. I mean, it was huge money by the time we got into 1989–90 and all the contracts just soared.
>
> Most general managers around the league didn't care what the hell they paid these players. All they wanted to do was keep their own jobs—and they kept their jobs by getting the right players and to hell with the budget. If the owner lost $10 million, that was his problem.

• • •

Two decades later, the players, the coaches and the owner look back on that championship era as the zenith of their lives, personally, professionally, collectively.

Ask Wayne Gretzky. "I wouldn't trade it for the world," Gretzky writes in the foreword to this book. "I wish it would have lasted another 20 years."

"Gretzky loves to sit and talk about those guys," adds Rod Phillips. "It was the best time of their lives, all of them. They were all young, they were all making good money, they were the dominant team and they just had so much fun. They partied together and their summer vacations were together. It was a great time.

"Their lives were changed by what happened. They've all gone on to have great success with other teams and other pursuits, but I bet if you lined them all up today and asked, 'What was the best time in your life?' they'd say without doubt those years between 1979 and 1990.

"It doesn't get better, you know?"

. . .

The departure of Wayne Gretzky in 1988, and to a lesser extent Paul Coffey a year earlier, were portents of what was to come for the Oilers, and for Peter Pocklington. The Oilers were not destined, after all, to keep winning for years to come, as many of them had predicted. Instead, by the time their championship days were over, most of them couldn't get out of town fast enough.

Peter Pocklington, too, would ultimately leave Edmonton, his reputation in tatters, his financial resources exhausted, his business empire in ruins. Yet he did everything he thought he could to avoid just such a calamity—beginning with his decision to sell Wayne Gretzky. Peter felt that sending his most prized asset to California would allow him to reinvest in his team, reseed its roster with up-and-coming stars, and continue to craft championships. Instead, the new beginning he envisioned turned out to be the beginning of the end for the Oilers' Pocklington era.

PART XVII

'And Peter Pocklington? . . . Good on you, man'

The Oilers can no longer afford their stable of stars and have parcelled them off to teams that are eager to have them and have the resources to pay them. Yet the players who replace the stars inspire little but indifference from the public. Soon, Peter Pocklington is faced with a decision: make a go of it in Edmonton or seek out another market for his team.

People will tell you Peter Pocklington is a charming guy. He is easy to like. He is polite, unfailingly positive and does not hesitate in offering an encouraging word at the opportune moment. He can be outgoing, generous in gesture and spirit, caring, respectful and kind. He is both a gentleman and, on occasion—particularly with his grandchildren—even a gentle man.

Yet few people—except perhaps those in the political realm—have been subjected to as much rudeness, suspicion, contempt, even vilification, as Peter Pocklington has faced over the past two decades. He continues to encounter it to this day.

Peter blames it on what he calls the culture of envy in North America; a culture, he says, that assumes the worst about successful people. But there is probably more to it than that.

As Nelson Skalbania says, Peter makes himself an easy target. Those who come to know him discover he can be demanding, judgmental, insensitive, forgetful, notoriously impatient, stubborn and infuriatingly inattentive. None of these are a crime. In fact, they are traits commonly held by many of us.

Yet for his more powerful critics—perhaps emboldened by vindictiveness and an acute sense of self-righteousness—Peter Pocklington's forceful personality was sufficient reason to seek his ruination. In Edmonton in the 1990s, those critics were people in positions of influence who subscribed to a notion shared by many in the city—they didn't like Peter Pocklington, they were eager to humiliate if not destroy him, and some of them were in a position to do just that. They wearied of his self-confidence, his perceived arrogance, his ultimatums, his wheedling and cajoling, his ability to get people to go along with him . . . sometimes, even the fact he could be charming was enough to piss them off.

In the 1990s, Peter Pocklington became a marked man.

• • •

The Oilers might not have been the most important piece in the puzzle that was the Pocklington business empire, but they were certainly the piece that commanded the most attention. And as long as they were profitable, they were also the most rewarding for the man who owned them.

But by 1988, the Oilers were no longer making money—and selling Wayne Gretzky provided only a temporary reprieve. By the early 1990s, player salaries had begun to balloon. The business of being an NHL owner was quickly becoming too rich for the likes of Peter Pocklington:

> From about 1988 on, we were losing $3 million to $4 million a
> year. And then it got really serious. The losses reached as high as
> $10 million a year.
>
> The payroll was to blame. By 1993–94, the cost of the players
> was 105 per cent of my gate. All the other costs we had were on top
> of that. When you lose $10 million a year, you can't make that up
> in Edmonton.
>
> So what are you supposed to do? Do you suck every nickel out

of every other business you own to run the Oilers? No. You start selling off your more expensive players.

Take Mark Messier, for instance. He wasn't past his prime yet, but in my opinion he was close to it. Once a guy is 33, 34, how many years does he have left? Mark was 30 when we traded him. If another team thinks he's got more to offer, then they should go for it and buy him.

. . .

The Oilers parcelled off their most expensive—albeit experienced— players one by one. Messier went to the Rangers. So, too, did Kevin Lowe, Craig MacTavish, Adam Graves and Esa Tikkanen. Jari Kurri went to Italy for a year, then rejoined Gretzky in Los Angeles. Huddy also went to L.A. Fuhr and Anderson were traded to Toronto; Joe Murphy and Steve Smith to Chicago. Craig Simpson was shipped to Buffalo, and Martin Gelinas to Quebec.

Three years after their 1990 Stanley Cup win, the Oilers won only 26 of 84 games. Rosters that were once filled with future Hall of Famers now featured the likes of Jason Bonsignore, Kevin Todd and Ralph Intranuovo.

There were games when the results were indicative of either a lack of talent or a lack of effort, and sometimes both—such as the night the Oilers lost 5–0 to the Tampa Bay Lightning, only 24 hours after the Lightning had lost 10–0 to the Calgary Flames.

"My dad once told me, 'Son, you can lead a horse to water, but you can't make him fuck the fish,'" coach Ron Low surmised afterwards.

A couple of minutes later, in an adjoining room, Sather confessed, "I can't keep beating a dead horse with these guys."

Interest in the team, and attendance at their games, began to wane. It wasn't long before the Oilers were playing in front of crowds smaller than 7,000.

Oilers' broadcaster Rod Phillips remembers the challenge of making the play-by-play sound exciting when a bad team was playing uninspired hockey in front of a small crowd.

"I can remember one night they were playing Ottawa, and there were around 6,000 people in the building," recalls Phillips. "On a night like that, you'd make a comment like, 'Small crowd here tonight. Doesn't look for it to be more than six or seven thousand people in the building,' and add something about it being a difficult time for the Oilers. But my job was to get on with the play-by-play, so there wasn't too much time for editorializing. It was a brutal game and you'd be trying to make it sound better than it was. But your heart was cold. You kept hoping the team would get better, but it was really a tough time. You knew the team was not going to make the playoffs. Those were dark days."

Those dark days were about to get even darker. The Canadian loonie began to sink towards the 60-cent level against the U.S. dollar. For most businesses, that might not have been such a bad thing, but in the hockey business, it was disastrous. While the Oilers' revenue was in Canadian dollars, their players were paid in U.S. currency. As the gap in the exchange rate widened, there were fewer American dollars to pay players. The financial losses mounted.

If the Oilers were to stay in Edmonton, they needed more sources of money. Peter's solution? He needed to gain control of Northlands Coliseum to trim his costs and generate more revenue streams. Either the deal gets done, or—he announced publicly—he would move the Oilers to another city. In return, he'd help pay for a major renovation of the arena.

> We were losing gobs of money. In '86 or '87, our total payroll was $7 or $8 million CDN. By '94 or '95, it was $45 million. With our players getting paid in U.S. dollars and the Canadian dollar sinking, we were in a jam.
>
> That's when I was forced to hold my nose and do that crazy deal with Northlands and the City of Edmonton. We spent $15 million updating the Coliseum. In 1994, the Chrétien government was making grants available for infrastructure projects, and the city was able to get $10 million for the Coliseum. But you couldn't do

the remodelling for that price. So I wrote a cheque from the Oilers for another $5 million. But I was allowed to keep the revenue from the concessions and the luxury boxes.

Anyway, when the money from the boxes came in, that added another $4 million in revenue. We did really well on the concessions, too; that was another $5 million. And we did a really good job setting up the building. We had the beer piped in through central lines down to the spigots, and automated the pricing and so on. So we did fairly well.

But we had to pay Northlands $2.8 million a year in rent, if you can imagine that. Remember they got that building from the city for nothing, and the renovations cost them nothing. On top of that, they got a free box and 75 free tickets, and all this crap—all because they happened to be Northlands.

The city did levy a ticket tax to help defray Peter's rental costs. And for $15 million—almost as much money as it cost to build the Coliseum in 1974—the building was completely rebuilt from the inside out with 39 additional luxury suites along the mezzanine to go along with 16 skyboxes, a new sound system and scoreboard, and all new seats.

But believe it or not, all the extra revenue that first year was spent on only three players. It was ridiculous.

It may have been the first time Peter had threatened to move the Oilers, but it wouldn't be the last. While he bargained for the Coliseum deal, he openly mused about moving the team to Hamilton. In later years, it was Minneapolis, and then Houston. But in his efforts to get the Coliseum renovated, he had no intention of making good on his ultimatum.

I wasn't going to do it, I wasn't going to move the team. I was using it for leverage to get people to come to the table. What other leverage do you have? What do you do when you got everybody

against you? I was one guy. What are you going to do? Have them
run over you while I lose a fortune? They didn't care.

I didn't want to move anywhere, though. I was committed to
dear Edmonton.

• • •

When the Northlands deal was finally struck, all sides cheered it as
the solution that would keep the Oilers in Edmonton. Yet, in the end,
it provided only temporary relief from what was becoming an
increasingly bleak economic picture for both Peter and the Oilers.
The renovations failed to lure back the fans, while the money owed to
the ATB—by now secured directly by the market value of the club—
continued to add up.

By late in 1995, the season-ticket base had shrunk to 6,000 seats.
Yet at the same time, the club was also beginning to develop into a
contender again. While that was good news for the Oilers' faithful, it
was bad for the payroll. In the '95–96 season, Doug Weight, the
Oilers' best player, racked up an impressive 104 points—and his
contract was coming up for renewal. He was going to expect a big
raise.

• • •

In January of 1996, NHL commissioner Gary Bettman came to
Edmonton at the behest of Peter Pocklington. While there, he
announced that help was coming for Canadian teams struggling
under the burden of a 60-cent dollar. The Canadian Assistance Plan
would pay each small-market Canadian team that qualified—Toronto
and Montreal did not—a subsidy to help them be more competitive
with American teams. The Oilers stood to get as much as $2.7 million
CDN. But there were conditions, said Bettman. The team must have
at least 13,000 season tickets. At the time, the Oilers had managed to
get the number up to only 6,800.

And there was more. All the luxury boxes would have to be sold, and all the board advertising, too. Without that support, Bettman hinted that the Oilers might not be long for Edmonton. Any small-market Canadian team that failed to qualify for the currency subsidy was not likely to survive, said the commissioner.

And he wasn't done. All this had to be accomplished by May 31, 1996, just five months away.

"In the final analysis, it's going to have to be Peter's decision," said Bettman. "At some point—I haven't done the math yet, I haven't looked at Peter's bank book yet, and I haven't given his constitution a test in terms of what his stamina is—but, at some point, the economics of this aren't going to work."

The media did not see encouraging signs in its assessment of the challenge facing Edmonton and the Oilers.

"Unless you believe in fairy tales, you can't really believe that this city is going to double its commitment to the hockey team in the next five months," wrote Cam Cole in the *Journal*.

• • •

This time, as the Oilers faced another do-or-die ultimatum, Peter did not make claims that he could get a better deal somewhere else. He already knew he could—in Minnesota. But what people didn't know was that he had already decided the team wasn't moving. For better or for worse, Peter was committed to staying in Edmonton.

At the end of the 1992–93 season, the owner of the Minnesota North Stars, Calgary developer Norm Green, moved that team to Dallas. After that, the Twin Cities of Minneapolis and St. Paul and the State of Minnesota began to cast about for a replacement. They had the arena. The Minnesota Timberwolves of the NBA had built the Target Center in 1990, and a few years later, the City of Minneapolis took it over. The facility could handle a hockey team and by mid-decade, they had set their sights on the Oilers.

By that time, Peter Pocklington was in the mood to be wooed. Fans in Edmonton were staying away from the Oilers' games, and the

ATB was getting cranky.

> Yeah, Glen and I flew to Minnesota. We met with the governor, Arne Carlson. He was a good guy—a Republican. They were interested, very much so. And it would have been easy to arrange the funds to pay off the Treasury Branch and be free and clear of that debt once and for all.

Clearly, it would have been in Peter's best interests to move the team to Minnesota but, in the end, he wouldn't do it. Sather remembers the day well.

"I got the sense he didn't want to move," Sather says. "We went to Minneapolis and looked at the Target Center, we had them raise and lower the floor—it goes up and down. We met with a guy by the name of Stan Hubbard (a broadcasting mogul based in St. Paul) who was going to put together a TV deal for us. It would have been a great deal. We even looked around at properties—where to move, where to live."

They also talked about how Bob Irsay, the owner of the National Football League's Baltimore Colts, had moved the team to Indianapolis in the middle of the night back in 1984.

"We talked about bringing the trucks in to move the stuff at night and how to get everything organized," Sather remembers. "But at the end of the day, on the way back to Edmonton, Peter said, 'I can't do it. I just can't do it to the city.'

"It was pretty honourable of him," says Sather. "Peter took the bullet for everybody."

• • •

The Quebec Nordiques left Canada for Denver in 1995. A year later, the Winnipeg Jets moved to Phoenix. The smart money was on the Edmonton Oilers doing the same in 1997 if the last-ditch season-ticket drive fell short.

And it wasn't going well. Two months after Bettman came to

town to draw his line in the sand, the season-ticket base had improved only marginally to 8,700. There was less than two months left to sell 4,300 season tickets.

Not surprisingly, Peter was being blamed for the sluggish response. And it wasn't just the average working-class hockey fan who wasn't coming to the party. The business community and the government sector were shunning the Oilers' owner, too.

"People hate Pocklington and they're willing to give up professional hockey to 'show him,'" wrote columnist Bill Sass in the *Journal*.

But Peter was not without allies. Mayor Bill Smith waded in on the subject in an interview with the *Journal*'s Robin Brownlee. It makes no sense to lose the team "for some crazy reason—like we don't like the owner," he said. "Move Peter's face out of the equation and put the Oiler logo in. That's my message."

Enter the Friends of the Oilers. A group of prominent business people was being assembled by Cal Nichols—who owned a chain of Edmonton gas stations called Gasland—to sell Oilers' season tickets to the mom-and-pop business community that was such a big part of the Edmonton economy.

At the time, Peter Pocklington—whether he was keeping his own counsel or someone else's he doesn't say—parked his ego and his customary bombast and fell silent. The community was left to its own conscience in deciding whether it wanted to keep its NHL team.

"The fact was the media was focusing on me rather than the campaign and what had to be done," Peter told the *Journal*'s Mark Spector. "It was the wrong thing to talk about and I immediately understood, let's bring in the folks who are going to do the job and get them to focus on where it has to be—buying tickets."

Not that Peter wasn't busy. He met behind the scenes with his own list of executives, such as Serge Darkazanli of the Real Canadian Superstores, who agreed to buy 1,000 tickets at a total cost of around $800,000.

He also lured Doug Piper ("The straw that stirred the drink," said Peter) from a ticket-promotion company in Portland, Oregon, to be the Oilers' marketing manager and to quarterback the ticket campaign from the club's end.

But there is no doubt Nichols' Friends of the Oilers made the critical difference. They undertook a community-wide campaign to sell several thousand season tickets, for no greater reward than civic pride and the satisfaction in a job well done.

And they succeeded. By the May 31 deadline, the Oilers season ticket total stood at 13,482.

To say the town was jubilant would be a gross understatement. A celebration was held at City Hall. The crowd that gathered welcomed the Oilers' owner with surprising warmth.

Mayor Smith thanked those Edmontonians who stepped up to buy season tickets. He thanked corporate Edmonton for its show of support. He thanked the Friends of the Oilers for helping to make the drive a success. And he had one more person to thank.

"And Peter Pocklington? . . . Good on you, man," said the mayor.

In turn, Peter thanked Piper, who taught a moribund front office how to hustle again. But he reserved special praise for Nichols and the Friends of the Oilers for saving his team.

"It was heartening, and humbling," said Peter of their efforts. "They sounded the clarion call and made sure everyone heard it. From the bottom of my heart, I thank all of you."

The last word was left for Gary Bettman, who spoke from his New York office. "There are a lot of differences between Edmonton on one hand, and Winnipeg and Quebec on the other. Markets, history, buildings. But the key difference is, in Quebec and Winnipeg, there was no longer anybody who could be considered a bona fide owner of an NHL club, no one who believed they could make it work. And that is the Pocklington difference.

"I've known since the very first day I met Peter that he wanted to keep that team in Edmonton."

•   •   •

The future was looking bright indeed.

The Oilers would begin the 1996–97 season with close to 14,000 season tickets, a higher number than half the teams in the league. All their corporate suites and board advertising were sold. They qualified for close to $3 million CDN in league subsidies. The team was on a stronger financial footing than it had been in a decade.

It would be a landmark season in other ways, too. Spurred by the play of Weight and goalie Curtis Joseph, the Oilers would again play before full houses and seize a community's imagination. They would return to the playoffs after a four-year absence, and—in true Oiler style—engineer one of the most exciting playoff upsets in NHL history.

But it would be Peter Pocklington's last season as sole owner of the Edmonton Oilers. The Alberta Treasury Branches was about to see to that.

PART XVIII

'Losing the Oilers was like having my heart torn out'

For the first time in a decade, the Oilers can look to the future with optimism. So, too, can Peter Pocklington. But that optimism is short-lived. It soon becomes apparent his bank doesn't share that optimism and is ready to take the steps to put Peter out of business.

Once it became evident the Oilers do-or-die season-ticket drive was a stunning success, Peter Pocklington began to look to the future with a measure of confidence. It was the first time in years. "We could have been up here announcing a move to St. Paul, Minnesota—or, God forbid, Nashville—just to survive economically," Peter told a congratulatory reception at City Hall. "But we can make it here now."

Within a few months, however, Peter would be reminded, yet again, what an expensive business professional hockey can be. While the ticket campaign generated about $4.1 million CDN in revenue, the money didn't stay long in the Oilers' bank account. That fall, Glen Sather announced two of the Oilers' best players, Doug Weight and Jason Arnott, had signed new two-year contracts. The total cost for the two stars, for just the first year alone—$6.2 million CDN.

The fact that the proceeds of a concerted community-wide sales effort, one that involved the volunteer labour and financial commitment of thousands upon thousands of Edmontonians, went into the pockets of just two hockey players—and, in fact, didn't even cover their raises—wasn't lost on anyone, least of all Peter.

That's how goofy it was in those days. I remember when we took over the Coliseum two years before then—we increased our revenue by $9 million, but the team costs went up $15 million. All the money we earned from those luxury boxes paid for only one player.

At the time, I would go to every NHL meeting and say, "For God's sake, let's get some business reality into our sport." But unfortunately, in the NHL, it took a 100-per-cent vote to change anything that had to do with economics. And of course, Bill Wirtz and Ed Snider (the club owners in Chicago and Philadelphia respectively) would never vote for anything like that. They made more money than God, so they didn't care. If they needed a player, they would just go sign him. All the arguments to show some restraint fell on deaf ears until they started to lose money, too. And it was years before that happened.

•   •   •

The Oilers may have faced financial challenges in keeping up with the more affluent teams in the league, but that was a problem faced by all small-market teams, and one the NHL could not ignore forever. In spite of that reality, capacity crowds were being brought to their feet cheering for a competitive, exciting, fast, playoff-bound team that seemed to exhibit all the traditional offensive traits of "Oilers hockey" in an era when the defensive trap was beginning to dominate the league.

The Oil were back.

The near-perfect end to their near-perfect season came in the first round of the post-season against the Dallas Stars. In Game 3, the first playoff game played in Edmonton in five years, the Oilers were trailing Dallas 3–0 with five minutes to go. But three Oiler goals in the span of two minutes tied the score, and a Kelly Buchberger goal in overtime gave the win to Edmonton.

The Oilers won two other games in overtime, too, including Game 7. Fans can still recite, in vivid detail, what happened on that hot April night in Dallas, with the series on the line: Curtis Joseph making a miraculous save on a Joe Nieuwendyk goalmouth shot, then Doug Weight feeding Todd Marchant for a breakaway goal and the series win.

"They were such huge underdogs in that series with Dallas," recalls Rod Phillips, whose radio call of the play has become the stuff of Oilers' legend. The *Journal* put Phillips's play-by-play of the Joseph save and Marchant goal on a tape that readers could hear by calling a dedicated phone number. "They had something like 100,000 hits on that telephone line because it was such an exciting play. The *Journal* people couldn't believe it. They were getting requests for that call for a year after that.

"Any time you win a seventh game in sudden-death overtime, that's what dreams are made of, for players and fans and cities. What a great series."

The town, in short, went nuts. If Curtis Joseph, or Cujo as he was known, had run for mayor, he would have won in a walk. The *Sun* and the *Journal* even photographed the all-star goalie wearing the mayor's chain of office.

"I thought we were going to go all the way," Peter remembers. "I thought we were going to win the Stanley Cup."

Well, they didn't, but no one would have blamed Peter at that point for thinking his hockey team had turned a corner. The team still lost $6.7 million that year, but with the Alberta economy again showing signs of life after 15 years of economic stagnation, those losses would be cut in half the following year. Moreover, his business fortunes appeared to be on the rebound as well.

Things were beginning to look up for Peter Pocklington. The Alberta Treasury Branches, however, had other plans.

•   •   •

The ATB was charging 19-per-cent interest on the Oilers' overdraft—and, well, the whole thing was the overdraft. So they nailed me for $20 million, $25 million in interest every year. Finally, I proposed a settlement.

By this point, Peter owed the ATB more than $120 million on a line of credit secured by the Oilers to underwrite losses incurred by the Oilers. Since $120 million was perceived to be the value of the club on the open market, the bank felt it was time to make its move.

Yet Peter had other business interests in his stable—successful, profitable enterprises. His Lethbridge canola margarine processor, Cambra Foods, was valued at $40 million. He had been offered $11 million US to sell the Trappers to a group in Portland. He owned developable land in Calgary worth $10 million, and had already received a $15-million offer for the property. He also owned Club Fit, a profitable chain of fitness centres. He proposed to use those companies as additional security and take out a mortgage with the ATB that would eventually settle his debt.

But the bank said no. Instead, they called his loan—a decision Peter maintains was politically motivated. The ATB, he claims was acting on orders from a Conservative government bent on revenge.

Whatever the ATB's motivation, Peter was faced with the inevitable: he would have to sell the Oilers.

•   •   •

Well, that was it, the ATB called my loan. What was I going to do? I had been putting tremendous pressure on them the best I could to find a resolution. And, to me, the best resolution would have been for the ATB to treat me the way they treated every other businessman they loaned big money to. Remember they wrote up hundreds of millions of dollars in deals to the forestry sector and so on. All they had to do was treat me the way they treated the Ghermezians at West Edmonton Mall: give me a proper mortgage at reasonable rates and I could meet it—instead of paying 19-per-cent interest on an overdraft.

That's all they had to do, but they wouldn't. They called in the loan instead. Believe me, you can't fight City Hall.

Why? It was the hatred. They knew that once I traded Gretzky, they could do anything to me and no one would complain. And I was controversial the way I settled the Gainers thing, and the way that it ended, and they were really pissed off about that. Remember, the provincial government had lost millions on Gainers after they took it away from me.

It got very personal. If the province had agreed to do what they shook hands on, we'd still have a Gainers. But I openly criticized the Conservative government for that and I shouldn't have. God forbid you should tell the emperor he's got no clothes.

So, I was going to have to sell the team. If I didn't pay them off, they were just going to put a bullet in my head—which they did anyway.

• • •

There was another option, but it wasn't one Peter would consider: taking on a partner. The NHL of the 1990s required owners with pockets deeper than Peter's, but recruiting one to help finance the Oilers wasn't on his to-do list.

"He could have added somebody else who had deep pockets, sold a percentage of the team," Sather remembers. "But in the end, he didn't want to do it. He didn't want to give up any part of the team."

Bill Comrie, owner of The Brick furniture chain, was mentioned as one possibility. He was on the record saying he had great respect for Peter and would do anything to help him out of his jam. Peter never asked.

• • •

In the first week of June 1997—almost a year to the day after most everyone in Edmonton thought the Oilers were going to stay in the city for good, Peter Pocklington announced he was selling the Oilers to settle his debt with the ATB.

Almost immediately, fears loomed that the club could be sold to out-of-town interests, though Peter did say he was "honour-bound" to find local buyers.

Nevertheless, within a week, two groups from Houston were publicly musing about buying the Oilers and moving them to the Texas oil capital. The first was headed by Robert McNair and Chuck Watson, two men who owned the Houston franchise in the International Hockey League. The other was the owner of the NBA's Houston Rockets, Les Alexander.

The McNair–Watson partnership had been rejected for an NHL franchise earlier that year—Nashville, Atlanta, Columbus and Minnesota's Twin Cities had been selected instead—but were reported to have the inside track on any future franchise. They were even proposing moving their IHL team, the Aeros, to Edmonton to replace the Oilers, should they depart.

The problem was the NHL wanted a new arena in Houston before there was any talk of a franchise and Alexander was likely closer to getting that done. Either way, the majority of the NHL's 25 other owners, 20 of whom were American, were keen on the idea of moving the Oilers to Houston. It was the ninth-largest market in the States, with a population of 2.9 million, three times the size of Edmonton. They would also provide a natural geographic rivalry for the Dallas Stars.

The people of Edmonton, however, were about to prove prying the Oilers out of their hands would be no easy task.

• • •

When Peter struck the deal in 1994 to take over the Coliseum, he signed an agreement with the city, Northlands and Economic Development Edmonton that kept the Oilers in town until at least 2004. If Peter no longer owned the team, anyone who bought it would also have to abide by that agreement. If a buyer was from out of town and did not wish to fulfil the agreement, a local buyer would be given 30 days to buy the team for a fixed price of $70 million US.

Such a group was quietly working in the background to assemble the money. The players included Bruce Saville, Jim and Harry Hole, Cal Nichols and Cathy Roozen—whose father, Dr. Charles Allard, sold the Oilers to Peter and Nelson Skalbania 21 years earlier.

However, if a local group didn't come up with the money, the ATB was free to sell the team to anyone, whether they would move it or not. That suited Alexander fine. "If the time passes and there's no local buyer, we believe we'll be the group that buys the team and moves them to Houston," John Thomas, a Rockets' executive, told the *Journal*.

Moreover, by the time the 1997–98 season had begun, the ATB had entrenched itself in the Oilers' operations. The bank appointed John Ramsey as the club's CEO with the mandate to find a new owner, but he also spent much of his time on day-to-day operations. Once it became evident some local groups had fallen short in raising the $70 million they needed to buy the club, Peter focused his efforts on working with Alexander—but only to keep the team in Edmonton.

By late October, they were ready to go public: Alexander would buy 90 per cent of the Oilers for $88.8 million US. He would agree to keep the team in Edmonton for three years. If the Oilers made money in that time, he would sell them to local interests in exchange for an expansion franchise for Houston. If they didn't, he would be free to move the Oilers to Texas. Either way, he figured he would get a team for Houston.

Alexander was prepared to leave the Oilers in Edmonton because he didn't have a rink ready in Houston that would be acceptable to the NHL. A three-year period would give him time to build one—either for the Oilers or for an expansion team. If he chose to leave Edmonton earlier, he could put the team into one of the four recently awarded expansion sites, then swap a franchise for Houston down the road.

During that three-year grace period, Peter would keep 10-per-cent interest in the club and would be the Oilers' alternate governor. He would also be paid any of the revenue the club might receive from the NHL in expansion fees during that time.

The proposal included the takeover of Coliseum Management Inc. (CMI), the company Peter formed to run the Coliseum. In addition, Alexander made it clear he wanted not only CMI's free rent from Northlands, but the $2.8 million in rent money the city was paying Northlands on Peter's behalf every year.

A meeting was hastily arranged for November 3, 1997, at City Hall, to be followed the next day by a news conference at the Coliseum, where the sale would be announced to the public. But storm clouds were gathering over the negotiations. Neither event would go as planned.

Rick LeLacheur was head of Economic Development Edmonton, one of the groups that had veto power over any deal that would violate the 1994 agreement. He announced that any new owner would have to abide by the location agreement to keep the Oilers in Edmonton until 2004. "It doesn't matter who owns the team as long as they leave it here," he said.

But Alexander wanted the location agreement trashed if he was to keep the team in Edmonton. He was particularly unsettled by the clause that would effectively allow local interests to buy the team from him in 2001 for $70 million—when he paid close to $89 million for 90 per cent of it.

And there was more. According to the Alexander proposal, if the attendance dropped below 12,000 in the first year, he would move the team the next season, not in 2001.

On November 3, the parties convened in a City Hall meeting room. The meeting was short. Alexander walked in and said he wasn't there to negotiate. He told the city representatives he needed the location agreement tossed out if his deal with Peter was to proceed. LeLacheur, Mayor Bill Smith and Northlands head Al Skoreyko said no. "My pitch was to 'honour the agreement,'" said the mayor. Alexander marched out in a huff, his army of aides trailing behind.

The news conference the next morning did go ahead as scheduled, but Alexander was a no-show. Peter stood there alone in front of a roomful of reporters. His hopes for selling the team, keeping it in Edmonton, staying involved, and paying off the ATB had just caught the first flight back to Houston:

What a character that guy turned out to be. I mean, he blew

Dodge! What a strange guy.

But, of course, the press conference went ahead, and people were there from all over Canada. So I did the only thing I could do: tell them the truth. "This is what happened. Sorry. I can't control other people," I said. I mean I felt like a total fool, obviously.

Because Alexander didn't have a rink where he was, he wanted to own the Oilers, to give him the leverage he needed to build the building for both of his teams in Houston—the Oilers and the Rockets.

And then at City Hall, they told him they wouldn't let him move it, under any circumstances, ever. They were just using his offer.

As he left his Edmonton hotel by the back door, Alexander refused to talk to the Edmonton media, but he was more chatty with the *Houston Chronicle*: "I was led to believe they were ready to address some of the larger issues, they would welcome me with open arms as the saviour of the team," Alexander said, "and the complete reverse was true. They were, to say the least, hostile.

"They were unbelievable. It was like they couldn't shake my hand."

But Peter told the *Journal*'s Jac Macdonald that "without question," he had painted an accurate picture for Alexander of what to expect. "He has seen all the documents, all the pros and cons, exactly what the local buyers have seen."

And therein lay the silver lining—the local buyers. As the smoke billowed from the wreckage of the Alexander offer, a group of Edmonton business people quietly formed a legal corporation with the single purpose of buying the Oilers. Their name: The Edmonton Investors Group.

• • •

With the Alexander offer dead in the water, the ATB running the Oilers, and the EIG's efforts to raise money far from the $70-million target, an air of uncertainty settled over the hockey club. If the EIG fell short, the Oilers would not be long for Edmonton.

"Oh, it was terrifying. I mean everybody in the organization was terrified," Phillips recalls. "We were all at a stage in our lives where, if the team left, there wasn't going to be any guarantees that we would leave with the team—and I don't think anybody really thought that they wanted to leave with the team.

"I certainly had no inclination to move my family and move with the team. That period was, for guys like me and people in the front office, a time of terrible pressure: 'What the hell am I going to do? I've got to find a job,' that sort of thing . . ."

Throughout that time, however—"Everybody was sick to death about that," Phillips said of the Alexander offer—neither he nor the others blamed Peter for what was happening.

"I knew Peter was trying as hard as he could to keep the team in Edmonton. And I knew that he didn't want the team to leave; I knew that in my heart. But it was still dollars and cents, and it looked like there was no possible financial way to keep the team here. There were lots of nights Debbie and I sat and talked about the fact that, you know, 'I don't think the NHL can make it here.' I was starting to come to think that maybe it can't survive in Edmonton."

. . .

With no one knowing what Alexander was going to do next, the ATB made its move. "Because Alexander's offer was off the table, they said, 'Well, you don't have an offer,' which is when they decided they were going to try and steal the team," says Peter.

On November 22, the ATB gave Peter until December 11 to sell the team, or they would put it into receivership. Said Darlene Dickinson, an ATB spokeswoman: "If they [Peter] have an offer in 20 days, we will grant them an additional 40 days [to finalize the deal]. If after 20 days there is no local offer, external offers will be sought." Furthermore, she said, if an out-of-town offer was made, local groups would have 30 days to submit offers of their own.

It was a move that would suit the fledgling EIG just fine. Rumour had it the group would wait for the receivership before making a move. This was one rumour that had merit. There were individuals in the EIG who refused to be in the same room with Peter Pocklington, never mind negotiate with him.

However, the deadline passed without the ATB taking action. Peter was still in charge, if only nominally. In January, the bank appointed Ramsey, the Oilers' CEO, to the club's board, joining Peter and Robert Kallir, the ATB's general counsel. The ATB now had the majority vote in directing the club's fortunes.

On February 11, the other shoe fell. The ATB announced Alexander had offered $82.5 million US for the Oilers, officially giving local buyers 30 days to come up with $70 million. "If I buy the team, it won't be playing in Edmonton next year," Alexander told the Houston media.

Peter was not part of that offer. "I don't really want to be involved if it's going to move," he told the *Journal*.

By that point, ATB president Paul Haggis said the bank was fully prepared to sell the Oilers to Alexander and move the team out of Edmonton. If Alexander would agree to make an $80-million offer, ATB officials even promised to pay him $4 million in compensation if the deal didn't go through. "Remember, our obligation was to collect on this loan," Haggis said later.

The time had come for the EIG to fish or cut bait.

•   •   •

Phillips recalls seeing Cal Nichols, who was quarterbacking the EIG effort, around the Coliseum in the days after February 11.

"I don't know whether we were pessimistic, but we just wondered, 'How do you find a whole bunch of guys to put up $70 million US?'

"We'd see Cal at the rink all the time and he was working his ass off. And every time we'd see him, we'd ask, 'How's it going?' 'Well, not too bad. Got some guys in Lloydminster and they're getting interested and—' 'Are you going to be able to pull this off?' 'Well, we got about $50 million so far, but we need another $30 million.'

"But he kept working at it and then all of a sudden, boom, they had the money. And that was like a thousand Christmases."

On the night of May 4, the Oilers shut out the talented Colorado Avalanche 4–0 to win their first-round playoff series in seven games. The next day, deadline day before the team would be handed to Houston, the papers were signed, the deal was done, and the Edmonton Investors Group was in as the new owner of the Edmonton Oilers. Peter Pocklington was officially out.

A consortium of 35 business people and corporations invested, raised and borrowed $70 million US—around $115 million CDN— to buy the Oilers and pay off the Alberta Treasury Branches.

By no means were the new owners guaranteed success. The challenges they faced were no different than those that ultimately destroyed their predecessor: a small market, a big-player payroll, the difference in value between the Canadian and U.S. currencies. But at the time, none of that seemed to matter.

"It was such a relief to know that if we did go down, at least we'd go down fighting," Phillips recalls. "Whether they could make it, we didn't know, but the thinking was, 'Let's give it a shot and see if we can survive.'

"That's, I think, when Gary Bettman told Cal Nichols, 'You guys have to ride it out until we get to our next collective bargaining agreement with the players. Then we'll fix the problem.' And that's exactly what they did after the 2004–05 lockout."

• • •

As Peter watched the Oilers taken from him, he said nothing. Others, however, were not so quiet.

Commissioner Bettman said Peter "brought the NHL to Edmonton and saw it through five Stanley Cups. His contributions to the NHL and hockey in Edmonton will always be remembered."

Two days later, Glen Sather spoke before a roomful of reporters and investors gathered to celebrate the passing of the torch. "I'd like to say congratulations," he began, "but first I want to say something to Peter Pocklington, who kept the team in Edmonton the last 20 years. I'd like to thank him publicly for his involvement in the team."

Cam Cole recorded the moment for posterity in his *Journal* column: "The stuff about Pocklington came from the heart," Cole wrote, "and the heart of Glen Sather was aching and he didn't care if the men who had bought the team and who had steadfastly refused to be in the same room with Puck throughout the negotiations were shifting uncomfortably in their seats."

> I owned the team for 22 years. It was more than a lifestyle for me. I loved it. It was my heart. It was like having your heart torn out. Not to be able to control the forces around me was pretty devastating. It was like the perfect storm. It all blew apart.
>
> It wasn't even a relief when it was all over. I was wounded. It took many, many years to get over the turmoil. It was a hole in my heart.

• • •

Peter has nothing negative to say about the people who made up the EIG—"They stepped up, and they didn't have to," he says—but it wasn't long before Sather faced his own frustrations with the new owners. For more than 20 years, the Oilers GM was accustomed to running the shop the way he saw fit, and was given the freedom by Peter to do just that. Suddenly, there were multiple owners eager to share their perspective on how to run things.

"I was dealing with 26 characters who knew diddly squat about the hockey team," Sather says of the EIG. "I admired them for putting up what they had to put up to buy the team, but they also knew it was a good investment."

Sather's relationship with the Oilers—forged over two decades—disintegrated in little more than two years, and the inevitable power struggles within the EIG leadership did little to help. Within months of the EIG takeover, Jim Hole and Bruce Saville were elbowed out of their leadership roles to make room for Cal Nichols. Saville resigned from the board. "I resented the fact that some of them started politicking around to change the power structure of the team when they got Hole and Saville out of it," Sather says. "And that was what really changed what I was going to do. I didn't want any part of that. So that's when I decided to resign.

"And there was such resentment towards Peter from those guys, it was just incredible. I didn't like being around them. I wouldn't go for a beer with any of them; I didn't want to socialize with them. There were two good guys, Hole and Saville, and they were doing it for the right reasons. I admired those guys and when they lost out, I couldn't see any sense of it. I knew sooner or later it was going to get emotional and I'd deck one of them, so I'd be better off to leave before I got into a lawsuit."

Kevin Lowe was the head coach of the Oilers that year, and he could see first-hand the relationship between Sather and the owners deteriorate. "I know exactly what happened," he says. "Glen's sort of view on the new ownership group was, 'Hey listen, I've run things for however many years and no one is going to tell me what to do,' and them saying, 'Yeah, we respect you but we own things now and we like to do things a little differently.' It was like that right from the get-go.

"It got ugly a few times, so that doesn't heal quickly, but I think it has now. As human beings, you know, you've got to move on."

Says Phillips: "I don't think Glen really liked some of the guys that owned the hockey team. He was going to run the team his way, and I don't think they had any problem with that. I think what it came down to was just a clash of personalities."

On May 19, 2000, two years and two weeks after the EIG took over the Oilers, Sather resigned. "And, you know, I didn't have a job to go to at that stage, but I was pretty sure I'd find one if I was going to look. It didn't take long."

The night Sather submitted his resignation, two NHL owners— anxious to have the first crack at signing him—met him at the Edmonton airport while he was on his way to his home in La Quinta, California. On June 1, he left Edmonton for good to become president and general manager of the New York Rangers.

. . .

By July of 1998, the ATB put Peter's holding companies, Pocklington Financial and Hartford Securities, into bankruptcy. What was once an impressive business empire was to be sold off, piece by piece—often at fire-sale prices.

The ATB sold Cambra Foods to Winnipeg-based grain merchant James Richardson & Son for $22 million, a fraction of its $40-million value. A thriving food-processing business was reduced to a milling station.

The sale of the baseball Trappers was a particular sore point for Peter. The ATB sold the team to the CFL's Edmonton Eskimos for the $5 million US it needed to recover its security in the team, a figure that was less than half what the group in Portland was prepared to pay. Five years later, the Eskimos sold the Trappers to baseball Hall of Famer Nolan Ryan for $10.4 million US—at the time about $13 million CDN—and the team was moved to Austin, Texas.

> That was my money. The Trappers would draw more fans over the course of a season than the Eskimos. Yet they were sold off for the sake of Tier 2 football. That's what happened in Edmonton. So do I have a sour taste? You bet I do. Not for the folks, not for the people, but for the politicians and the bank.

The ATB wasn't done. Receivers went into Peter's penthouse offices in the Sun Life Building and carried off anything that wasn't nailed down—and a few things that were. His chain of fitness centres, Club Fit, was sold off. Eventually, Peter would sign off on an agreement settling his debt with the ATB.

Finally, in October of 1998, after 27 years in Edmonton, Peter set out for Indian Wells, California, leaving Edmonton for good.

. . .

As Peter took his leave, the hostility that had stuck to him like gum on a shoe stayed behind, where it has continued to fester to this day.

But there are people in Edmonton who look beyond the conventional wisdom that suggests Peter Pocklington was some sort of renegade capitalist out to exploit and impoverish the good burghers of Edmonton.

They speak of the legacy he left his adopted hometown.

Kevin Lowe: "Five Stanley Cups is pretty big in a short period of time, you know, and as much as some politicians refuse to admit it, the Oilers really did a lot for this city. They put it on the map, worldwide. I guess oil has as well. But I talk to a lot of Americans, and they have no idea there is this much oil up here. But they know there's a hockey team because of Gretzky. I think Peter and Glen were huge influences on us, thinking big, thinking globally and not thinking small."

Charlie Huddy: "He did a lot of good for the city. He should be proud of what he did."

Bob Kinasewich: "People have been blinded by the press as to the good that he did, and to the fact that there were outside factors that contributed towards the downfall of his business interests."

Glen Sather: "Peter's legacy? That one's complicated. I know what it is with me—it's being a great friend. I'm not sure what it is with everybody else. I think he's an enigma to most people. But I think people don't understand all the humanitarian things he did over the years, the money he gave away to people that nobody knows about, the charities he started, even the Glen Sather Sports Medicine Clinic at the University of Alberta. That was Peter's idea; it certainly wasn't mine. I'm proud it's named after me, but Peter's the guy it should have been named after. Then there is the Jamie Platz YMCA, the school lunch programs. Look at the Junior Achievement program he started. Think of all the guys who have gone on and built businesses and been successful because Peter helped them out. He did a lot of good things in Edmonton. He brought that city some personality and character in those days."

Failing in business is something that can happen to anybody. It's happened to me, it has to everybody. It's something I share with young people. They have a new entrepreneurial school in Palm Springs where I speak occasionally. Other than "You become what you think about," and "Here's how you create wealth," you have to learn from your mistakes and don't be bruised to the point [where] you don't get up again. If you're going to climb a mountain, and you slip and bruise your legs, you have to keep getting up if you're going to get to the top.

I've learned a heck of a lot more from failure at something, losing something, watching it self-destruct, than I have from the shining periods of watching Stanley Cups. That was almost ordained. It was really the Great Spirit bringing us along on that trip. But the ones I failed at, boy!

PART XIX

'You can't live in the past'

The time comes for Peter Pocklington to say goodbye to the Oilers and to the city he has called home for close to three decades. Yet, while a new life in California beckons, so does the old game he has come to love and the desire to do it all once more, with feeling.

In October of 1998, Peter and Eva Pocklington boarded a jet and left Edmonton—the city that had become home to them both—once and for all. In doing so, they hoped to get away from the vitriol, the open hostility, the ongoing disparagement, the lingering resentment, and the anger a community had been hurling at them for the better part of a decade.

They also left behind the hockey team whose fortunes Peter had guided for more than 20 years, a point that Glen Sather touched on at the time in an interview with the *Journal*'s Jim Matheson.

Peter's departure, Sather told Matheson, "is sad for me because we've been friends and he's been great to work for, for 22 years. I think he's been maligned, to say the least, in Edmonton. In my mind, that's not right for a guy who kept hockey in Edmonton for a lot of years under trying circumstances. He's asked for nothing more than [what] the new ownership is getting. He just wanted a chance to survive."

Sather was confident, however, that his friend would persevere. "Peter's mentally as tough as anybody I've ever met, but it's been a tough, tough time. A lesser person would have collapsed under this," he said. "If I know Peter, he'll look at the positive side. He'll try to find something that's constructive and exciting to do. He won't sit back and be depressed with this. He'll get on with his life."

The Pocklingtons did get on with their lives in Indian Wells. For Peter, the move was a chance for a fresh start in what he hoped would be a more welcoming business environment.

* * *

Life away from the glare of public scrutiny did have its attractions. Nevertheless, it presented challenges for the Pocklingtons.

Their greatest personal crisis came when Eva was almost killed in a car crash on May 25, 2001.

She was driving in Palm Desert, not far from their home. As she turned left on the advance green off Highway 111 onto El Paseo Drive, an upscale shopping district, two men in a stolen car ran the red light coming the other way and broadsided her car.

I came in from golfing and someone said, "Your wife has been in a bit of an accident. You have to get over to the hospital." They wouldn't tell me any more than that. So I got to hospital and she was on a gurney in the emergency room. She had a broken neck in two places, broken pelvis in two places, she was scalped, 70, 80 stitches in her head, her teeth were knocked out, ankle broken. She was a mess.

But she recovered and you'd never know she had been in an accident.

Something like that changes you. That really would have changed me if she hadn't made the cut, obviously. But I knew she'd make it, because that's just the way she is. We are a lot alike, Eva and I. We're both strong people and self-reliant and we're never going to let anybody dictate to us how we are going to live and not live. Our core beliefs are very similar.

I admit she is more sensitive than I am. I'm really a buccaneer, but tender underneath. But we think the same way. We even know what each of us is thinking. She will start a sentence and I'll complete it before she's through. That's how close we are.

If Peter hadn't confronted his own mortality before, Eva's car crash certainly compelled him to do so.

As I've said before, a brave man dies once, a coward dies every day. I'm not afraid of anything. I will get nailed one day, I'm going to die, but it doesn't bother me. You've got to live life with strength and goodwill and being very strongly positive every day. To my mind, every day can use a blessing.

I guess I'll keep working until I die. I don't really call it work because it isn't work. I really enjoy it.

But when my time does come, cremate the body and scatter the ashes in Maui. It's a pretty special place. I feel connected to the universe there.

　　　　　•　•　•

Rare is the person who engenders fulsome praise from just about everyone who speaks about her, but Eva Pocklington is that kind of person.

"She is an absolutely lovely person," says former prime minister Brian Mulroney, "and a huge influence for good in Peter's life."

Oilers' broadcaster Rod Phillips also sees Eva as a moderating influence in their marriage. "It's a great love story. There aren't too many people in this world who don't have some enemies, but I doubt if Eva has one, because she is just that kind of person. She's just really thoughtful and really classy."

"There isn't anybody who doesn't like Eva," adds Sather. "Never met anyone.

"Peter and Ann and Eva and I, we would do a lot of things together. We enjoyed their company, and I assume they enjoyed ours. We were around them a lot, and our kids liked them. I can remember Daryl Katz dating Peter's daughter, Jill," he adds with a laugh, referring to the Oilers' new owner.

Bob Kinasewich calls Eva "an absolute princess." And, he adds, "Peter is totally devoted to her. Anything she ever wanted, she got—but I never found her very demanding, quite frankly."

Yet Kinasewich remembers the family's strength was most evident when things weren't going well. "I think Eva has tremendous intestinal fortitude, to have put up with the crap and the publicity and things like that," he says. "I think Peter tried to shelter her from some of the financial difficulties.

"You know, with Peter, everything was rosy. 'How are you doing, Peter?' 'Aw shit, couldn't be better, absolutely great.' 'What about that thing that went sideways.' 'Oh, thank God, got rid of it. I'm on to bigger and better things.'

"Life with Peter was 'tremendous,' everything was always 'tremendous.' Peter was a very generous guy and Eva, she was just as generous."

Peter says that, as a couple, he and Eva are well grounded, which has helped them face some of the more difficult challenges in their lives. And, as sentimental as it might sound, it all begins with love.

> If you love yourself, you can love others, and that's the premise I've always ordered my life on. So I don't carry grudges and hurts about somebody else. If they screw up, they screw up, but keep going.
>
> It doesn't mean you have to accept the negative people, the ones that you don't like being around, but I don't hate anybody—even the people who used to go after me with guns and knives in newsprint, and the bankers.

•   •   •

The Pocklingtons' six children and 12 grandchildren continue to make the trip to California to see Peter and Eva, but rarely all at once. That suits Peter fine: "A family reunion is just a good name for a bad party," he says. "I'd rather spend close time with each of them on a personal level so you can relate, rather than annoy."

Daughter Leslie is a realtor and developer in Collingwood, Ontario. Daughter Molly is a homemaker in Toronto. Son Peter, a financial consultant who once ran the Club Fit chain in Edmonton, recently relocated from Phoenix to Oakville, Ontario. Zach, an executive with a medical supplies company, also lives in Oakville. Jill resides in New York on Long Island. Darren works with his dad, Brian Hughes, at Hughes Petroleum in Edmonton.

Peter is reluctant to draw too much attention to his family, however. He is protective of the relative anonymity they enjoy:

> I never wanted to bring the family into any of it. It's their lives, after all, and they chose to be silent. They're not interested in my crazy antics. I know there have been times when my kids would have loved some of the shine maybe, but I thought it was too dangerous. There are a lot of nuts out there.
>
> Besides, look at the youngsters of all these high-profile people who do make a noise. They make complete fools of themselves. Take the Hilton sisters and so on. You don't live vicariously through people in your family who have a high profile. It just doesn't work.
>
> The only things my kids were given were an education and a new car and that was it. They're totally on their own, and they're all successful.
>
> The way we treat the grandchildren might be different, though. I spoil the hell out of them.

One of Peter's indulgences for his grandchildren is to help finance their college education. Last year, he contracted with a sports memorabilia website in Montreal to auction off his five Stanley Cup rings as well other Oilers mementoes he had put in a family trust 17 years ago. The auction garnered bids totalling more than $300,000.

"The collection should be put to good use, rather than letting it collect dust," Peter said at the time of the auction. "It's a sad moment, but I also find it rewarding to see my loved ones helped in this way."

. . .

Putting those rings into a family trust in 1992 may have been one of the more judicious steps Peter could have taken.

Six years later, there were reports the Alberta Treasury Branches was not satisfied with confiscating the paintings off Peter's walls and claiming his other personal possessions. They wanted the rings, too.

"Even a lawyer or a bank can't be that unfeeling," wrote Terry Jones in his column in the *Edmonton Sun*. "If there is one lawyer or one bank president who really wants to kick Pocklington five more times when he's down . . . that's simply sick."

But a source within the ATB's legal team confirmed they were indeed after the mementoes, worth an estimated $75,000 at the time. That was beyond the pale for some Edmontonians.

"That would be awful," said Jim Hole, at that time head of the Edmonton Investors Group, the Oilers' then-owners. "He's entitled to those Stanley Cup rings. They belong to him.

"This team would not be here today if it weren't for Peter."

Because of the family trust, the ATB's efforts were ultimately in vain.

•   •   •

Hockey, the game Peter loves, continues to beckon, and he has his own ideas on where it would work best.

> I look at cities in the following way: they are either inner-looking or outward-looking. Edmonton is an inner-looking city—there is bugger-all to do a mile outside of Edmonton. Los Angeles is outward-looking. All you do is look around, and you've got the ocean, the mountains, the desert—all kinds of distractions and hockey is not one of them.
>
> But you look at cities like Edmonton, Calgary, Toronto, Montreal, even Ottawa, they are all definitely inward-looking cities. Only Vancouver is an outward-looking city, but because it's in Canada and has a good-sized population, hockey still does well. But basketball didn't do well in Vancouver. So you can have an

outward-looking city in Canada and still do well in hockey.

But if you're in the U.S., you definitely have to be inward-looking. Look at Chicago, or Boston, or Manhattan. New York is an inward-looking city, and it has a great tradition in hockey. You look around, all you see is tall buildings. You can't ski in New York, you're not going boating, so what are you going to do? Go to a hockey game, go to a concert, go to a basketball game.

Peter's friends and associates couldn't be blamed for thinking he would be crazy to want back into a game that had done so much to financially ruin him. But Peter insists the year-long lockout that cancelled the NHL's 2004–05 season changed the rules. With the salary cap—and, of course, a sound economy—hockey is a good business to be in again.

"It's certainly fun and you can make some money at it," he says. "I should have made my move before the lockout was settled because I knew it would be successful."

If Peter was ever to put another NHL franchise in Canada, he likes Hamilton. He isn't as enthusiastic about Winnipeg. While he considers both cities inward-looking with suitable NHL-calibre arenas, Peter says the Winnipeg market is too small. There are only 1 million people in all of Manitoba. In his opinion, that's just not enough to support NHL hockey these days.

Hamilton, on the other hand, is the geographic centre for a market of 2.5 million people that includes London, Kitchener–Waterloo and St. Catharines–Niagara. And that doesn't include the 5.5 million people living next door in the Greater Toronto Area.

In 2009, BlackBerry co-founder Jim Balsillie offered $212.5 million to buy the Phoenix Coyotes out of bankruptcy and move them to Hamilton. While his plan was enthusiastically received in Canada, the NHL establishment was considerably less enthusiastic. For one, moving an existing team into the Central Ontario market would mean forgoing the revenue the other owners would receive from granting an expansion franchise for the area. Moreover, some U.S. owners were not enthusiastic about yet another Canadian team based in a city most Americans had never heard of. It wasn't Balsillie's first crack at moving a team to Hamilton. In 2007, he went after the Nashville Predators. To prove Hamilton's suitability to the NHL, he collected deposits for 13,000 season tickets and 70 corporate suites within a matter of days.

The Predators were the team Peter also coveted at the time because of the lacklustre support they'd earned in Tennessee since the franchise began playing there in 1998. "Nashville doesn't work," Peter says. Though Nashville is about the same size as Edmonton, "there is no market there. They are more interested in guitars and drinking beer than they are in hockey."

At that time, however, the NHL appeared more determined to beat the dead horse in Nashville than convince its American owners to accept another Canadian team. Balsillie's $238-million US offer was waved off in favour of one for $176 million from local Nashville investors. But the plan to keep the team in Tennessee had a bad aroma for more reasons than just the arithmetic. The locals were backed by California shooter William (Boots) Del Biaggio, who was subsequently charged by the FBI with fraud and later declared bankruptcy.

Moreover, the *Nashville Tennessean* subsequently reported, Craig Leipold, the Predators' owner, and Los Angeles Kings owner Philip Anschutz secretly loaned Del Biaggio $17 million to do the deal without the knowledge of either NHL commissioner Gary Bettman or even Del Biaggio's Nashville partners. Once free of the Predators, Leipold then bought the Minnesota Wild.

That said, Peter's interest in the Predators did not involve a move to Hamilton. Rather, he had his eye on what was then the fastest-growing city in the United States: Las Vegas.

"Vegas is kind of exciting because you could sell out the place," Peter says.

The challenge facing him was raising $175 million to buy the Predators, getting an arena built in Vegas, and outmanoeuvring the other bidders interested in the Nevada market. At the time, he assessed his chances at maybe 20 per cent.

"When you get bidders with deep, deep, deep pockets, it's tough," says Peter, "but I was hopeful I could do it."

Among the other bidders was television and movie producer Jerry Bruckheimer. However, Peter is an acquaintance and former neighbour of Anschutz, who in 2008 pledged to build a new arena for Vegas through his company, Anschutz Entertainment Group. Prior to that commitment, any prospective new owner would have needed assurances the State of Nevada would help finance a new arena before an NHL team would agree to move—and that's where Peter's hopes for Vegas ultimately foundered.

It would have taken two years to build a new arena, so Peter had struck a tentative deal with officials at the University of Nevada Las Vegas to park the team temporarily in the Thomas and Mack Center, home of the university's men's basketball program. The facility's ice plant had been ripped out, however, so it would have to be reinstalled. At least 200 luxury boxes would also have to be built to keep the team financially viable during the wait for a new arena.

Still, "I'd move the team there—they have 16,000 seats—but only after we were sure the state would help build a new arena," says Peter. "If you move in beforehand, and then they tell you they don't want to help build a building, then they have you."

As it turned out, Peter never had the chance to play poker with the state. The Nevada legislature meets only on odd-numbered years for a maximum of 120 days. They ended their 2007 session without even considering funding for a new arena. "The government didn't seem to want to get involved," says Peter, and the idea of the NHL in Las Vegas died—at least for the time being.

Peter responded by reminding himself never to fall in love with any deal:

> I guess I've never been in an unrequited love situation. But if it doesn't work, it doesn't work. There are thousands of opportunities around. "There is a freight every five minutes" is the way I look at life.
>
> I never get too discouraged. I might be pissed off for a day, but after that, forget it—on to the next deal.
>
> But if it ever comes about that I do get back in the NHL, I

know it's going to be a lot of work. It's a big responsibility. If you go to a city and promise them you'll give them the best you have, it means you've got to work at it.

It could still come to that. The NHL teams in Atlanta, Miami–Fort Lauderdale and, yes, Nashville, were struggling before the economy tanked. After the team in Phoenix went bankrupt, all bets were off.

"Florida in particular is a mess. The Panthers don't work and the people in Miami don't give a rat's ass if they come or go," says Peter. Miami, he says, is an outward-looking city. "They are more interested in jai alai and horse or dog racing."

Eventually, the other NHL owners could decide Balsillie and his millions have taken on the sheen of the proverbial gift horse, and whatever perceptions working against Hamilton could suddenly evaporate. Meanwhile there are other markets in play, too—Kansas City, for one, as well as Vegas.

There is the possibility the last chapter in Peter Pocklington's life as an NHL owner is yet to be written.

• • •

Daryl Katz, the Edmonton billionaire whose family built the Rexall drug store empire, has been the Oilers' owner since February 2008. He was a regular at Oilers' games during the team's 1980s dynasty, and came to know many of the players personally.

Today, Katz represents the ideal of the modern NHL owner. He is keen, respectful of the team's heritage and—perhaps most important of all—extraordinarily wealthy. His has a profile that, in many ways, is the antithesis of the fly-by-the-seat-of-the-pants style that was prevalent in Peter's heyday.

There is no way of knowing, of course, how well Peter Pocklington and Daryl Katz would work together should they ever find themselves sitting across the same NHL boardroom table. Nevertheless, Katz is extraordinarily positive in his assessment of his predecessor's stewardship of the Oilers.

"We wouldn't have had all the Stanley Cups and we wouldn't have had the Oilers as we know them today without Peter," Katz told the *Journal*'s David Staples after he took ownership of the Oilers.

"Peter is a very aggressive guy, an aggressive businessman, and I think he had some bad timing relative to some things, but it shouldn't diminish at all what he did for the hockey team and what he did for the city of Edmonton."

Staples writes that Katz considers himself a diehard Oilers fan, one who witnessed the departure of Gretzky, Messier, Lowe and others in sales and trades. Yet, while most fans reacted with disgust, Katz did not. He was starting his own career in business at the time and had an appreciation for what was happening.

"It's a business. . . . When Wayne went, it probably had to happen for the team and for Wayne and for the league."

Katz told Staples he could see it coming. "You're saddled with being in a small market and look at it. Could you imagine having six or seven or eight guys like that and you've got to sign them all? You can't sign them all."

Ultimately, he said, the team's overwhelming success contributed to the selloff of players.

"I think the number one most passionate fan, the guy who sweated it more than anyone else at the time, was Peter. He had as much to do with the Cups and the success as anybody and I think he got kind of a raw deal from a lot of guys. I wouldn't hold anything against him."

• • •

Peter says Katz's ownership of the Oilers should be good for the team and its fortunes, "especially given how tough it is to win one Stanley Cup, let alone five."

As well-intentioned as the EIG may have been, "community ownership doesn't work." It would often take weeks, sometimes longer, for decisions to be made, he says. "The speed of the ship is the speed of the boss," Peter adds, "and that's just the way things are."

Peter is also encouraged by news of a possible new downtown arena in Edmonton—and he's confident it can be built without tax dollars. "There are other ways to raise the money," Peter says. "Tell the mayor that one phone call to me and I'd raise the dough for him. I know where he can get the money."

He adds a word of caution, however, for the new Oilers' owner. "You're holding the team in trust for the community. If you do a good job, they love you. If you don't, they'll put a knife in your back."

● ● ●

In 1998, as Peter prepared to leave Edmonton, he mused publicly about what happens when those knives come out. "I have trouble getting a fair hearing in Edmonton—I guess because of 20 years of terrible press," he was quoted as saying.

It's not uncommon for high-profile individuals to take issue with uncomplimentary media coverage, whether they've earned it or not. But Peter might not have been far off the mark. The barrage was unrelenting and no denunciation of Peter was beneath his critics. With nary a nod to the libel laws of the land, he was branded a liar, a cheat, a robber baron, a scoundrel, a scam artist and a bully.

Peter was "the most hated man in Edmonton," wrote Scott Haskins in the *Edmonton Sun*, though that was more an observation than an editorial comment. It may have been one of the kinder statements.

When Glen Sather left the Oilers' organization, Haskins' *Sun* colleague Graham Hicks wrote that Sather and Pocklington were "arrogant and cocky" and their attitude "permeated the organization."

More recently, Hicks wrote there were examples too numerous to mention of Peter "being willing to exploit whoever he was doing business with.

"Pocklington had a win/lose philosophy of business—that it was his job to get the best possible deal, and if you were dumb enough to be taken advantage of by him, well that was your problem, not his."

When Peter first announced he would be leaving Edmonton, *Journal* columnist Cam Cole asked, "Is that a threat or a promise?"

Added popular *Journal* columnist Linda Goyette: "Wherever Peter Pocklington is going, he will get what's coming to him."

To Goyette, Peter was "a blunt bully," "a rogue capitalist," and "Edmonton's Lucifer."

The hostility did not escape Peter's attention. "I've got to say, reading a lot of that crap, I wouldn't have liked the guy either," he laughs.

• • •

Peter's media critics frequently took issue with his threats to move his teams out of Edmonton in order to secure the improvements he considered necessary to public facilities. But as Peter has said, threats and ultimatums were the best way he knew to get the necessary parties to the negotiating table—and he always invested his own money to help pay for those improvements.

In due time, some of those renovations were hailed in the media. Of the 1994 reconstruction of the Coliseum, Hicks wrote in the *Sun*, "Peter Pocklington's renovations a few years back did the trick of keeping the building up to date, for a fraction of the cost of a new one."

In another column, he wrote that the rebuilt Telus Field was among "the best sports facilities in North America."

Peter's real difficulty—it's unfair to call it a shortcoming—is one that has haunted him from the moment he first stepped forward to help buy the Oilers. It's his unyielding candour whenever he is within earshot of a reporter. Cole once referred to it in the *Journal* as speaking "to delicate issues with an astonishing indelicacy." They are traits that, in the parlance of the journalism trade, make Peter a "great quote," but they have usually not served him well over the years. For every reporter who might be willing to protect Peter from the fallout of his own indiscreet comments, there were 10 others prepared to seize on every impolitic remark or injudicious observation like a starving dog on a bone. They would wait for him to screw up.

Peter would respond to the resulting scathing coverage by

becoming even more blusterous, more outrageous, railing against the treatment accorded him and the critics dispensing it. That in turn would generate even more scornful coverage.

In the end, Peter was like the listing battleship on which all guns were trained. Whether he deserved to be sunk was immaterial. More important was getting on with the job of sinking him.

• • •

When Peter left Edmonton, he was belatedly reticent to talk about his tattered public image. His friends had no such problem.

"People in Edmonton don't know all the little things Peter's done," Sather told the *Journal*'s Matheson at the time. "All the donating of money, keeping it quiet in a lot of cases: the scholarships to all the University of Alberta hockey players; the $1 million he gave to the Jamie Platz YMCA; he bought a breast-imaging machine for the Cross Cancer Institute when they couldn't afford it; setting up the Glen Sather Sports Medicine Clinic; all the Junior Achievement dinners he's put on for kids. They've raised millions."

Bill Tuele, the Oilers' public-relations director at the time, expressed the same sentiments to the *Sun*'s Haskins: "For him to be excluded from the list of Edmonton's top 100 citizens is unbelievable," said Tuele. "He got things done. He turned this city around."

The opinions of those who were closest to Peter at the time have not changed in the intervening years.

Sather says Peter may have earned the scorn directed his way in the wake of the Gretzky sale, but "some of the other stuff, I think he had a bad rap."

Says Sather: "Peter was a good man for Edmonton.

"People talk about Bill Hunter and Zane Feldman bringing the team there, but it was a WHA team that they brought, not the NHL team. Peter brought the NHL team there. Peter was the one who stuck his neck out."

Mulroney speaks to Peter's daring spirit as well. "Peter is an exceptional guy, entrepreneurial, vigorous," says the former prime minister. "He is very courageous. He doesn't waver, and he pursues his objectives with tenacity. Peter is warm-hearted, generous. He's done great things. I believe he's won more than he's lost in his life."

Wayne Gretzky feels the same way. "At the end of the day, you've got to treat people well. That's what I always kind of believed. And I always felt that Peter treated people well. You know, business is business, bad things can happen, a guy gets mad. But as far as helping people, he was always there helping people. That was never an issue with him."

Rod Phillips: "Peter's been blamed for things that were out of his control. He just said a lot of things a lot of people didn't want to hear. They didn't want to hear it and didn't want to understand the problem. He was kind of perceived as the mean rich guy, breaking unions and taking food off people's table—but that wasn't fair to him, either. He was trying to survive and get his businesses to survive.

"Peter's legacy should be as the man who brought NHL hockey to Edmonton and made it hugely successful. If he hadn't bought the team from Nelson Skalbania in 1976, I think there is probably a pretty good chance the team would have folded. When he bought the Oilers, that is the day that saved hockey in Edmonton. Then he made the right decision to get a dynamic guy like Glen in front of the organization. That's what they say good executives do, right? Hire somebody you trust and let them be successful. Is that not true?"

. . .

In time, the two best friends, Peter Pocklington and Glen Sather, went their separate ways. "It's kind of sad that we don't see very much of Peter and Eva any more but we were really close friends for a long time," Sather says. "It's just a matter that everyone has a different chapter in their life. It doesn't mean that your relationship changes. Maybe the frequency of the relationship does. I don't think anything else has to change."

Contrary to rumours, however, both men agree there was no falling out. "Different paths. He got out of the hockey business, I moved on. It's the way life is," says Sather.

"He's got his own life in New York," Peter says of Sather. "He's into his own thing and I'm into mine."

• • •

Among the "things" that involve Peter's time now is charity work in southern California. It is a focus of his attention that he finds infinitely more rewarding than what has transpired in his business life.

He served on the board of the Betty Ford Center in Rancho Mirage for several years and, though he stepped down recently, he was grateful for the experience.

One of his more intriguing ventures is focused on the Watts neighbourhood of South Central Los Angeles. It's a community with more than 1 million people and very little in the way of health-care facilities.

Peter was initially approached by the administration of Charles Drew University of Science and Medicine, which was established as a private, non-profit medical school in the 1960s in response to the absence of health care in the area. The only hospital in the neighbourhood reportedly severed relations with the school in a dispute over accreditation. Charles Drew officials wanted to establish a string of health clinics in the area, and they approached Peter to help make it happen.

Whether he and the university will continue to work together on the project remains to be seen, but there is no doubt Peter views the prospect of bringing medical care to a dramatically underserviced area as something of a legacy project.

"We'll have to see how it goes," he says.

• • •

Peter looks back on his time in Edmonton, and the successes he enjoyed there, as a mix of serendipity, determination and faith. "A lot of these things didn't happen because I was the smartest guy in the world. They happened because I believed they were going to happen—

and I was good at picking up opportunities."

Terry Jones, while still writing for the *Journal*, picked up on that theme shortly after the hostage-taking incident in 1982 that so easily could have ended Peter's life.

"There is something I think Edmonton would want Pocklington to know today, which sets him apart from the Harold Ballards, Nelson Skalbanias, George Steinbrenners and many of the other sports owners who find themselves making headlines every day," Jones wrote. "What sets him apart is the city itself and the way he relates to it. This is his city and he's helped make it.

"Peter Pocklington, we don't tell him often enough, has meant more to this city because of the professional sports franchises he has brought us, which are major factors in helping us through the grand transition, as I have so often put it, from being a pimple on the prairie to being major league."

There can be no doubt that Jones, and other members of the Edmonton media, came to view the Pocklington era differently in the years to come. Does Peter still bear the emotional scars of those times in Edmonton that weren't as successful—and when such accolades vanished? "No, I put that behind me," he says.

"You can't live in the past."

PART XX

'In the States, they'd sue you as soon as look at you'

Peter Pocklington had left Canada for what he hoped would be greener pastures in the United States. Yet he eventually discovers that America's take-no-prisoners capitalism is difficult for even an ardent free-enterpriser like him to stomach.

During the first four years after Peter and Eva Pocklington had left Edmonton, they split their time between their home in Indian Wells and another they owned in Toronto. By 2002, they had decided their future was to be found solely in the sunny climes of southern California.

Peter hoped he would find a more welcoming business environment in California than the one he knew in Alberta. Regretfully, he would discover it was anything but.

He did enjoy his minor successes, though the most noteworthy had its roots in Canada. That was Medatron Medical, a Quebec-based supplier of medical equipment, garments and supplies for hospitals and health clinics throughout North America.

The company was run by Peter's son, Zach. As was the case with many Canadian enterprises doing business in the States, its greatest competitive advantage was the exchange rate between the Canadian and U.S. dollar—because of it, American customers could buy from Medatron for a discount that ranged from 25 to 40 per cent. Ironically, the exchange rate was finally working to Peter's advantage, the reverse of his experience with the Oilers. This time, the expenses were in

Canadian loonies and the revenue in the higher U.S. dollars.

When the gap in the currency values began to disappear, however, the Pocklingtons knew it was time to sell. The company was bought by an American company, Medline. Zach now runs Medline's Canadian division; it did about $80 million in business last year.

There were business failures, too, though not all were particularly devastating.

For example, there was Law America, a prepaid legal services plan. In exchange for a modest fee of $30 a month, a customer was given access to a wealth of online counsel for whatever legal problem was confronting him.

> That was something we tried to sell because of the litigiousness of the folks in America. We set up lawyers to look after every account we gave them in return for a $6 retainer every month per customer. We thought we could sell hundreds of thousands of these plans at $30 a month on the customers' credit cards. So we did a TV infomercial—and we did sell thousands of them.

The fly in the ointment? The customer would commit to paying $30 a month, but once he used the legal service, he cancelled the plan.

> If someone who bought the plan talked to the lawyer and got a little advice, he'd say, "What do we need to keep paying $30 a month for?" and cancel. We weren't getting any return.

Law America was shut down after only six months. None of Peter's other American business ventures would wind up so tidily.

Ultimately, Peter's legal and financial woes would grow more contentious than any he confronted with the demise of Law America— and by the spring of 2009, they were drawing considerable media attention, and even threatening his liberty. In the course of defending himself from the civil litigation and criminal charges he now faces, Peter makes a number of assertions and accusations about the people with whom he was doing business. None of them have been proven in court.

. . .

The genesis of Peter's troubles came in 2005 when he first gained majority control of an American nutraceutical company called Naturade.

The company, based in Irvine, California, has been in business since 1926, but it's doubtful anything in its history would be as colourful—or as distressing—as what transpired in the few short years Peter was involved.

Naturade markets more than a dozen natural food supplements and herbal remedies, including such well-known products as Colostrom, through pharmacies and health-food stores. It attracted Peter's attention because, despite its history and reputation, it was an underperformer in the marketplace.

In 2005, Peter acquired majority control of Naturade in exchange for a $2-million guarantee. His plan was to buy other, smaller companies and, in Peter's words, "bolt them" onto the larger firm. "That way," he says, "you can eliminate the overhead from the smaller company, and it's new-found cash flow for the larger company."

Finding the money to finance the purchase of the smaller companies, however, proved futile.

> We spent a year trying to raise capital. The only way you can raise capital down here is: No. 1, do it privately, which is a pain in the you-know-what—I don't like asking friends for investments like that; and No. 2, go to hedge funds where they want 80 to 90 per cent of the company. It wasn't worth it.

The trick, therefore, was to finance the acquisition of smaller companies the same way he gained majority interest in Naturade— that is, without resorting to a cash deal. It was a strategy that ultimately led Peter to consummate the purchase of a Florida company called

Ageless Foundation with its owner, Naomi Balcombe.

To buy Ageless at the most advantageous terms he could negotiate, Peter says he agreed to give Balcombe a personal guarantee, rather than one through his company. It was a concession that would ultimately come back to haunt him.

At first blush, Ageless seemed to be the perfect fit for Naturade. Its primary product was a drink loaded with the sort of vitamins and nutrients that are supposed to help people live longer—thus its name, Ageless.

> I think we paid $1.1 million for Ageless and we hoped the money it earned would add $700,000 to $800,000 to Naturade's bottom line. If it does that, you can afford to pay one and a half times the gross when you buy it.
>
> The problem was that Ageless turned out to be not what I expected it to be. The products had turned bad—no one would buy them—and the sales turned out to be roughly a third of what they were claiming from prior years. Unfortunately they had not kept up with their product quality and a lot of what had been shipped to stores months before had spoiled.
>
> So then we had to find another two or three manufacturers and write off all the product that we had purchased from them.

That was just the beginning of Peter's problems with Ageless. He claims Balcombe's company was being sued. "So Naturade ended up defending itself against lawsuits we had known nothing about."

Peter says he tried to reach some kind of accommodation with Balcombe—she wanted her money; Peter wanted some renegotiation that reflected the cost of the product that had spoiled, as well as the expense of defending Naturade against the litigation inherited from Ageless—but in his words, it was "to no avail." Finally, Balcombe sued Naturade. The company responded in kind.

It wasn't all bad news, though. At the same time, another company Peter had added to the Naturade stable was thriving and Naturade itself was beginning to turn the corner.

And that's when Peter decided it would be a good time to sell the company.

. . .

Peter says he didn't know a lot about Adam Michelin, but he knew the California entrepreneur was offering a $5-million deal for Naturade—$3 million in stock, $500,000 in cash, and a management contract for $1.5 million over five years, payable to Peter's holding company. It constituted a handsome return on Peter's initial investment and that of his partners.

Moreover, Peter says Michelin agreed to assume responsibility for the litigation pending against Ageless, as well as relieve Peter of his personal financial culpability for the deal he had made with Balcombe.

But then Michelin did something that—for lack of a more descriptive phrase—took Peter's breath away. Within 30 days of taking over Naturade in 2006, Michelin put the company into Chapter 11 bankruptcy protection—before Peter and the other creditors had been paid a dime.

> That bankruptcy screwed me and everyone else, including
> Naturade's accounts payable, for the money he owed us. And doing
> this seems to be perfectly legal in the States.

Michelin's intent, says Peter, was to acquire a debt-free company at little or no cost, secure the licensing for its product line, assume control of its multimillion-dollar revenue stream and, in Peter's words, "make a good bottom line."

Peter took the only recourse he felt he had available to him—he sued Michelin personally for $10 million. Michelin responded by declaring personal bankruptcy, blowing Peter's lawsuit out of the water. Naturade subsequently went into Chapter 11 again in 2008 and this time, says Peter, Michelin was dismissed from the company by its new owners.

Nevertheless, Peter remains gobsmacked by how easily his company was taken from him without recourse.

Doing business in the U.S. is a helluva lot different than doing it in Canada. You couldn't get away with that in Canada. You wouldn't do it. You wouldn't want to do it.

If I was going to do more business in the States, I wish I'd done it when I was 25, not 65. At 25, I was obviously more resilient. I would have learned the ropes, the ropes I had to learn.

As it is, I learned most of my business experience in places like Tilbury and Chatham, and Edmonton in the early days. People dealt on a handshake. You made a deal and everybody stuck to it. You didn't have to have 10 inches of paper and nobody put things in Chapter 7 or 11 and on and on and on.

I bought half-a-billion dollars in real estate from Nelson Skalbania over 20 years, and most of it was on handshakes. You can't do that in California.

To add further insult to monumental injury, Naturade's initial bankruptcy left Peter accountable for the legal commitments a Michelin-run Naturade was supposed to assume from him—and it wasn't long before Naomi Balcombe came looking for her money. She was granted an $800,000 personal judgment against Peter by a judge in Miami.

• • •

If Peter's harsh experience with Naturade was a harbinger for even greater challenges he was to face, so was an even earlier acquisition. In 2002, shortly after he and Eva settled permanently in the Coachella Valley, Peter parlayed his love of golf into a majority interest in a golf equipment company called Golf Gear International.

The experience was not a positive one.

Golf Gear was a publicly traded company that had been operated by its founder, Don Anderson, from its base in Garden Grove,

California, since 1989. In the 13 years since, it had not made a nickel. Still, it was "a tiny little company with great technology," says Peter, so when Golf Gear began casting around for investors, he signed on with a majority interest.

Golf Gear's ace in the hole was a driver with a titanium insert forged into its face. The club held enormous sales potential for golfers seeking to add distance to their drives.

When Peter gained control of the company, he raised a few million dollars in convertible debentures—notes that can be converted to equity—then negotiated a licensing agreement with Nike. That allowed Nike to sell the titanium driver in stores as its own brand.

But within a year, Peter maintains the company was faced with an internal crisis.

> We found out that someone was stealing from the company. He was going to Taiwan, where the clubs were being manufactured, and they would give him a bill for Golf Gear for $85 to $90 per club. But he had worked out a deal with the Taiwanese where he was actually buying the clubs for only $45—and once the company paid them, they were giving him the difference in cash.
>
> When you're buying hundreds of clubs, that difference added up in a hurry.

Peter says Golf Gear's board of directors fired the alleged embezzler as soon as the deception was discovered. The executvie responded by suing both Peter and the company for $15 million.

> We danced around for a few months and then we had a forensic auditor come into the company and found that this guy embezzled a lot of money. He dropped his lawsuit because we said we would charge him with embezzlement unless he did.

That wasn't the end of it, Peter says.

That fired executive had brought four other partners into the company, each of whom, like him, owned only 1 or 2 per cent of the stock. Collectively, they accused Peter of mishandling the company, and in 2006 they sued Golf Gear for malfeasance.

That was bad news for a couple of reasons. If Golf Gear was to grow and compete with its competitors—Tailor-Made, Callaway, Cleveland, Titleist and the like—it needed an infusion of capital. Indeed, that was why it struggled before Peter became involved. But the company also needed money to defend its patents, particularly those related to its titanium-forged heads. Well-heeled competitors with financial brawn and legions of lawyers to back it up were borrowing liberally from Golf Gear's technology and if the company wasn't prepared to defend its patents in court, no one else was going to step forward to do it.

But Peter soon learned it was tough to attract investment while fending off lawsuits, frivolous or not.

> When you're trying to raise money for a public company that's full of lawsuits, it isn't going to happen. So my investment company funded it over that period of time for over $1 million. Plus it was going to cost probably $2 million in legal fees to defend the patents we had, to go after the big guys.
>
> The board continued to defend the company against the lawsuits for up to a year but we finally saw it was going nowhere. Plus spending money to defend patents for a dead horse didn't make sense, so we put Golf Gear into Chapter 7 bankruptcy. It's gone, liquidated.

• • •

As Golf Gear's board prepared to bury the company in early 2007, they began casting about for an alternate plan. Peter had his eye on Sonartec Inc., a golf equipment company in Carlsbad, California, that had earned accolades for its metal woods and wedges.

Sonartec's product line had even attracted the attention of golfers on the professional golf tours. Among those who had used its clubs: World Golf Hall of Fame member Nick Price; Todd Hamilton, who won the 2004 British Open using a Sonartec hybrid; and Zach Johnson, who used one of Sonartec's fairway woods when he won the Masters in 2007.

Yet according to a report in *Golfweek* magazine, the company had failed to achieve commercial success of any significance in the seven years since it was founded. Sonartec's owners, Toru Kamatari and a group of partners in Japan, had begun to cast about for a buyer.

Peter had taken out convertible debentures—in effect, a mortgage—on Golf Gear in return for the money he had invested in the company. Those debentures were secured by Golf Gear's patents.

> So the board agreed to a deal I put together to buy Sonartec. I was going to transfer the Golf Gear patents to Sonartec and put in some money, which I went out and raised, and we closed the deal. It took six or seven months, but it was done by June of 2007.

However, Peter had his misgivings about the wisdom of this particular acquisition.

> I wish we never did the deal. It seems strange but when a deal is that tough, and it's uphill the whole way, I should have just walked away. But it made such great sense to go ahead with it.

In the end, Peter and his board agreed to pay $500,000 in cash for Sonartec and an additional $500,000 a year for three years at zero interest, as well as providing a $500,000 line of credit. That was on top of the Golf Gear patents Peter agreed to sign over to Sonartec that were valued at $1 million.

But Peter's misgivings about the deal were justified. If due diligence had failed him when he acquired Ageless Foundation, that failure was even more pronounced with the purchase of Sonartec.

According to Peter, the laundry list of problems tied with Sonartec was a lengthy one. The nature of those problems and how he attempted to resolve them constitutes the thrust of his defence against the accusations subsequently leveled against him in court by Kamatari.

Because the documents supporting his defence have not yet been filed in court, they cannot be disclosed publicly. But Peter is confident in his ultimate vindication.

Peter says in the end that Kamatari was fired for cause, though Kamatari disputes this.

> We stopped paying for the company, then we got Kamatari and his partners into mediation to settle our differences. We tried to make a deal with them. We sat down with the mediator and said to them, "Here's what you've done. We're willing to go ahead with this purchase if you do what I understood you were going to do in the first place." They refused and then they started suing everybody.

Peter put Sonartec in Chapter 11 bankruptcy protection in the hope of reorganizing it. "It was the only way we could defend ourselves," from the lawsuits, he says.

"It's too bad. They were great clubs and it could have been a great little company. But at my age, life is too short to fight."

• • •

Kamatari and a Japanese partner, Hidetsugu Koyama, were claiming they were still owed $1 million each for Sonartec, but by the summer of 2008, their legal actions had stalled.

According to Brent Jang in the *Globe and Mail*, that's when Kamatari and Naomi Balcombe joined forces. Their objective was to nail Peter Pocklington. As a first step, Kamatari's lawyers registered Balcombe's Florida court judgment against Peter in California. They then went to federal court, *ex parte*—that is, without legal notice to Peter— persuaded a judge that, because Peter is Canadian he was a risk to flee the country, and were granted the right to move against Peter.

What followed attracted international media attention.

On July 29, 2008, U.S. marshals raided the Pocklingtons' Vintage Club home. Two more raids followed on August 6 and 9. In all, 250 items, most of which belonged to Eva Pocklington, were taken to satisfy Balcombe's court order. The collective value of the 56 items taken in the first raid alone were estimated at more than $1 million. Among the assets seized: two hockey sticks autographed by Wayne Gretzky, numerous Buddha statues, Inuit soapstone carvings, two sculptures by French artist Antoniucci Volti, Christofle silverware, pieces of the Berlin Wall, a set of Rosenthal white china plates, five Andy Warhol prints of Mick Jagger, and a cannon shell fired in the 21-gun salute at Gerald Ford's funeral that the former president left in his will for Peter.

Also taken from Eva's closet: Yves Saint Laurent evening gowns, Chanel women's shoes, Hermes purses, and Louis Vuitton bags. "I'm not a cross-dresser," Peter told Jang. "They can't take my wife's articles." Peter threatened a lawsuit of his own, for $5 million, alleging the goods were seized wrongfully. "We're going to get it all back, and then we're going to sue for $5 million," Peter threatened at the time.

The legality of the seizures aside, the resulting media attention quickly drew the attention of other creditors, including the Alberta government. The province had been trying for years to recover from Peter as an individual $2 million still outstanding from loans it made to Gainers in the 1980s—"I never got a penny of that money," says Peter, "but they still got a $2-million judgment against me"—as well as an additional $10.5 million in interest, calculated at a rate that can only be described as usurious.

As the sharks circled, sensing all this blood in the water, Peter felt he had no choice but to declare personal bankruptcy. In his filings, he listed his net worth at $2,900 US and his liabilities at $19.7 million. Balcombe and Kamatari did not react kindly to that development. A complaint filed by their lawyers afterwards called Peter "a professional con man."

Said the complaint: "Plaintiffs are an unrelated group of victims who have never encountered anyone as blatantly dishonest as Pocklington."

What these experiences have taught Peter, aside from the fact such a checkered track record does nothing to enhance the notion of ethics in business—though he is convinced he did nothing unethical and, in fact, considers himself the wronged party—is that the United

States is an extraordinarily litigious society. Sportswriter and pundit Al Strachan suggested as much in an interview on the Canadian sports channel The Score: "This is the U.S. court system; 5 per cent of the gross national product is litigation."

In a $14-trillion economy, that translates into a $700 billion industry.

When Peter left Edmonton in 1998—in the wake of a business failure that would have been the undoing of most people—he was determined to succeed in California in a manner he felt he was never allowed to in Canada. Yet, ironically, he has since come to prefer the business environment in his homeland to the Wild West capitalism that seems to reign supreme in the United States.

> This country is nuts. I don't know how people put up with this down here. I really don't. The things going on in the States would shock you. It's have gun, will travel.
>
> I sure miss Canada. Somebody described Canada as decaf coffee compared to the U.S. and it's absolutely correct. In the States, they'd sue you as soon as look at you; it's just crazy. And I like Canada from the point of view that, when I was there, at least when you shook hands on a deal, it was a deal. Here, unless you bring out the lawyers, that's not necessarily so—and even then it doesn't matter, they still change the deal on you.
>
> Canada is certainly a more civil country.

EPILOGUE

'What else are you going to do? You can never give up'

An early morning knock on the door lands Peter Pocklington in a California jail cell and on the front pages of newspapers across Canada. But the experience fills him with resolve; not only to restore his reputation but also to crusade against what he views as judicial maliciousness.

Peter Pocklington filed for bankruptcy two days after the third and final raid on his home in August of 2008. By that December, however, he was having second thoughts.

Peter told Brent Jang of the *Globe and Mail* he intended to have the bankruptcy dismissed in January. "It's a filing, and it can be withdrawn," he told Jang. Ultimately, though, he chose not to. "Well, there was no point," Peter says. "It had gone too far"—so he kept it going.

That said, if he had to do it over again, "I never would have declared bankruptcy." He did so only to free himself from what he considers a host of scurrilous lawsuits: "I mean, it was really just to save myself hundreds and hundreds of thousands of dollars in legal fees."

Peter maintains he did not declare bankruptcy to hide assets, or that he transferred ownership of those assets to his wife with the intent of defrauding the bankruptcy courts. Rather, most everything he shared with Mrs. Pocklington was placed in her name in 1998, shortly after the couple left Edmonton. "We could do that because

California is a community property state," he says. Any suggestion that it was done to perpetrate a fraud 10 years later is "all nonsense."

Nonsense or not, transferring his assets to his wife became part of the ammunition the lawyers for Naomi Balcombe and Toru Kamatari drew on in their efforts to demonize Peter Pocklington and challenge his bankruptcy before a U.S. grand jury. In California, asserts Peter, the facts need not get in the way of an innovative legal strategy.

> In California, you can say anything you want in a public document. It then gets into the public domain and everybody thinks it's correct. As a friend of mine, Bill Tuele, told me, it's frontier justice.
>
> They told the grand jury that this guy Pocklington has $20 million or $30 million or $50 million offshore and he's declared in this bankruptcy thing that he doesn't have any assets. The grand jury looks at their "evidence," and decides, "Well, if he has $20 million in liabilities, he obviously has all kinds of money because he couldn't have liabilities without the money." I don't really know how that follows but—anyway, that's what happened.

Among the assets listed in Peter's bankruputcy filing: $200 in cash; memorabilia, trophies and photos worth $500; clothing and shoes valued at $300; a $500 watch and golf clubs also valued at $500.

According to a story by Darcy Henton in the *Edmonton Journal*, it was this gap between the assets and liabilities that tweaked the interest of the public bankruptcy trustee. The FBI was called in to investigate.

What followed in the early morning hours of March 11, 2009, was something Peter never anticipated: the FBI breaking in the door of the Pocklingtons' recently rented home in Palm Desert. They were there to arrest him.

"We were still in bed. They broke the lock and came in," Peter's 87-year-old mother Eileen told Henton. "I heard all this banging. I think, 'What on earth are the neighbours doing? Bang, bang, bang. . . . Little did I know.'"

Peter was led away in handcuffs. He was arraigned, then he spent two nights in the Riverside County jail. It is an experience Peter refuses to talk about publicly.

The lawyers prosecuting the case had hoped to keep Peter in jail for even longer—at least until he was tried on the charge of bankruptcy fraud—because Peter was deemed a flight risk. The trial was scheduled for May and later delayed to August. But when Peter was brought before a judge two days after his arrest, a $1-million bond had been posted on his behalf, ostensibly by his friend Glen Sather, whose lawyers handed over the deed to a property in Minnesota.

Peter was returned to his family wearing an ankle bracelet so the FBI could monitor his movements. Moreover, his travel was limited to the area between Los Angeles and Phoenix, and only for business or court purposes.

Nevertheless, he was free once more, and Peter returned to Palm Desert filled with a fresh resolve: to not only exonerate himself and clear his name, but to launch a crusade against what he claims is the indiscriminate incarceration of individuals—sometimes, to his mind, at the whimsy of the U.S. justice system.

He cited an example: a couple in northern California that had been given approval from the state and their municipality to cultivate marijuana for medicinal purposes. But the couple was found to be in violation of a federal law that did not recognize the state's jurisdiction and they were sent to prison anyway.

> Of all the people in all the jails in all the world, 25 per cent of them are in American jails—even though the U.S. accounts for only 5 per cent of the world's population. This is just madness. I don't understand how it can be happening. It's fascism.

. . .

Despite what he sees as overzealous prosecution—he might even say it has crossed the line to persecution—Peter does have faith the U.S. justice system will establish his innocence. He says the prosecution's case against him is so weak, it will never stand up to judicial scrutiny.

For instance, he points to the accusations levelled against him over the listed value of his memorabilia at $500.

In making their case for bankruptcy fraud, his accusers point to the fact Peter's five Stanley Cup rings that were put up for auction in 2008 attracted a winning bid of $272,829 US—though the sale was never consummated.

How can his memorabilia be valued at $500 when those rings are still in Peter's possession? they asked.

"But the rings weren't that memorabilia listed in the bankruptcy," Peter responds. "That's the problem, you see—people look at things and say, 'Whoops, that's not right.' Well, it is right."

The memento in question was a present from President Ford. The rings weren't listed because, as has been outlined before, they were put in a family trust in 1992 for the benefit of his grandchildren. They are now in the safekeeping of the auctioneer, Marc Juteau, in Montreal.

And why wasn't the deal consummated? Peter points to a column written by Terry Jones in the *Edmonton Sun*. Jones wrote that another set of Pocklington Stanley Cup rings had been auctioned off in 2001. Peter says those rings were made for his late father and they were auctioned by his estate.

> The people that made my rings certified they were the real items. But the guy who was buying them got cold feet. He went away. In fact, all the bids went away because of Terry Jones. I'll never talk to that prick again. He is the most arrogant sportswriter I know.

Jones's column was only about rumours that were already circulating in the collections community, but that makes no difference to Peter. He already had little regard for the columnist. This latest episode merely reinforced Peter's desire not to have anything more to do with him.

• • •

Another point of contention is the accusation that Peter was drawing an income as high as $50,000 a month from offshore trust accounts. Not true, says Peter.

> Any money that I lived on was money I brought into the U.S. from Canada when I first came here. I lived off my capital. When I invested that income here in California, I drew off the capital to live on. I never had an income in the U.S.
>
> My offshore companies were trusts, and I didn't own them. I wasn't a beneficiary, I wasn't a director, period. They were set up to hold shares in Golf Gear, shares in Naturade, units in Sonartec. That's all that was ever in those trusts.

Nor, he says, did he ever have cash-flow problems—at least until the past year, when the costs of defending himself in court began to mount.

Peter fell behind in his mortgage payments on his Indian Wells condo and when he was unable to sell it in the moribund U.S. real estate market, he turned it back to the bank. He and Mrs. Pocklington moved to their rented home in Palm Desert in September.

•   •   •

Then there is the matter of Ed Moroz.

The Edmonton construction company owner and restaurateur is the son-in-law of Charlotte Cooper, a friend of some 50 years' standing with Eva Pocklington. He and Zach Pocklington, along with a third investor, Ryan McCann, were partners in an Internet search engine portal called Sherpaonline.com in 2000, at the height of the dot-com boom. McCann, a friend of Zach's, had founded the company a year earlier.

Peter says he invested $100,000 US in the venture, as did Moroz. McCann also had money in the company.

By 2001, when the dot-com boom went bust, so did their company. "Those little Internet companies collapsed—thousands of them, hundreds of thousands," says Peter. The money invested by Moroz, McCann and Peter was lost. Peter says he offered Moroz shares in another venture they could undertake together as a way to regain his lost investment, but Moroz declined. Instead, he sued Peter to get his money back.

Peter returned to Edmonton in September 2005—the first time he had been back since he left seven years before—for the court case. Moroz argued that since Sherpaonline was supposed to go public, he thought Peter would hold the money in trust until then. But the company never did go public before the dot-com bubble collapsed, and when Moroz asked for his money back, Peter had to tell him it was gone.

Peter testified he never promised Moroz would get his money back if the company failed, and that Moroz was told his investment was in a private venture. Yet the judge ruled in Moroz's favour anyway, saying he found Moroz's testimony more reliable. The judge ordered Peter to repay Moroz his $100,000 as well as Moroz's legal costs, a total that amounted to around $200,000 CDN.

Three years later, Moroz went to Palm Springs, still looking to collect his money. (In order for the judgment to be enforceable in California, Peter would either have to voluntarily turn over the money, or Moroz would have to argue his case again in a California court. Peter chose the former.) Peter met Moroz at a storage facility and let him take some art valued at $80,000, a rug and a desk. It was later argued in court Peter had hidden these assets in his bankruptcy filing, yet, again, he points out they belonged to Eva.

But why would Peter agree to give Moroz anything?

"Charlotte told Eva it was her money that they put into this Internet company with Zach," recalls Peter, "so I was trying to mitigate the loss to Charlotte. I would never do business again with the guy."

In March, as Peter was led into that Riverside courtroom on the day of his arrest, Moroz was there to watch it happen.

"He had handcuffs on and arm restraints on, and I think there was some justice in it. He wasn't a smirky, little Peter Pocklington he always is when he gets into a courtroom," Moroz told the *Journal*'s Henton.

"I think you can count Peter's friends on one finger. He has nothing and nobody." Two days later, one of those supposedly non-existent friends posted a $1-million bail.

Ed Moroz is certainly not the first person to lose an investment in a business venture. He wasn't even the only one who lost money on Sherpaonline.com. He is, however, one of those rare individuals who sued one of the other partners to get his investment back—and won.

"Even Moroz's lawyer testified in court it was an investment," claims Peter. Yet, when Peter attempted to make good on at least part of the court judgment, the gesture was ultimately used in the criminal case against him. Moroz, reports the *Edmonton Journal*, was co-operating with the FBI investigation.

"Moroz is just a mean-spirited guy," says Peter.

·   ·   ·

Should Peter emerge from court an exonerated man—and he is confident he will—the slate will be wiped clean. The criminal case against him will have been dismissed and the civil prosecutions wiped away by a bankruptcy that can then proceed.

If it doesn't play out that way? That's a scenario Peter will not entertain. But either way, he refuses to allow the events of the past few years to get him down.

> There have been days over the years, in Edmonton and in California, when I think what the blazes am I trying all this for?
>
> But what else are you going to do? You can never give up. When you're going after a goal, you slip and bump your knees and if you don't get up, you're defeated. You just have to keep getting up, scale the mountain and, by God, find there is a bigger peak to climb.
>
> As an entrepreneur, as a dreamer, a visionary, a builder, you can never give up. There are times you'd like to—I'm as human as anybody—for maybe 10 minutes. But then you get your backside in high gear and move on.

There are days and, to be sure, nights when self-doubt does creep into Peter's mind. He says at times like that, he finds reassurance by quoting to himself a passage from William Shakespeare's *Measure By Measure*:

"Our doubts are traitors, and make us lose the good we oft might win by fearing to attempt."

I've had my ass kicked many times, but at the end of the day, life is short and as long as I can feel good about how I acted, that's all that matters. I don't really care what anyone else thinks.

And where will Peter Pocklington go from here? "When another door opens and there is a breeze, I'll go for that."

SOURCES

The authors acknowledge use of the following sources and thank their authors and publishers:

The Glory Barons: The Saga of the Edmonton Oilers, by Douglas Hunter; Penguin Canada, 2000; pp. 21, 30.

The Rebel League: The Short and Unruly Life of the World Hockey Association, by Ed Willes; McClelland & Stewart, 2005; pp. 32, 42, 45, 46.

Memoirs: 1939-1993, by Brian Mulroney; Douglas Gibson Books, 2007; pp. 105, 111, 112.

In My Own Name, by Maureen McTeer; Random House Canada, 2003; p. 105.

The Business of Professional Sports, by Paul D. Staudohar and James A. Mangan; University of Illinois Press, 1991; pp. 118.

A Matter of Trust: Greed, Government and Canada's $60 Billion Trust Industry, by Patricia Best and Ann Shortell; Penguin Canada, 1986; pp. 118, 119.

INDEX

Nixon, Richard, 176, 184-85
Norris Trophy, 81
North American Soccer League (NASL), 54, 156, 157, 158, 159
Northlands Coliseum, 35, 64, 157, 190, 233-34, 242, 246, 248, 270
Northlands Sportex, 141
North West Trust, 20, 118
Nova Bancorp, 120

Oakland Athletics, 153
Oakland Stompers, 156
Ogden A's, 152-53
Omega program, 77-78
Ontario Hockey League, 38
O'Reilly, Bill, 119-20, 121-22, 123, 124
Orlich, Dan, 154-55
Orr, Bobby, 82, 195, 197
Oswald, Lee Harvey, 176, 177
Ottawa Civic Centre, 113
Ovenden, Norm, 219

Pacific Coast League (PCL), 54, 152-53, 155
Paiement, Wilf, 67, 69
Palmateer, Mike, 65, 67
Palm Dairies, 54, 126, 127-28
Patrician Land Corp., 53, 118, 121, 123
Patrician Oil, 54, 126
Pavarotti, Luciano, 174-75
Pearson, Scott, 198
Pelé, 156
Petro-Canada, 108, 114
Petrovic, Mirko, 85-92, 93-95, 96, 98-99, 100
Philadelphia Flyers, 67, 242
Phillips, Debbie, 52, 199, 250
Phillips, Quinn, 52
Phillips, Rod, 31, 32, 35, 39, 47-48, 52, 71, 72, 81, 82, 132, 151, 167, 199-200, 204, 212, 217, 227, 228, 232, 233, 243, 250, 251, 252, 254, 260, 272
Phoenix Coyotes, 79, 215, 264, 267
Picture Butte, 148
Pilous, Rudy, 42, 43, 44
Piper, Doug, 238-39
Pittsburgh Penguins, 35, 81, 82, 213, 214
Platz, Jamie, 170
Plummer's Lodge, 179
Pocklington, Basil (father), 24, 25, 26, 184
Pocklington, Eileen (mother), 24, 25, 26, 288

Pocklington, Eva (wife), 15, 17, 19, 20, 21, 26, 49, 50-52, 61, 75, 83, 86, 87, 88, 89-90, 91, 96, 97, 101, 141, 162, 163, 168, 173, 184, 187, 191, 258, 259-61, 272, 280, 284, 285, 286, 291, 292
Pocklington, Jill (daughter), 50, 51, 187, 260, 262
Pocklington, Leslie (daughter), 51, 96, 261
Pocklington, Molly (daughter), 51, 96, 261
Pocklington, Nancy (sister), 25
Pocklington, Peter Jr. (son), 51, 96, 261-62
Pocklington, Zach (son), 50, 51, 86, 159, 262, 275, 276, 292, 293
Pocklington Chair in Free Enterprise, 169
Pocklington Financial, 88, 180, 255
Pretty Woman, 127
Price, Nick, 283
Prix de l'Arc de Triomphe, 219
Progressive Conservative Party, 101, 104, 105, 111-14, 117, 138, 149, 244, 245
Pronger, Lauren, 211
Provincial Bank, 28

Quebec, 109
Quebec Nordiques, 34, 188, 232, 237

Ramsey, John, 247, 251
Ranford, Bill, 227
RCMP, 183
Reagan, Ronald, 185
Real Canadian Superstores, 238
The Rebel League (Willes), 32, 42, 45-46
Reisman, Heather, 119
Reisman, Simon, 119, 179
Rendezvous '87, 61
Renfrew Park, 97, 153
Revson, Peter, 187
Rexall, 267
Reynolds, Burt, 76
Reynolds, Marilyn, 88
Riis, Nelson, 212
Rio Balsas, 162-64, 165, 186
Robinson, Max, 96
Robitaille, Luc, 198
Roozen, Cathy, 247
Royal Bank, 91
Ruth, Babe, 194, 217
Rutherford, Jim, 67
Ryan, Nolan, 255